Alexander the Great is said to have sat down and cried because he had no more worlds to conquer. The lot of present-day adventurers is equally hard, for there are very few parts of the world left unexplored and few journeys that really justify what it takes to make them. The travels of John Hillaby are a remarkable exception. A tireless Yorkshireman who lives in London, he has been described as one of the world's greatest walkers. He journeys alone and on foot, describing what he sees with fresh understanding. He strode the length of Britain through Europe from the North Sea to the Mediterranean and across parts of boreal Canada and tropical Africa. Mr Hillaby is, moreover a distinguished natural historian who for years wrote for *The Guardian* and *New York Times*.

The author has written three books which have become best-sellers: *Journey Through Britain*, *Journey Through Europe* and his latest, *Journey Through Love*.

John Hillaby

Journey to the Jade Sea

PALADIN
GRANADA PUBLISHING
London Toronto Sydney New York

Published by Granada Publishing Limited
in Paladin Books 1973
Reprinted 1974, 1975, 1977, 1979

ISBN 0 586 08140 2

First published in Great Britain
by Constable and Co Ltd 1964
Copyright © John Hillaby 1964

Granada Publishing Limited
Frogmore, St Albans, Herts AL2 2NF
and
3 Upper James Street, London W1R 4BP
1221 Avenue of the Americas, New York, NY 10020, USA
117 York Street, Sydney, NSW 2000 Australia
100 Skyway Avenue, Toronto, Ontario, Canada M9W 3A6
110 Northpark Centre, 2193 Johannesburg, South Africa
CML Centre, Queen & Wyndham, Auckland 1, New Zealand

Made and printed in Great Britain by
Richard Clay (The Chaucer Press) Ltd
Bungay, Suffolk
Set in Monotype Ehrhardt

Granada Publishing ®

Contents

List of Illustrations

How It All Began

I knew where I was going. The hill station of Wamba, the place where this journey began, lies on the western edge of the deserts of North Kenya. To the north the mountains slant down to a strange lake. I had been to Wamba once before. The circumstances are unimportant except that towards the end of a long tour, conducted by friends in the Game Department and arranged, thoughtfully, for comfort, I became so fed up with looking at spectacular scenery through the dusty windscreen of a Land-Rover that I got out and climbed a chunk of ancient rock called Lolokwi, largely to stretch my legs.

What I saw from the top made a profound impression on me. The deserts of the Northern Frontier District have an apocalyptic quality; they are utterly stark and relieved only by the stumps of worn-out volcanoes. What life there may have been there has long since been burnt out by the sun. The N.F.D. is not only one of the hottest and driest places in the world; when the wind picks up the sand it must be one of the most violent. From the top of Lolokwi the impression is of an uninhabited corner of hell.

Without giving much thought to ways and means I told the warden who accompanied me that if he could name a worthwhile objective I would return to Wamba as soon as I could and cross the desert on foot. To my surprise he was not particularly surprised and said that Lake Rudolf would be a good place to head for. For an hour or two he told me about the green lake among the geysers and lava fields, the lake known as the Jade Sea. From what he said of its varying moods, sometimes tempestuous, sometimes womb-like in its oceanic peace, it seemed wholly appropriate that Rudolf should have been named after the neurotic Crown Prince of Austria who committed suicide at Mayerling after shooting his mistress through the head.

This then is the story of a fortunate journey towards the strip of water that lies across the border of Kenya and Ethiopia. I say fortunate because to reach Rudolf and return via the Chalbi and the Turkana shore we covered about eleven hundred miles on foot and we covered them without serious mishap, at least to ourselves if not the camels. I had almost no qualifications for making a foot safari, certainly nothing in the way of previous experience. It was the first time I had been into the bush without a European on hand. I knew nothing about guns and gear and as for the camels, those gangling, good-natured beasts, I had seen them previously only through the bars of a zoo. The fact that we were able to get through difficult country with a minimum of replacements was due largely to the skill and resourcefulness of four Africans whose names and character will, I hope, become affectionately familiar as we move along.

What is harder to explain is why I decided to make the journey and what, if anything, I hoped to gain from it. Peter Fleming has spoken for the majority of us when he said that the trouble about journeys nowadays is that they are easy to make but difficult to justify. Only a few places remain untrampled and they are those that are inaccessible on wheels.

Essentially, I walked into the N.F.D. for the hell of it. I was tired of city life and heartily ashamed of having done nothing in the way of physical exertion that I could look back on with satisfaction. If this widespread brand of revolt in a middle-aged man is the sign of an emotional second adolescence I wish only that I could have more of it and had made the decision to break the pattern of chronic boredom earlier than I did. As a writer and naturalist I had travelled widely without seeing very much at close quarters. In Nairobi and elsewhere the big agencies sell safari, expensively, but as simply available as oysters on the open shell. Bush experience can be bought complete with kit, transport and guides at a cost of between £1,400 and £2,000 per person per month. I had to watch my pocket. I borrowed six camels, hired others and bought a few for less than £5 each. The men received sixty shillings a month and when I eventually got the feel of a distinctly unfamiliar rifle I shot most of what we ate. Looking back on the trip I regret little except my initial incompetence.

I am tempted to say that bush experience can be picked up pretty quickly but, remembering the stupid things I did during the first week or two, I would advise anyone as inexperienced as I was to watch local *expertise* and try to improve on it. In this way – and I wish I could make it sound less sententious – I found it not too difficult to live in reasonable comfort. Some things, of course, can't be picked up quickly. There is no short cut to the language problem or the difficulty of getting used to the sun. I tackled both problems together by baking myself on the deck of a Nile stern-wheeler and arguing in elementary Kiswahili with anyone who came up to tell me that I was mad. The result was that before I reached Wamba I could put simple questions to Africans who couldn't speak English and, equally important, I could walk about with nothing on except a pair of shorts and a bush hat decked out with an ostrich feather which, I discovered by accident, helped to keep the flies off.

As far as the walking part of a foot safari was concerned, I put in a great deal of time on the South Downs before I left London and each day I walked to my office in the city from Hampstead. There is not very much more I need say about that. I like walking.

Gear, especially important things like rope and sacks for the camel loads, can be bought in one sitting at any one of half a dozen stores in Nairobi, but a word of warning here. The man in charge of an expedition needs good advice before he starts and I had the very best available from that prince of modern travellers, Wilfred Thesiger. He advised me, among other matters, to carry a lot of medicine instead of useless trinkets and knick-knacks, and to wear tennis shoes rather than bush boots. I should like to mention three other men who, for different reasons, proved reliable friends. The first is Ian Grimwood of the Kenya Game Department to whom all conservationists are deeply indebted; the second is Peter Saw, a young warden in the N.F.D. The third is my old friend, David Wood of *The Times*.

To reach Wamba I flew to Khartoum and sailed up the Nile as far as Juba in the Sudan. After a period of acclimatization among the white rhino of West Nile, a game warden ferried me down the length of Lake Albert and passed me on to a colleague who was on safari in Semliki. I made my way, slowly, around the borders of Uganda; I skirted the Ruwenzori, the Mountains of the Moon, drove north and eventually spent a couple of weeks in Karamoja where the Turkana were at odds with the Dodoth. Two companies of the King's African Rifles had to be flown in to sort them out. From that point onwards I thought only of what I should do when I eventually got to Wamba where I hoped to pick up a string of camels. They told me that everything would be in order when I got there.

As I spoke almost nothing but a loose form of up-country Kiswahili for several months, I shall borrow a few words here and there in describing my relationships with those on whom I depended most.

The Shake-down

At Wamba almost everything went wrong. The local game warden had gone home on leave. Eight camels hired on my behalf had been left to the care of an idle fellow who had allowed them to champ away at the wrong sort of browse. By the time I arrived, all of them were very, very sick and one had died. They said it was mange. Another warden, a very distinguished man, came in from an adjacent station and tried to hire some beasts from the local Veterinary Department, but he doubted whether even healthy animals could carry as much gear as I had brought from Nairobi. Resolving to jettison about forty tins of corned beef, two dictionaries and some historical works on the discovery of the Northern Frontier District, I faced other problems.

The most pressing was the question of an escort. Because the Marille tribesmen from Ethiopia were said to be on the rampage with guns, the District Commissioner insisted that if I wanted to travel beyond a point less than one-third of the way up the east shore of the lake I must be accompanied by armed men and 'somebody reliable'. I referred this unexpected set-back to my resourceful friend, the game warden, who said, good fellow that he was, that he thought he could bring in a squad of *askaris* from Marsabit, a mountain post out in Rendille country. I turned to my staff.

Everyone wanted to say something. A man introduced as my syce or chief camel leader seemed to be distinctly surly. A red-painted fellow, with bones like napkin rings in his dangling ears, he tried to explain through a giggling interpreter that he had wife trouble and was unanxious to leave a girl worth at least sixty cows to the attentions of a rival brave. I had to say something. I had been told that the Swahili for 'yes?' (*N'dio?*), 'good' (*M'zuri*) or 'maybe' (*labda*) were effective substitutes for almost any positive statement of opinion. Diffidently, I tried

M'zuri. To my dismay the man also said 'good' and went back to his red-painted paramour. Clearly I needed another camel leader.

If I understood them aright, two other men on my pay-roll were complaining that they had been told that the safari would last at least three months. They had hoped, they said, to be back in Wamba in about three weeks' time. Ignoring the interpreter and muttering what I hoped was Swahili for 'Yes, three months, definitely,' I passed on. They looked horrified.

A third fellow, a man with an atrocious tic like a wink, was anxious to sell what appeared to be the middle portion of a fair-sized snake wrapped up in cocoanut fibre. 'Kamba?' he kept asking. 'Kamba?' Not knowing what *kamba* was and suppressing a ridiculous desire to wink back, I turned it down. Did I mention that I had diarrhoea? If not, I do so now.

Even the weather was wrong. As far as I could foresee, our route north took us through two ranges of mountains, the Matthews and N'dotos. Providing the going was firm and dry, I gathered there was nothing particularly difficult about the trail. But on that first frustrating morning in Wamba, the tops of the Matthews were hidden in lines of leaden clouds, lit by blinks of lightning. The game warden, informative as ever, said rain was probably coming. Perhaps floods, too. Camel driving might be difficult on wet ground. Had I considered starting from Laisamis, a drier locality heaven knows how many miles away to the east where I might be able to pick up a bunch of bigger, stronger animals? It had not even entered my mind and was unlikely to. But besides diarrhoea I had an acute attack of nervous indigestion and an ominous feeling that brave words spoken far away about undertaking a long trip entirely on my own were no more than brave, idle words.

Perhaps all safaris start this way. Somewhat despondently, I sat down among the food and gear piled up on the game warden's verandah. Trying to ignore the snake-seller who crouched down at the foot of the steps looking up at me like a faithful dog, I opened the only package which seemed important at that moment, the one that contained half a dozen bottles of Scotch.

Apart from two tin trunks, a roll of bedding and a tent in a large green kitbag, almost everything I had bought had been done up in old cardboard boxes of the kind found around the dustbins of a grocery store. There were about twenty and most of them contained food.

Thesiger, who is something of a stoic, had advised me to avoid fancy tinned stuff and buy as much rice as I could carry. I bought sixty pounds. Memories of school dinners. It seemed a mighty amount of rice. I had also started out from Nairobi with about forty pounds of sugar; from the crunch on the floor it was apparent that the abrasive processes of a foot safari had already begun. I traced the leak back to a hole caused by the protrusive leg of a badly packed Primus stove and, for want of something better to do, I looked over the rest of my stock. Very soon I started to pick out dried limes, one by one, from among about fifty packets of soup. Clearly, there was a great deal of sorting out to be done.

The groceries can be dismissed briefly. To begin with I separated oddments such as curry powder and pellets of yeast like swanshot from basic supplies of tea, sugar, dried milk and flour. It was important to keep all food apart from sharp-edged kitchenware and a vast amount of rope. Thesiger had warned me that camels were intolerant of tins and boxes but they could carry almost anything stowed away in floppy sacks or kitbags. Bags formed well and they could be lashed around the animals' flanks or laid across their backs.

I had bought thirty empty sacks, twelve kitbags and forty calico bags about a foot square. By putting the food in labelled bags and the bags in labelled sacks, I managed to reduce the whole load to about fourteen hundred pounds. This included half a hundredweight of dried camel meat (emergency supplies) and two hundred pounds of maize meal (*posho*) for the men. It was doubtful whether a string of mangy camels could stand up under this load but I couldn't think of anything else I could leave behind. However, I had forgotten we needed at least sixteen gallons of water, a large box of ammunition and about £150 in cash, mostly in small notes and East African shillings; this for wages, additional food and the hire of camels and guides.

Somebody came up behind me. I shut the cash box guiltily and turned to find a bullet-headed man who wore only a faded rose-coloured blanket, patched like the sail of a barge. 'Effendi,' he began, opening his hands in an expressive gesture of welcome and respect.

I recognized the man, vaguely, although I could not remember his name. He was one of the camel leaders, presumably the man hired to stand in for the fellow who had gone back to his wife. I was somewhat disconcerted by being addressed as *effendi*. I had no desire to wrestle with Arabic as well as Swahili of which I had learnt a basic minimum on the way down through Uganda.

But Karo, the son of Lapali, was not a Muslim. A wandering Samburu, he had been to many places including gaol. He proved to be a man of infinite resource and not a little cunning. When we had trouble in the camp, Karo was usually at the bottom of it; yet when I had trouble from outside it was to Karo that I turned. Nevertheless, his presence on that hot and harassing afternoon in Wamba proved something of an embarrassment as I had the utmost difficulty in understanding what he was talking about.

I went through a series of conversational openings which I had carefully rehearsed in advance. First a hearty *Jambo* to which he replied no less cordially. How were his affairs? His affairs, he said, were well. Was he from Wamba? No? Then where was his *manyatta*, his homestead? He said it was near Mount Kulal, far away to the north where the Samburu merged with the Rendille. Eventually, I asked him what he wanted.

This question tended to wreck the rest of the conversation because Karo the son of Lapali answered in a torrent of Swahili. I nodded without knowing what it was all about. When he shook his head and shrugged his shoulders I did the same. In fact, if he hadn't pushed his right hand forward as if to grasp a crisp twenty-shilling note, I might have made the mistake of saying 'good' for the second time in one afternoon, thereby parting with yet another £1 to an incorrigible cadger.

I shook my head slowly, sorrowfully. Karo also looked a little sad; then his face lit up in a huge grin. 'Good,' he said. 'Good!' Thinking that I had got round one minor staff problem, I felt pretty good too. Karo stayed for about half an hour and looked at everything laid out on the verandah floor. He fingered the sacks, squeezed the bags and peered into everything that could be opened or unfastened. I was surprised that he could even identify the dried camel meat and those useful bill-hooks called *pangas* which were wrapped up in straw, but he probed about and pronounced everything 'good' or 'very good' or 'not *very* good'. The condemnation was mild enough and rare but it seemed so absolute in its implications that I was tempted to throw the inadequate articles away. They included most of my rope.

As I had bought about three hundred yards in Nairobi, this was a distinct disappointment. Some of the sisal was rough to the touch; I felt somewhat diffident about it, but Karo seemed more concerned about the soft cotton stuff, the very best I could buy. After watching him hold a length between his teeth and nod his head approvingly, I gathered that it would make good ropes or halters for the camels. But I could not understand why he frowned when he threw a loop round his bare waist and pulled it from side to side, like a tailor with a tape measure. 'Not very good,' he said.

'Why not good?'

Karo got down on his hands and his knees: obviously he had become a camel. He groaned as a camel would groan as it lifted a load and then, as he rose on to his toes and his finger tips, he allowed the rope to slip round his waist until he was holding it with one hand in the small of his back. Without knowing much Swahili, I realized that cotton rope was liable to slip and was not good enough for a camel girth. Yet the problem remained. I had no other rope. I shrugged my shoulders. Too bad! What was I expected to do?

Karo continued to speak rapidly. I caught only one vaguely familiar word out of the babble of explanation. It was *kamba*. But what was *kamba*?

Kamba was rope.

Outside in the dusk the snake-seller with the atrocious tic moved a step nearer, expectantly, and Karo motioned him on to the verandah. What had appeared to be a snake wrapped in cocoa-nut fibre was a tight, cylindrical coil of pliant bark fibre rope, plaited by the vendor's wife. They were camel girths. They cost five shillings each and I bought seven lengths, one for each camel. They were about the most useful things I bought in Wamba and their utility was undiminished even when I learnt some time afterwards that the vendor's wife was Karo's sister. The wandering Samburu would go to extraordinary lengths, even to do someone a good turn.

Late that night I sat in the game warden's house, half listening to a professional argument between my host and a white hunter who had looked in on his way up country. It had something to do with the local close seasons for hunting. My mind was on other matters. I was due to leave at eight o'clock the next morning. The warden had managed to hire two camels from the Veterinary Department. He felt that five of my original string of animals, the beasts with mange, were probably just strong enough to reach a point in the mountains where I could replace them with eight others hired from the forestry service.

These replacements would take me to yet another point where I had a rendezvous with the armed *askaris* from Marsabit who, they assured me, would have first-rate camels of their own. I could borrow these animals for as long as I wanted them. It sounded very complicated. One of the points was not even on the map. There was still some doubt about replacing my head camel leader although several men were said to have applied for the job. Everything seemed to turn on the following day.

At this point I was aware of more apprehensions than a little Scotch would allay. My gear had been substantially reduced in weight by throwing out some massive tarpaulins, a great deal of tinned food and four metal jerricans. But there was still the threat of bad weather. I could hear an occasional rumble of thunder from the hills, and wondered whether the sick camels would succumb to storms. And what could I do about mange? If a few days of neglect could upset camels in this way, how far would they get under unfamiliar camel leaders and a person who knew as little as I did? Far from knowing how to look after a camel, I had yet to see one.

I asked about the men who had objected to a safari likely to last longer than three months. Apparently I had made another mistake. The warden explained that the question put to me that morning was whether the safari would last more than three weeks (*weeki*): the men were anxious to get long-term employment. It seems that I had shaken my head and by confusing the word for month or moon (*m'wozi*) with *m'waka* (meaning year) I had said 'Yes, definitely three years'. Their dismay had been understandable.

Outside in the dark the hills were lit by flashes of lightning. Perhaps I should not be able to leave Wamba. Perhaps the whole idea of a safari on my own had been a mistake from the beginning. Yet if I called the journey off I had to decide then and there, since we were due to start in about eight hours' time. Would things be different in the morning? Were the camels really sick? Question after question spun round in my head like waltzing mice. So much depended on the next day. Tomorrow and tomorrow . . .

To my surprise the day dawned like any other. Doves droned from the tops of the acacias; a metallic-green starling looked at me sideways through a bright yellow eye and walked off, chuckling. At half-past six only the birds and I and a lethargic houseboy were up and about. I fidgeted and looked at my watch; he laid out breakfast with the alacrity of a two-toed sloth. As the game warden and a white hunter who had come to see me off were still in bed, I had time to take another long and unloving look at the great plain of Wamba. I liked it no more than I did the previous day: miles and miles of desolate scrub with a backcloth of blue mountains.

At seven o'clock I tried to put breakfast forward by half an hour without disclosing how nervous I felt, how urgently I wanted to be out and away, anywhere. The feeling of complete dependence on the opinion of authority was an embarrassment. The warden clearly knew too much; the hunter was laconic. For these people safari had become an orderly business as stylized as packing a weekend suitcase, looking up a train and ordering a taxi to the station. They *enjoyed* their breakfast; they ordered more coffee and chatted about totally unimportant things like home leave and the exorbitant cost of fishing tackle. I fed my dyspepsia on unchewed toast and made it worse.

By eight o'clock there was still no sign of the local tribesmen who had been hired to get me over the mountains and into the desert. They had probably deserted, and, like as not, taken most of my gear with them. Nonsense, the warden said. What I needed was another cup of coffee. The camels had to be rounded up and driven in from some browsing grounds at the back of the warden's house. It might take hours. Breathing an overbreathy whistle, as if the whole affair were completely under control, I sauntered over to an immense pile of boxes and fiddled about with my unused guns.

Fascinating and rather fearful-looking things. I picked up the twelve bore. What had the instructor said? Left hand on the fore-end; the right behind the trigger guard. Keep both eyes on the target and *push* the gun forward. Forward at what? It seemed easy enough on the range in London but neither the warden nor the hunter knew that my first live shot on their territory would be literally my first. Never before had I used a gun or a rifle seriously. As the most inexperienced leader of a safari in East Africa I began to wonder if two lessons had been enough. I picked up the Winchester, pulled back the bolt with a hollow *clack* and got an irritated, schoolmasterly look from the warden. 'Better be careful,' he said and went on talking about the price of spinners. Blast him.

At a quarter past eight came a sudden babble of voices and bellowing of beasts from the compound in front of the house. The warden rose to look out of the window. 'Your camels,' he said, 'have arrived.'

Apprehension promptly turned to a mild feeling of panic. Up to that point I had been a traveller only by dubious virtue of preparation. Innumerable problems had arisen, but I had been comforted by the thought that at any moment and at relatively small cost I could call the whole expedition off. Now I appeared to be in charge of a circus of dilapidated animals and men. I had hired it at long range and at the very least I was obliged to see it through the first act. The camels were being driven down a little hill at the back of the house by an excited mob of villagers. They may have been sick animals, but my first impression was of a troupe of comedians. They lurched about as if they were drunk. One of them seemed to be partly paralysed. It tried, repeatedly, to kneel down but as soon as it leaned forward, the ridiculous back legs began to wobble and it almost fell over. Two others tried to bolt back to wherever they had come from and were being systematically thrashed. Another blew immense frothy bubbles which burst and clung to its jowl like shaving lather. The rest were simply skittish. They pirouetted from side to side, snatched at leaves and swung their huge necks round in half-hearted attempts to bite their drivers. All of them either bellowed like cattle or made a curious high-pitched whistling noise.

The camels wheeled in front of the house and at the command 'Toa! Toa!' they flopped down, apparently already exhausted by a journey of a quarter of a mile. A tough little man in the peaked cap and uniform of a game scout shouted something incomprehensible and then marched stiffly towards me. This was my headman, Lelean. He gave me a crashing butt salute and said we were ready to load. I nodded, not having the heart to use even one of my carefully rehearsed bits of Swahili.

Looking back on the business of loading, I think now that we must have established an all-time record. The details are a little vague because I took almost no part in it and was surprised by everything I saw. Somebody produced a bundle of mats; somebody else untied a bundle of sticks about eight feet in length and no thicker than bean-poles. The mats or *herios* were thrown over the backs of the camels, one fore and one aft. The sticks were matched, divided into groups of four and, by the deft manipulation of the bark rope woven by Karo's sister, a double-V of framework was built up on each flank. These were the wooden supports, the *miti* or sticks, to which the loads were lashed.

Then a succession of boys, most of them unknown to me, scampered up the verandah steps, grabbed a bundle each and staggered back with it towards the camels. There were no questions about whether my gear was good or bad, useful or unnecessary. If a bundle stood on the verandah floor it obviously had to be loaded and I had a feeling that if the warden had left a filing cabinet or a miniature piano lying about it would have been hauled off and lashed down as nimbly as a sack of maize meal.

This was an aspect of responsibility I chose to ignore. I was obliged to. Almost everything that could be moved rapidly disappeared. Like bailiffs, the boys simply took the stuff away. I was worried that the camels seemed to be grossly over-loaded but as they bellowed when anyone approached them, empty-handed or not, it was difficult to form an opinion.

I wandered among the loading parties, trying to give the impression of an old safari hand, prepared to be a bit indulgent on the first day. Nonchalance became something of a strain. As the loads mounted, the lower portion of the camel's bellies became more and more distended; some were distinctly pear-shaped. I thought that at least two of the creatures would never be able to rise again. But somehow they all managed it.

When most of the shouting was over and the villagers stood back from the trussed beasts, Lelean marched over and gave me another crashing salute. 'It is prepared,' he said. This time I ventured a carefully phrased 'Good! Let us go'. Farewells were exchanged. The camels were kicked in the rear. They rose to their feet, noisily, and then babbling, bubbling and breaking wind, they staggered forward on the long journey towards the Jade Sea.

First Day Out

Within ten minutes we were out of sight of the village and making for a gap in the mountains as clear cut as the rear sight of a rifle. The going was easy, the scenery superb and the sky pale blue with no more than a wisp of genial cloud. Looking back on the disordered events of departure, I can remember nothing more clearly than the enormous sense of relief that the preliminaries were over and done with. Now I was on my own; I felt as if I had run away from school. Even the camels looked less grotesque than before. They might have mangy sores but at least the worst of them were hidden away under the loads. There was no more bellowing; the animals strode out handsomely to the accompaniment of a rhythmical *tonkitty tonk* from a loose piece of kitchenware buried somewhere inside a sack.

I wondered, momentarily, what the other sacks contained and what, if anything, had been left behind on the verandah in Wamba. But substantially I didn't care a damn. I felt a little self-conscious about striding ahead of the column, but as the men waited until I walked ahead I could think of no good reason for falling behind, at least none that I could put into Swahili. In imagination I was already far ahead of the column and getting to grips with the desert.

Away to the right the west face of the Matthews rose like a wall and disappeared into the distance. The range, I knew from the map, extended for about forty miles and then merged into the N'doto hills. The mountains stretched as far as the South Horr Gap and beyond, to the very fringe of the Jade Sea. I could recognize the topmost peaks of Waraguess, high above Wamba, but Lolokwi, the mountain I had climbed the previous year when I swore I would return to the desert, was already far behind. Each step forward was a step into new country.

I should have liked to continue north and thereby avoid crossing the mountain barrier, but somewhere on the far side of the Matthews lay the forestry station where, with any luck, I hoped to get fresh camels to carry us on to the next stage.

On the pretext of tying a shoe lace I bent down and waited until the camels came up. I felt that at least I should have a look at what I had hired. The first three were roped together and led by someone I could not recognize. Karo brought up the remainder and gave me a huge grin as he drew level. I rose to my feet and waved. This was a bad mistake. The first camel shied violently and dragged the others off the path. The animals bellowed and kicked and it was some minutes before they quietened down. Clearly one had to be careful about making sudden gestures in front of camels. I walked on behind them feeling a bit of a fool.

It then became apparent that all camels attract flies and camels with festering sores attract more than most. The hindquarters of the beasts were covered with large flat-bodied creatures that promptly transferred their attention to my bare legs. After an unsuccessful attempt at beating them off I dropped back about a hundred yards. This obviously worried Lelean who stopped the camels and respectfully strode back, motioning me to my rightful place at the head of the column. I was obliged to walk in front of everyone else and look at the scenery.

Wamba is renowned for its wild life and our path through the bush was like a road through a zoo. Knowing nothing about the habits of rhino and other creatures that tend to lurk unseen, I was probably the happiest and most feckless game-spotter in the Northern Frontier District. Little antelopes bounced into the scrub as if on springs, while groups of zebra allowed us to get within a hundred yards before they nodded their heads and galloped off, barking and bumping into each other as they ran. Large, cow-like eland lumbered along the high ground accompanied by black blobs of ostrich. Remembering that I had to provide the men with meat, it was some comfort to know that we should be within the boundaries of a reserve for at least another ten miles. On the first day out I wanted to conceal the fact that I knew almost nothing about how to use a rifle.

Two hours passed before Waraguess crept up to us, slowly, and we began to walk in the shadow of the Ol Canto pass. According to the game warden, the V-shaped gap rose gently to a shoulder and I envisaged an equally gentle descent on the other side. The camels shambled along like cart-horses; there seemed to be no good reason why we should not carry on until we got within sight of a suitable camping place.

Lelean thought otherwise. He made it clear that we ought to halt to adjust the loads. He wanted to get through the pass by nightfall because we were in elephant country and, as I learnt to my cost later on, a good camel leader steers clear of elephants. We halted for about a quarter of an hour which gave me an opportunity of looking at the men.

Among a motley of local unemployed, five were on my pay roll. They worked; the others leaned on their spears and watched them. Lelean, my headman, was the most active of all. With his black, close-cropped head and bustling manner he looked like a bumble bee, buzzing from camel to camel, testing load-ropes, readjusting the wooden supports of the harness and talking to everyone. Karo, the man who carried off the rope-trick, seemed to be getting in his way and I wondered how long it would be before there was trouble between them.

My head syce, the man with wife trouble, was responsible for the camels. After a talk with the warden and the offer of an extra shilling or two, he had after all agreed to come along as far as the forestry station. By name, Munta, he walked for the most part by himself, rarely joining in the general chatter. Perhaps his thoughts were elsewhere; he had reason enough. He proved a splendid camelman. I noticed not only that he walked alone, he seemed to be talking to himself. He spoke Samburu. The words trilled and clicked and the phrases ended in a little uplift of the voice, as if each were attached to a question mark. Munta kept the camels quiet by chatting to them and they invariably brightened up when he was about. For the rest, I had a young Turkana cook and an old man, an assistant camel leader called Goiti, who was so unobtrusive that for days on end I forgot he was there.

We stopped for the second time about midday. The sun burned down high and bright. I felt as fresh as they come but I became a little anxious about the track. The Ol Canto had narrowed to a defile with steep sides, overhung with black rock; oppressive country by any reckoning. No sound except for an occasional echoing cough from the baboons on the hillside. Overhead an eagle hung like a cross nailed to the sky.

At two o'clock I realized we had reached the crest of the shoulder but, instead of the gentle downward slope I had hoped for, it looked as if the plains ahead were at least fifteen hundred feet below. The warden had said the going would be easy and the open flowing contours of the map confirmed this. Thinking there might be an easy way down invisible to me, I sought Lelean's advice.

He was voluble and reassuring although there was much he said that I didn't understand. Yet there was anxiety in his voice when he suggested, largely by gestures, that the two of us should go ahead and look for an alternative trail. The camels, he said, would follow. As I saw it, there was little else we could do unless we all turned back.

I am not by nature a chatty person, certainly not in a strange tongue and after about ten minutes our slender reserve of small talk about the heat (very hot) and the baboons (much noise) expired. Lelean seemed to be fascinated by the fact that I wore canvas tennis shoes. This was something I could talk about. I explained, laboriously, that on this safari I intended to wear nothing else. He bent down, fingered the soles and said they were good and very strong but the canvas, he thought, was not strong enough for a man with feet as soft as mine. With a stabbing movement of his forefinger he indicated where I was liable to be pierced by thorns. This had occurred to me and on the way up to the pass I had experimented, cautiously, by walking through one or two low-lying acacia bushes. The shoes seemed resilient enough. But good or bad, I was committed. After trying out various sorts of footwear I had put my faith in Thesiger who recommended canvas shoes without socks. I had bought a dozen pairs in Nairobi, numbered them and intended to wear a different pair each day. Lelean seemed impressed by a white man with twelve pairs of shoes but he was sorry, he said, that I had wasted my money. Until I remembered that the Samburu are usually on the make his comments both worried and depressed me. I felt better when he mentioned in a roundabout way that if I decided to wear something more substantial, the men would be glad to have them.

The track got worse. The pass opened out a little. In places there were alternative paths, but they tended to run parallel where herdsmen had tried to avoid the massive rocks and gravel screes swept down the mountain by the floods of the previous year.

What worried me was the absence of any appreciable slope: the plains were still far below us. It was clear that at some point we should have to descend.

We reached the lip of the cliff at half-past two. The track turned abruptly. Suddenly, as if curtains had been swept aside, we seemed to be looking over the edge of the world. The frontier plains stretched out towards Ethiopia, a boundless expanse of sand and lava dust, broken only by the wrecks of ancient volcanoes, some with exquisite breast-like cones, straight-sided and nippled with rosettes of magma; others had been worn down by the winds until, like the flat backs of a school of whales, they seemed to be swimming away, line astern, across a sea of sand.

Fascinated as I was by the devastated landscape I became morbidly conscious that, somehow, five men, seven camels and fourteen hundred pounds of baggage had to be inched down the side of a cliff.

At least the way down could be seen; it was a zig-zag track which began at our feet and ended on the banks of a stream far below. The remains of the old track curved away to the right. It curved gently, following the contours of the hill – a splendid track in all respects except that the middle portion had been carried away by a landslide. I looked at Lelean who shrugged his shoulders and said nothing until the camels arrived.

During the descent I winced each time I heard an agonized roar. The sound usually came from places far above us where Munta was leading four camels and Karo three. The camels roared whenever their spindly legs and heavily-cushioned feet became jammed between boulders or scraped by rocks. Most of the hangers-on from the village had left us at the top of the pass, but on Lelean's advice I retained four of the toughest at a shilling

25

a head to act as road-makers on the way down. The procedure was simple in practice but desperately slow and calculated eventually to cripple the animals unless the going improved lower down.

Somehow we had to get the boulders out of the way. Some had been washed down by the rains and blocked the track. A few were pushed over the edge to the prejudice of Lelean and myself who were usually somewhere below, marking the trail. But the majority of the rocks had been buried for centuries and the task of getting over or around them was made doubly difficult since they were buttressed by screes of pebbles carried down by flood-wakes.

The road gang filled in the crevices with small stones and put larger ones on top. If the ramps were firm enough the camels could be hauled over them, forcibly, by a great deal of tugging and thrashing. But if the gaps between the rocks were too wide or too deep to be filled in, as they often were, the camels had to be persuaded to step from one rock to another. It was like leading a drunk over dangerous stepping stones. Each footfall was an event. One man held the head rope; another pushed, gently, from behind. The camels groaned, deeply, sepulchrally – they had an impressive vocabulary of groans – and then ponderously, uncertainly, they staggered forward until the obstacle was overcome and we could jog along the path to the next pile of rock. Seldom was there more than ten minutes of easy going between obstacles.

Munta got us out of some of the worst of our difficulties. On one fearful occasion a camel mounted a ramp, swayed precariously at the top and fell into an unseen hole below. It remained upright, suspended by its load, but its legs appeared to be pinned in a narrow crack between two slabs of rock. The creature bellowed piteously, the more so because the men thrashed it from behind and hauled on a head-rope that was already stained with frothy blood.

Munta became indignant. He pushed the men aside and began to soothe the beast by stroking its neck and talking to it, rapidly. It ceased to bellow but it stretched its neck forward until, like an immense turtle, it rested with its chin on a rock. It sighed deeply and I thought it was dying. Munta made a clicking noise with his tongue, the noise used to make a camel stand up. It heaved a little but soon subsided again. Two men untied the burden and Munta strove to get beneath the animal. By tugging on a twisted leg and shoving under its massive breastbone, he induced the camel to rise unsteadily. But only on three legs. It looked as if the knee of the forelimb had been crushed.

I wondered if I would have to shoot the animal and, if so, whether it would be better to use the shot gun or the rifle. And if I shot it, what should we do with the meat? It was extremely doubtful whether the remaining animals could carry any extra sacks, let alone a dismembered fellow. This gruesome train of thought was broken by a piercing whistle from the injured beast. Munta had pulled the bent limb down to the ground. It was straight and by something just short of a miracle, the camel not only stood on its four legs but was able to walk with no more than a slight limp. Pausing only to reload we struggled on, sending scouts ahead to look for the next obstacle.

Towards sundown Lelean pointed to a green patch some hundreds of yards below, where a small plateau led into a sub-sidiary valley. He thought we might camp there; at least it would be a convenient place for a rest. Through glasses it looked inviting. The animals were desperately tired and the roars that echoed through the hills had given way to low, mournful bellows, like a distant herd of cattle. In addition to being thrashed and hauled along on tight ropes they had to be repeatedly couched and raised again as the loads were tightened or re-adjusted.

Camels, it can be seen from a glance, are heavily made at the front; they have huge heads and muscular necks but they are somewhat feeble about the hindquarters. Such natural dispro-portion tends to make them pitch forward when they walk, especially on a downhill track. To rectify the balance, Munta had lashed down most of the burdens with a bias towards their tails. When the animals were plodding downhill they were in fine trim but when they staggered up the ramps their loads tended to slip off their backs.

I found Munta reloading the leading camel when I walked back to tell him that with any luck we should be resting within an hour. At least, that is what I should have liked to have said. What emerged was 'We rest little close by', he nodded without looking up and went on tying elegant knots in a piece of plaited bark rope. I tended to forget how tired the men were; I tended to forget how tired I was myself.

The last incident of an eventful day occurred when we were within sight of camp and mindful only of food and rest. We had been without food for more than ten hours. The green patch proved to be a dry watercourse, almost at the foot of the pass. Karo was singing; some of my kitchenware was still beating out a resonant *tonkitty-tonk* and it looked as if the worst of the Ol Canto was over. I thought we had found an excellent place to camp but Lelean seemed anxious, first because there was no browse for the camels and second, and more ominously, because he had noticed an abundance of elephant droppings under the trees. Karo arrived first with three animals and started to untie a precariously balanced load. He worked fast. Thirty yards of rope had to be disentangled from the crossed sticks and loads. He laid a sack containing a tin box on the ground and began to untie a kitbag, a folding table and chair and a roll of groundsheets. Suddenly he stopped, lifted his finger and looked at me. A metallic call of *tek-tek-tek* came from the bushes beneath the trees. He had heard guinea-fowl. As I fumbled for a cartridge, Lelean slipped off behind the trees to drive the birds out into the open where I should be able to catch them on the wing. Events thereafter became somewhat confused.

Lelean disappeared. The twittering ceased. I pushed the safety catch forward and crept towards the tallest tree but instead of the expected flutter of birds, a big bull elephant strode out of the bushes. It saw me. It raised its trunk and screamed, shrilly. There was no mistaking its intention. It was scared and it promptly turned and made off.

But if the elephant was scared, the camel standing half undressed among a mound of gear was terrified. It reared up and rushed off towards the far side of the dry river bed with a length of rope and a box trailing from one leg. At a point where it tried to climb out of the gully, it tripped and fell over, with its legs splayed out like a star-fish.

Karo pulled the rope clear of its thrashing legs but though it repeatedly jerked its neck up in the air, not even Munta could make it stand up. Watching where he lightly massaged the animal,

I gathered that if a bone was not actually broken, the shoulder had been badly sprained.

In camp that night, the first of nearly a hundred I spent in the bush, I was too tired to write more than fragmentary notes in my diary. It became an inventory of first experiences ending '. . . one lamp broken, one camel lame, one probably crippled and one day done'.

Ordeal By Combat

I awoke to the unfamiliar sound of doves. The birds murmured so contentedly that I lay abed, enjoying the comfort and thinking about the disordered events of the previous day. They might have happened a long time ago. I believe I was happier and more care-free than I had been since I arrived in Africa. This was largely because the men seemed quite competent to handle any situation that arose.

Looking back I know now that I was unnecessarily concerned about being asked for an opinion on things I knew little about. It took me some time to realize that I would not be asked 'What shall we do now?' The question was too complicated to put into Swahili. When minor crises arose, and they arose more often than I care to remember, Lelean wanted no more than a confir-mation of his own opinion. With raised eyebrows and partly outstretched hands, he would say 'Yes?' I gave up trying to think of a choice phrase. Pausing only as if considering all aspects of the matter I usually answered 'N'dio – yes'. Thanks to Lelean leadership was not as difficult as I had imagined. I sniffed at the air and wriggled back among the sheets.

Listening to the gentle *doo-doo-doo* of the doves, I thought about how we had pitched camp the previous night. As we lurched in at dusk there seemed to be a dozen ways in which the camp could be laid out in relation to the hobbled camels, the fires, the men's lines and my tent; yet once I had agreed to the site suggested at the foot of an isolated tree, the tent sprang up, un-bidden, with two men lashing it down outside and two within. Mezek the cook arranged my own gear. He unroped the boxes and laid out groundsheets, table, chair and a washbowl on a tripod. While this was being done I sat on an upturned box, sipped a Scotch and watched the fires being lit, downwind. Within a quarter of an hour the ground was cleared of scrub and the camel mats piled up on the poles of the harness until they resembled an Indian tepee.

As far as I can recall that first night I gave only three or four orders: one concerned the camel mats; I wanted them stored even further away from my tent as they were wet with sweat and attracting clouds of flies. I also took command of the jerrican because the men wasted water. This done I ordered dinner: roast guinea fowl on a large plate of rice, a tin of tangerines with cream and two cups of coffee. The bird was a parting gift from the warden at Wamba.

'Jambo!'

Mezek brought me back to the realities of the day with a pot of tea. I returned his greeting and listened without much attention to what he was saying. It sounded as if the camels had run away during the night. I stared at him incredulously.

'Run away! Where?'

He shrugged his shoulders and repeated that they had gone. As there was a suggestion of a smile on his face, I slipped on a pair of shorts and walked out into the camp with no particular sense of apprehension. In some ways I was surprised by my own complacency. For days I had thought about very little else except the camels; I should not have been in the least surprised to learn that one of them had died. Instead, they had run away. Doubtlessly we should find them or someone would bring them back. That was the way things were on safari.

Lelean related briefly what had happened. The animals had been penned up in a *boma* built of thick branches of thorn scrub. Because they were tired and two were lame they had not been hobbled. At one point in the fence they had found some fresh green leaves and had promptly eaten their way out. Five were missing; the two sick beasts were still squatting down, dribbling and moo-ing, mournfully, like cows. By pattering his fingers on his arm, Mezek indicated that the old man Goiti was running after the fugitives and, no doubt, would soon be back. At least he hoped so. I hoped so, too. But in the soft, lemon-coloured light of that first morning I was not unduly concerned about anything connected with misfortune.

Goiti drove them in as I was shaving from a mug of coffee-coloured water (we were drawing on local supplies) and I began to rehearse what I should say to him. Clearly an occasion for a dressing down but as I held up the unused hobbles I could think of nothing better to say than 'This is bad. This is *very* bad.' Convinced as I was that life on the whole was pretty good I said it with no particular conviction. I lit a cheroot and gave the order to move.

By eleven o'clock we had covered about six miles. The going was irksome rather than arduous. We slouched over a plain dotted with little prickly bushes, rather like low gorse. The prickles raised a network of scratches around my bare ankles and I was obliged to hop and skip in the manner of a Scottish reel. This rather amused the men and irritated me.

The camels were extremely tired. The injured beast had an atrocious limp but managed to stagger along without a load on its back – it was a relief to find that it could walk. The other animals bellowed whenever the headropes tightened; two of them repeatedly flopped down on their elbows and had to be thrashed to their feet. I changed the leading animal several times in the hope of finding a beast which could be led rather than dragged along. As Lelean assured me that we should reach at least two wells before nightfall, I ordered the men to pour away sixteen gallons of water. I was sorry to lose good water, but it reduced the loads by nearly a hundred and seventy pounds. Behind us Waraguess still dominated the horizon, but it was behind and not in front and the Ol Canto pass was out of sight.

During the afternoon we came across an immense caravan, slowly winding ahead, like a trail of ants. They were Samburu moving towards their dry season grazing grounds in the Losai Hills. The tribesmen were accompanied by more cattle, sheep and goats than I had ever seen before. A few camels jogged along but they were not of a kind I should have cared to hire, even to supplement our own; they were scrawny beasts, emaciated by the loss of blood which is drawn from them once a week and drunk mixed with milk. Each family walked beside its own donkeys to which they had lashed everything lashable. As we drew near I peered inside the panniers on the donkeys' backs. The uprights were distinctive objects, made of wood and thongs, not unlike two snowshoes, one on each side of the animal's flanks and joined at a point above its back, in such a way that it gave the impression of a big tent.

Inside these contraptions babies howled, goats bleated and puppies yapped. All the inmates were trussed like chickens, immovable except for their wobbling heads. When I tried to take a photograph of living cargo mixed up with mats and cooking pots, the indignant father dragged the donkey along so fast that I feared for the safety of the child's wildly wobbling head. One blind old woman stumbled along with head bowed, her hand on her daughter's shoulder; another dragged a foot that was almost severed at the ankle; it left an almost circular impression in the red earth. I had the feeling that if either of them had stopped they would have been left alone, probably to die. The caravan swept on with a disturbing sense of urgency. 'Over endless plains, stumbling in cracked earth. Ringed by the flat horizons only.'

The Samburu are a curious people. Closely related to the Masai in almost everything including hypertrophy of the ego, they are exceptionally good-looking, arrogant and lazy. Condemned to a life of incessant wandering they take their leisure seriously, existing for days on the principle of least effort. When I met the Samburu alone I sometimes had the impression that they were staring at me but their eyes showed that they were staring forward and I happened to be in the way. Like the Masai, the tribal braves or *morans* of the Samburu crop their hair except for a top-knot on the crown which is usually decorated with a bobbing feather. They also plaster themselves with brick-red pigments and stand with one leg curled around the other, leaning on their spears. The Masai have a splendid contempt for almost everything that can be lumped together under the name of civilization but the same cannot be said of an increasing number of Samburu, who, through contact with insidious tourism, are becoming understandably avaricious.

Nobody seems to know where these so-called Nilo-Hamites came from or when they swept down, conquering every tribe they met on the way. With their straight noses and thin lips they look like dark Europeans and one theory is that they entered Africa from the eastern end of the Mediterranean, possibly inter-marrying with the northern negroes. Until the British took away their shields – but, significantly, not their spears – the Masai were among the greatest warriors in East Africa. The Samburu were almost certainly fighters, too, but they broke away from the

Masai – the word *Samburu* means 'butterfly' – and settled in the vicinity of Lake Rudolf.

They have remained there ever since, moving up into the hills during the dry season and coming down again for the rains. It has been suggested that by burning the bush and over-grazing the meagre vegetation the pastoralists are responsible for the present desolation of the Northern Frontier District. This seems a most unlikely explanation for an enormous expanse of waste land. North Kenya has probably suffered from a widespread change towards arid conditions and if the land continues to be neglected as badly as it is today, it is possible that the whole of Kenya will be reduced to a desert.

The Samburu wound over the top of a hill and disappeared from sight with a tinkling of camel bells. It was sad to think that they might be the last of their race but, like the Red-men of North America, they need more space than governments are prepared to give them. Pastoralism is an expansive means of livelihood and the last resort of a doomed race. We crossed their tracks about two days later. I should not have known who they were, but among the evidence of a large number of sheep and cattle Karo showed me the distinctive circular footprints of the maimed old woman.

We began to look for a camping site about four o'clock in the afternoon. As it was not too hot and I had become adept at skipping over acacia bushes, I wanted to march on for at least another hour, but Lelean had his mind on the camels. He emphasized that one was sick, another lame and all of them 'wanted to lala'. This seemed insufficient reason for a halt of more than a few minutes but feeling that I might have misunderstood him, I looked the word up. It means 'to rest or sleep'.

The best place for a *lala* seemed to be a patch of bare ground about the size of a football pitch. Almost entirely surrounded by prickly scrub, I wondered whether it might not be perhaps too bare. It looked like the sort of place where we should find rhinoceros. Nevertheless, as Lelean had chosen the site, it remained only for me to select a spot for my tent. Remembering the routine of the previous evening, I went through the motions of testing the wind with a pinch of dust and dug my heel into the ground at a point where I would be upwind of the camels and the cookhouse fire. The men, as usual, did the rest.

One of the camels wandered into the middle of the arena, shuffled its back legs and began to urinate, prodigiously. Almost immediately a column of large black ants poured out of a hole in the damp earth and hurried off, presumably in search of drier quarters. When another camel started to scratch itself like a fox terrier we found an ant column underneath its belly; as we began to debate whether we should reload and move on somewhere else, at least two other columns emerged from the ground and that settled it.

Lelean found a new site nearby. It was still on bare ground and I was not particularly enthusiastic about his choice but after repeatedly digging a stick into the ground, he assured me that the site was a hundred per cent ant-free. *Kabissa*, as he put it. Leaving the men to erect the tent for the second time that evening, I walked over to inspect the ants on the abandoned plot.

Five bands of vicious-looking creatures scuttled backwards and forwards like armoured columns, looking for a weak point to attack. The bands were about two yards in length with big-jawed soldiers on the outside and workers between them. The marauders were army ants or *siafu*, probably the most formidable insects in Africa. They have been known to devour a large python which was so gorged after a meal that it could not escape. A warden had told me that if a horse is left tethered among these ants it will be eaten and left a skeleton where it stands. This may or may not be true. In the Congo some years ago I met a Wanande hunter who owed his life to the fact that if a soldier ant once closes its pincer-like jaws on a piece of skin it is very difficult to prise them apart.

This was on the western flank of the Ruwenzori, the range known as the Mountains of the Moon. The hunter had been employed as a guide. At supper one night I noticed that his upper arm was furrowed by a scar which stretched from his shoulder to his elbow. The story, as he told it, was that he had been walking through a forest track some miles from his village when a leopard sprang out and pinned his dog to the ground. The hunter lunged at the leopard with his spear and wounded it but before the animal made off it raked him with its claws. Blood poured from a large, loose flap of skin below his shoulder. Realizing he was in danger of bleeding to death, the hunter looked round until he found a trail of army ants. By holding the big-jawed specimens over the wound, one by one, he induced them to close their pincers on the flap of skin, in such a way that they clasped the edges of the wound together. Once the bodies had been nipped off, he was left with a row of 'stitches' composed of ants' jaws.

The *siafu* of the Congo are forest ants, existing in hordes a hundred thousand strong. Those at my feet were desert nomads, smaller in numbers but equally fierce. They have no permanent nests. They never settle down. Like the Huns and the Tartars, they sally forth on one raid after another. The *siafu* are an outstanding example of a society which has defied the law that says that no large association of individuals can exist exclusively as carnivores. Because they literally clean up their hunting grounds they are condemned to incessant nomadism; they are constantly obliged to seek fresh territory. *Siafu* pause only to raise their young. Every thirty or forty days, depending on the species, the queens lay a large batch of eggs. The legions come to a halt and forage locally, tending the new-born larvae. Within a short time, the ranks are reinforced by more young adults and the whole army moves off once again, as if under the influence of some mighty force stronger than themselves. It would be accurate to describe their nomadism as blind destiny because, although the ants sometimes cover great distances on their foraging raids, the majority of them are blind. The men pointed out that each column was led by one or two diminutive ants which they called *kiongozi* or guides. My impression was that the columns were not composed of individuals; they were the cells of a restless super-insect which, for want of a better word, we call the colony. Further speculation on this point was interrupted by a shout from Lelean.

Two men were inside the tent, holding up the poles while Lelean and Karo hammered in the pegs from the outside. They had evidently stirred up yet another colony of ants which promptly bit the feet of the men inside. The canvas sagged and the whole tent began to plunge and rear like a circus horse before it finally collapsed and the men inside scrambled out.

After two attempts at sharing living space with the *siafu* we gave up and pitched camp among some acacia bushes. They might scratch but they couldn't bite.

At five o'clock that afternoon Lelean suggested that we should hold a *baraza*, a public pow-wow. From the hang-dog way in which he looked over his shoulder towards the men's lines I suspected that he wanted support for something he was not prepared to ask on his own. Reminding him he was headman and that it was his job to speak for them all, I asked him what he wanted.

Out of a long rambling speech I managed to extract only three words. The men (*watu*) were hungry or, more literally, they had no food (*hapana chakula*). A pause while I tried to remember the word for 'why'.

'Kwa nini hapana chakula?'

The unexpected answer was 'because of the elephants'. Lelean explained that when the camel had tripped up the previous night it had rolled over on the men's ration bags. They had lost their *posho* (maize meal). This sounded highly improbable. I had doled out two day's ration which, as far as I could remember, they kept in separate bags. However, the effort of unravelling the problem was scarcely worth the sum involved. The men's basic rations cost about five shillings a day. I said that in future all rations would be handed out on a weekly basis. If they lost them they could not expect any more.

'Call the men!'

They lined up and I gave each man seven pounds of *posho*, two pounds of sugar, a quarter of a pound of tea and a small portion of fat. I repeated the little speech about everyone looking after their own food and asked if they wanted anything else.

An idiotic question. In a chorus they said they wanted more food. They had to work hard. More than anything else they wanted some vegetables and by vegetables (*m'boga*) they meant meat, that is something which could be added to a bowl of *posho*. They reminded me that I had agreed to give them at least one animal a week.

'No animals here,' I said firmly.

Another stupid remark. 'Yes,' they chorused. 'Yes, yes, yes!' Lelean had cunningly chosen a site where there was a great deal of game. Everyone – everyone, that is, except myself – had seen a group of gazelle on a nearby hill. I looked at them with profound distaste. Through field-glasses I also spotted a couple of oryx, a group of unidentifiable antelopes and a small herd of zebra. I put the field-glasses down and nodded, sadly. It was quite clear that I had been pushed into the vegetable-shooting business.

I take no pleasure in recalling subsequent events and intend to relate them as briefly as possible.

First, the approach: it took us about a quarter of an hour to get within four hundred yards of the gazelle. Lelean loped ahead with the rifle; Karo followed him carrying the shotgun and a sharp *panga*; I did my best to keep up with them.

Second, the surprising fact that we made little or no attempt to seek cover. Both men crouched as they ran but they seemed quite unconcerned by the fact that the animals had spotted us. We reached a straggly tree, the only substantial piece of cover within sight. Lelean handed me the rifle and whispered 'Shoot quickly!'

I shook my head. The range was about three hundred yards and far beyond my competence. Banging away on a rifle range before I left for Africa, I had acquired a distinctly limited skill. The sights of the Winchester had been zeroed at a hundred yards. With a little lift and a lot of luck I might have increased the range by half, but three times the distance was out of the question. I said 'Too far. No good.' Whatever happened during the rest of the safari, I was anxious to hit something with my first shot.

The men looked so disappointed that I looked around for ways of getting within range. A gully led off to the right. With any luck I could get into it unseen. Telling the men to wait, I pulled back the safety catch and set off on a distinctly uncomfortable stalk.

After a great deal of crawling about I closed the distance to about a hundred and fifty yards. I had my eye on a big animal, a buck with a fine spread of horns. By poking the rifle through the lower branches of a bush, I reckoned that I should be able to hit it in the shoulder. Putting on my spectacles, I peered at the animal. It seemed blurred and curiously distorted. My glasses were misty. More fiddling about. I cleaned them; I got the buck in the sights for the second time and squeezed. Nothing happened. Dreadful feeling. I had forgotten to release the safety catch. In pushing it forward I made a slight noise. The buck slewed round until it was facing me.

I squeezed again. Tremendous crash. My glasses fell off and from the puff of dust I realized my shot had gone wide. The animals promptly plunged off into the bush.

Lelean ran up, excited and somewhat indignant. He said it had been quite wrong of me to crawl up the gully. The animals became wary and had time to spot the hunter. Sketching on the ground with his forefinger, he explained that one should approach the animal obliquely, drop behind a bush or a tree and fire without hesitation. As the gazelle were still within sight, I handed over the gun and stood aside to see how it was done.

On the whole his performance was worse than mine; instead of missing once Lelean missed four times, and emptied the magazine. Through field-glasses I watched him lope forward like a dog; I began to appreciate his point about the oblique approach. With little or no cover it was necessary to lull the animals' suspicions and give them the impression that the hunter was about to pass them by. When he reached a bush about two hundred yards from a buck, he knelt down and fired. The shot went wide. It was possibly more accurate than my own attempt at a lesser range but it was still undoubtedly a miss. His second shot raised a cloud of dust ahead of the galloping animals and his third and fourth attempts at long-range bombardment were even less accurate.

The score was five shots with nothing to show for it. I was anxious to supply the expedition with meat, even if I had an occasional miss. On the other hand, I had no wish to cripple what I fired at and I certainly had no compunction about handing the rifle over to Lelean if he were a better shot than I was. It looked as if the problem could be settled only by some competitive target practice.

I pinned four pages of my notebook against the trunk of a tree with thorns and we hammered away at it, four shots each, at a hundred paces. I got three indifferent inners after correcting from a bad miss and Lelean missed four times. What I did not realize at the time was that bullets carried in the unprotected magazine of a rifle get hot and tend to fly high when fired. What I had established was that I could shoot slightly better than Lelean. There was no enthusiasm about our return to camp, empty handed. I ate a tin of corned beef. The men boiled up a few handfuls of dried camel meat. It looked dreadful.

The Samburu Woman

At the end of the third day it was obvious that the injured camel could no longer keep up with us. It lurched about like a drunk and when it fell down it was difficult to get it up. Camels rise by throwing their weight forward in the manner of an elderly person rising from a chair. The head is thrust forward with a jerk until the whole weight of the animal is balanced on the hard pad at the base of the chest. This enables it to lift its hindquarters into the air. It then unfolds one of its forelegs until the foot is flat on the ground and it can heave itself up.

Munta, the camel man, was gentle with the sick animal. Instead of giving it a clout with a stick or a kick in the hindquarters, as the other men did, he talked it into rising and helped it with a push from the rear. Even so it groaned deeply and the groan rose to a throaty roar as it transferred its weight to its front legs. Some bone or joint in its shoulder was either broken or badly strained. I had thought that if it were relieved of its burden for a few days and allowed to amble along at the end of the column, snatching a bit of browse here and there, it might recover sufficiently to carry one or two of the lighter loads. But it was either unwilling or unable to walk for more than two or three hours at a stretch. Thereafter, it flopped down and showed every sign of taking a prolonged *lala*. With no burden on its back, a camel can fold up, rigidly, like a camp bed or a trussed chicken. The invalid was particularly adept at curling up and repeatedly brought the column to a standstill. The question was whether to stop for a few days and give the animal a complete rest or march on without it.

Munta thought that if the beast were to be given the rest it required, we should have to stop for at least a week. I turned to Lelean. He suggested that we should ignore the forestry station up in the hills and make for the big waterhole at Rodosoit where it had been arranged that we should pick up a fresh string of animals. I asked him how long it would take us to march to Rodosoit. He thought about two days: it was not very far. Alternatively, he said he could march to Rodosoit with one or two men and bring the fresh string back to the camp. Listening to the proposals, I was aware that I was becoming something more than a supernumerary, accidentally endowed with the role of leadership; I was taking at least some part in the ordering of day-to-day affairs, that is without having to rehearse a command or wait for the opinion of others. In the exhilaration of the moment I probably made a number of decisions more hastily than I should have done.

The most disturbing news was that Munta, the man who understood camels, wanted to go home. I tried to persuade him to stay and hinted that there would be a lot of *bakshishi* when the journey was over. But he was adamant; the woman in Wamba was still on his mind. Holding up five fingers he indicated that in five days he would be back where no red-painted rival could slip in unawares. Eventually we agreed that he should take the injured camel back to a nearby Samburu *manyatta* where it would be left in charge of a man who was responsible to the Veterinary Department from whom it had been hired. I paid him off and gave him food for the journey. A brief handshake and a wave concluded the deal. With six beasts in reasonably good condition for short hauls we once more made our way due east across the prickly thornbush.

The midday halt brought us into hummocky country, relieved by clumps of fresh-green bushes with pendulous branches resembling cascade willows. The boys called them 'the food of the rhino' and hinted that they should be given a wide berth. When the march was resumed at three o'clock I carried a shotgun, intent on making amends for the sorry outcome of the previous day's hunt. Lelean accompanied me as guard and guide and we walked about a half a mile ahead of the rest of the column.

Later during our long journey I used to look back with longing on our days on the edge of the mountains and wish that I could see something less harsh than endless horizons of sand and lava dust. But there in the shadows of the Matthews I wanted to get to grips with the desert. We had crossed the mountains. As I understood it from Lelean, the next obstacle was the lava wall around the south end of the lake where the winds from Mount Kulal blew for days on end. The early explorers had told how their pack animals had been bowled over by gusts of up to eighty miles an hour. I wanted to get to the wall as quickly as I could and put it behind me. It was not that I was tired of the mountains; it was disappointing to know that for three days the relationship of the peaks behind us had remained unchanged; it looked as if we had made virtually no progress.

There were guinea-fowl ahead. I recognized the metallic group call and hurried towards the sound. Unfortunately, the birds saw us before we got within easy range and a flock of some thirty or forty bounced out of the top of one of the rhino bushes. The flock parted in mid-air; one group planed to earth not far to our left while the others flapped off furiously, grinding out protestations. I took a chance on a long shot and got one full in the breast but missed a second. 'Very bad,' said Lelean. I glanced at him. His face was expressionless.

The dead bird was a helmeted guinea-fowl. The ridiculously small head was topped with a horn which gave it a grotesque appearance, like Punch. But the starlight stipple of the powdery blue plumage was superb. Lelean's interest in the bird was more practical. He felt the breast bone, said it was a youngster and hoped I would shoot several more. After chasing the scattered flock for about half an hour I managed to bag another one and by then it was apparent that Lelean had lost the way. 'Very bad,' I said drily, but the irony was lost on him; with his head down like a fox-hound, he quartered the ground, looking for our own tracks in an effort to retrace our steps. It was not difficult (for Lelean) to point out where we had walked but it was both tiring and irritating to go back over the encircling movements of the bird chase. Eventually we reached a point where we had to decide whether to go back to where we had parted company with the camels or strike across country in the hope of intercepting the caravan. We struck across the country.

During that brilliant sunlit afternoon I had my first experience of keeping out of the way of animals in the wild. Up to that point we had kept to plainly marked trails. Here it was a question of making a trail of our own. Lelean set the pace and took the lead. He was normally a fast walker and I was somewhat disconcerted to find that in his efforts to catch up with the others he sometimes broke into a trot. It was noticeable, too, that, although he was making for a rocky mound on a crest ahead where he hoped to get a view of the whole plain, his path was far from straight. He made elaborate detours round clumps of trees and dense scrub. On several occasions he promptly moved off a path where tracks showed it had recently been used by rhino and once he pointed to where a beast had rubbed its horns against the red column of a termites' nest. As a farmer might show a townsman over his stockyard, he indicated places where we might encounter buffalo or elephant; through bushes I got a fleeting glimpse of the horns of waterbuck; the animals themselves were usually invisible, at least they were to me.

I noticed that very few animals roamed through the bush at random; by far the majority seemed to be confined to tracks as rigidly defined as a set of railway lines. It was equally evident that no one could ensure against the possibility of the totally unexpected encounter. We had a ludicrous illustration of this when I was jerked out of a totally irrelevant train of thought by a prodigious snort from the middle of a thicket. Lelean spun round, slammed a round into the breech of the rifle and half crouched with the weapon cocked. But instead of being charged, a frightened bushpig scuttled out of the far side of the thicket and made off, its tail high in the air. Only once were we confronted with an animal that showed the least sign of aggression, and that was a rhino at a distance of about a hundred yards. Lelean stopped abruptly, pointed at it and motioned to me to be quiet.

The beast stood with its back to us. There was a chance that we might have sneaked off unseen but the animal either heard us or got wind of us and spun round on its back legs with the agility of a boxer. I was surprised by the delicacy of its footwork. Lelean immediately began to talk to it. I don't know what he said, but it was clear that he told it to go away quietly and I was considerably relieved when the animal lowered its head and trotted off.

What would have happened if we had met the animal at close quarters I can only guess, but my feeling is that it would have charged only if it were injured or if we had stood in its way. By far the principal occupation of all animals in the wild lies in finding safety. Flight, not aggression, is the dominant reaction and the one to which sex and hunger are subordinate. The desire for food or a mate can be put aside. An effective flight has to be undertaken at once; the alternative is often death and most, if not all, animals spend a great deal of their time in fleeing from man, the most destructive animal of all. Gazelle ran away when we got within two hundred yards; they were in the open and unprotected. With more cover at hand, the waterbuck were less shy and allowed us to approach within seventy or eighty yards; some of the smaller antelopes, especially the little dik-diks, were even more tolerant.

The distances at which animals begin to run away are called flight-distances. They are less self-evident than they appear to be. Lelean could judge some of them to within twenty or thirty yards; competent animal trainers know them to within a few feet. These distances are among the most important laws of survival.

The bush or the forest is a mosaic of strictly defined prowling grounds in which each kind of animal has its own place. The pig we disturbed was under a thicket; it might have shared the shade with a rhino but not with an animal that habitually rooted about in the ground and certainly not with a flesh eating animal. During the day the killers either keep out of the way or else, like lions, they loll about in the open, entirely disregarded by their prey until they stretch themselves at dusk and start to hunt.

Animals rarely fight; they kill to eat and although they challenge each other during the mating season, the aggression is ritualized into a bluffing match in which the weaker give way to their betters. However, I doubt if I should be able to write with such confidence about the innate fearfulness of animals in the wild if I had been in the bush on my own. The confidence came from Lelean. Knowing that I was interested in the movements of animals he began to show me what he could do.

We had been walking for about an hour when he discovered a young buffalo under a tree. It was a cheerful little fellow, almost fully grown but not old enough to show much sign of aggression. As we were in a patch of open country and there were no signs of any other members of the herd, Lelean began to walk towards it. The buffalo promptly slipped into the shade of the tree and peered at us, anxiously. We were inside the flight-distance. When we got within a hundred yards the animal seemed to be trying to make up its mind whether to run away from the shelter of the tree or fight it out. It lowered its head as if to charge. When Lelean stopped it raised its head and looked even more puzzled. By taking a single pace backwards or forwards, Lelean seemed to be exercising complete control over its defensive reactions. Watching him, I was reminded vividly of the famous animal trainers of the circus world, expecially those who perform with lions and tigers. From the spectators' point of view it looks as if the trainers are either giving verbal commands or exercising some mesmeric influence over the animals. In fact, they are drawing on their immense knowledge of the reactions of animals towards an aggressor. When they advance within the limited flight-distance of the circus ring, the animals retreat. When they can retreat no further, that is when they reach the far side of the ring or come up against the bars of the cage, the animals turn round and advance.

A great deal of nonsense has been written about the training of circus animals, especially the big cats. There is no brutality in flight-distance control. It enables animals to be led on to pedestals and induced to jump through hoops judiciously placed in their natural flight lines. Much of the trainer's whip-cracking and posturing is good showmanship, designed to impress the spectators. What is rarely appreciated is that although the animal trainer maintains a position of absolute authority, he never interferes with the animal's instinctive reactions and when two or more mutually aggressive animals, such as lions and tigers, are kept under control at the same time, the act becomes an orchestration of insight and artistry.

We left the puzzled young buffalo to work out the anomalies of the flight-distance for himself, and faced up to the fact that we were lost. It was apparent that Lelean, for all his skill, was not much good in country where he had neither tracks nor landmarks to guide him. After a somewhat uncomfortable half-hour in which we sought advice (unsuccessfully) from a young Samburu shepherd who was dandling a young Samburu shepherdess under a tree, the situation resolved itself by a spectacular upheaval of guinea-fowl.

About fifty birds rose into the air at our feet. I pulled down three by firing into the blue. It was almost impossible to miss. I reloaded and got two more. In the silence that followed came a faint shout from a point beyond a rocky mound ahead. Karo was calling. He was looking for us. He said the men had pitched camp near 'very good water' and with a glance at the seven birds he added that everyone would be very glad to see us.

As an example of good water a pool about the size of a village pond used by the Samburu as a cattle watering place was a distinct disappointment. Warm, frothy and of the colour and consistency of cocoa, the water was the filthiest I have seen outside a common sewer. To make matters worse the camels had already waded in and were adding to the dung floating on the surface. I ordered them out and told Lelean to dig a channel from which he drew off about a quart of something slightly less opaque than chicken soup. When I tried to filter it through a fanciful Swiss pump, the porcelain strainers clogged. Mezek watched the whole performance without comment before announcing that he had already drawn about a gallon from the middle of the pool to make tea. It was gritty but by no means unpleasant. I drank two quarts and tried to forget what I had been told about the dangers of dysentery.

Tea time was any time. Mezek usually brewed enough to fill at least two pint mugs for breakfast; he served up another quart during the midday halt and brought more when we pitched camp for the night. I drank about a gallon between dawn and dusk. Of all the sessions, I looked forward most to the sundowner. It was pleasant to look back on the events of the day and it was doubly pleasant to relax comfortably on a chair which, together with a little table, had become the possessions I valued most.

The chair was a folding affair made of aluminium tubes and some bright, red-striped plastic material. The warden in Wamba had told me that on safari it would be unlikely to last more than a week. It was certainly an awkward object to pack and I had given instructions that both the chair and the table were to be wrapped up in two thicknesses of sacking before they were lashed down with the rest of the loads. Had anything happened to either of them I should have felt that I had lost an intimate friend.

In camp that night I was obliged to display my meagre knowledge of medicine for the first time. It was about eight o'clock in the evening. The light of our huge fire had attracted little groups of Samburu from the adjacent *manyatta*. Most of them were *morans*, the tribal warriors who stalked across the compound with the dignity of cranes. They stuck their spears into the ground and sat down in front of the fires. As Lelean, Karo and Goiti were Samburu they could always rely on a supply of food whenever they encountered their fellow tribesmen. I was surprised that these impoverished people could afford to slaughter a sheep or a goat whenever a stranger turned up, but presumably the custom tended to even itself out in country where most of the able-bodied men spent most of the year on the move looking for fresh pastures; it certainly gave them an excuse for a feast. What I did not know was that Lelean had procured a large goat on the strength of my unproven skill as a medicine man. When I had finished dinner he brought the herdsman to the door of my tent. The man, he said, was 'very sick'. I tried to remember my homework.

'This sickness it is where?'

The man sighed and stroked his body from his forehead to his navel.

This was discouraging. I flicked over the pages of a dictionary, looking for the word for 'pain'. It was *uma* which also meant fork, sting or thorn.

'Have you a fork in your head?'

He shook his head.

'In your chest?'

No forks there.

'In your belly?'

His face brightened. Holding his hands over his bare stomach, he opened and closed his fingers spasmodically. He was transfixed with forks. 'Many, many,' he said. They were biting and clawing at him. They were very bad. He had had them for three days. Suspecting worms, I tried another tack.

'Much lavatory?'

He shook his head violently.

'No lavatory?'

He nodded and began a ludicrous mime in a crouching position which made it abundantly clear that he was suffering from acute constipation. I gave him a substantial dose of Epsom salts.

Four cases of diarrhoea received kaolin; the headaches got an aspirin each; I gave two sulpha tablets to an old man with many forks in his chest and much coughing while daubs of iodine sufficed for the superficial cuts and scratches.

From the purely manipulative point of view the most difficult case was a little chocolate-coloured piccaninny with enormous eyes who clung so tightly to his mother that I was obliged to treat him upside down. The father explained that the child had got a thorn in the ball of its heel. He had tried to cut it out with a piece of tin but had made a bad job of it. The mother unwrapped the child from a blanket but it refused to be detached from her warm, comforting bosom and I had to swivel it round on a nipple until one leg was high in the air. The child scarcely stirred as I tweezered out the thorn and put on a dab of iodine.

It soon became apparent that the ritual of treatment was as important as the remedy. After applying iodine with the dark blue wing feather of a guinea-fowl, I threw the feather aside and used a swab of bandage to paint the next patient. The man shook his head and pointed to the discarded feather. Not only had it a potency of its own but I was able to make even more of it by painting magical circles and crosses instead of merely dabbing the stuff on.

My last case was a woman called Malaya. She was of such outstanding beauty that I was somewhat taken aback when she sauntered into the little halo of yellow light from the oil lamp. I say sauntered because in her movements there was something of the casual grace of the trained mannequin. The illusion was heightened by her theatrical investment in a piece of cloth which was wrapped tightly around her thighs and fell in classical folds to her ankles. Apart from jewellery it was all she wore: the Malaya was copper-coloured, straight as a reed and bare from the waist upwards. The symmetry of her conical breasts was emphasized by the curved shadow of an enormous necklet of woven wire that hung over her shoulders. Her arms were held limply, but like a ballet dancer the fingers were curved as if to emphasize her figure. Lelean brought her forward but instead of saying what was the matter with her as he had done with the others, he whispered 'She is a Malaya' and gave the impression that there had been an argument about whether the woman had any right to join in the queue of patients.

For a moment or two she looked at me without speaking. Then she said she wanted medicine – not ordinary medicine but powerful *dawa* 'to bring a child'.

Not knowing what to say and feeling somewhat disconcerted about the whole business of quackery, I fobbed her off with a couple of bright red vitamin tablets. It was not until I asked questions about the girl the next day that I learnt that *malaya* meant whore.

Moon Over the Matthews

A safari, like any other form of prolonged exertion, is characterized by persistent *ordinariness* which is difficult to describe. George Orwell points out that autobiography is only to be trusted when it reveals something disgraceful. A man who gives a good account of himself is probably lying, since almost any kind of life when viewed from the inside is simply a series of defeats. During a very ordinary day's march between the cattle watering point and Rodosoit, the place where I hoped we should find the fresh camels waiting for us, I began to regard my apparent inability to use a rifle as a major defeat. The deficiency was driven home when the men pestered me to shoot anything within sight that moved. I shook my head when we came across herds of gazelle; they seemed to be miles away. When the men pointed out a solitary buck on the skyline I refused even to load the rifle. The animal looked as if it could run and the day was too hot for athletics. I was also feeling slightly unwell due, perhaps, to the soupy water drunk the previous day.

However, when two little sandgrouse leaped into the air almost at my feet, I went after them with the shotgun. After all, sport was sport and we needed something for the pot. Instead of flying off they circled round like toy aeroplanes. I took a swing at the nearer one when it was probably too far away and missed. I waited until both birds were not only in line but close enough to be hit with a brick. I missed again. 'Very bad', said Lelean. I glared at him and trudged after the camels. The birds had not even the decency to fly away.

At this point I should like to be able to say that I followed them and brought them down with a well-timed right and left. What actually happened is more prosaic.

After a great deal of twittering, the birds circled round once more and pitched down behind a bush. I ran after them and stood there, gun cocked, waiting for them to take off. Nothing happened. I peered over the top of the bush to find that they were bobbing up and down, billing and coo-ing. Did I tip-toe away from this touching little scene? I did not. I fired through the bush at point-blank range with both barrels and, to my surprise, got five birds. For a moment the air was alive with startled sandgrouse. The courting couple had alighted in the middle of a flock.

The landscape that morning was among the dreariest I have ever seen. We plodded up and down a series of bare ridges, littered with the charred stumps of trees. In the hope of raising a bit of grass, the vegetation had been fired by the Samburu. There was no grass, no scrub: nothing but a rubble of shattered rock that tinkled under the camels' feet. As we coasted down a slope resembling the spoil head of a colliery, one of the animals tripped and fell and began to dash its head against the ground. Goiti tried to restrain the frenzied creature and was knocked over as it thrashed its head from side to side. The fit was over in a few seconds and the camel rose to its feet, shivering violently. It was not badly hurt but I was obliged to paint an ugly gash under its ear with Dettol. Perhaps camels suffer from a Dettol-deficiency. The animal tried to lick off the antiseptic with some remarkable elongations of its tongue and what it couldn't reach was soon licked off by the others.

Ahead of us Rodosoit began to flash in the sun but far from being the spectacular place I had imagined from the bottom of the valley, it was a drab collection of mud huts on the top of a ridge of cinders in front of which the camels eventually flopped down. The daub walls of the *duka*, the local store, had crumbled to such an extent that the proprietor had patched them up with sheets of tin that flashed like a heliograph. Seen against a background of palm trees and distant hills, the squalor was somehow improbable and so, too, was our arrival; I had the feeling of being irrelevant to our surroundings. It was as if we had been at sea for a long time and no longer cared whether we reached a once long-sought harbour. And yet as I glanced at the dusty contents of the *duka* – the piles of blankets and sacks of sugar, the carbolic soap and the virility pills ('Rich gentilmens in Calcutta use nothing else') – I felt that we had at least got as far as Square

Two. Lelean reminded me that I had agreed to buy four pairs of khaki pants for the men. I had been defeated once again, this time in a begging campaign.

Karo had sidled up to me the previous day with the complaint that his blanket was threadbare at the point where it covered his backside. My recollection was that he normally wore a somewhat dilapidated pair of shorts but he insisted that he had nothing else to wear and, as he put it, he wanted to walk without shame among the people of Rodosoit. I made the ridiculous mistake of giving him one of my own pairs. Within five minutes Lelean turned up with a similar story. He said he had worn out his government issue in my service and could he please have what I had given to Karo. When Goiti and Mezek appeared on the scene I didn't wait to hear their story but promised everyone a new pair, emphasizing that it would be the last they would get from me. The lesson cost me thirty-seven shillings.

The proprietor of the *duka* was a thin-faced Somali, smooth and black as a stick of liquorice, who seemed to be cut off from his customers by a barricade of skinny bosoms. They belonged to the tribal matriarchs who leaned forward over the counter with arms folded and discussed the gossip of the day. As far as I could determine they bought nothing for cash but after interminable monologues punctuated by long drawn-out bleats of 'Aiee', they produced little bags of *posho* or emaciated chickens and tried to exchange them for something else. Most *dukas* operate on a complicated system of barter. A group of old men tottered round, cadging tobacco and the haughty, spear-carrying *morans* smudged me with red ochre as they brushed past. Outside on the verandah the girls of the town hung about in twos and threes, spitting out of the corner of their mouths and shaking their shoulders seductively whenever a *moran* passed by. It was an attractive little shake which made their necklets tinkle.

Stretching over the barricade of bosoms I asked for drinks all round for the men. They liked Pepsi-Cola which normally costs about a shilling a bottle. Out of their salaries of fifteen shillings a week, the men usually bought two or three bottles at every *duka* we stopped at. I disliked the stuff myself; I was inclined to speculate on the profits of the industry but I was obliged to drink it when the alternatives were muddy water or an astringent form of lemonade made in Nairobi.

The Somali was even smarter than I thought. Interpreting 'drinks for the men' in its widest sense, he gave a bottle to every man in the store and told me I owed him thirty shillings. Another minor defeat.

After buying a gallon of paraffin and six tin mugs which can be used for almost anything on safari, I walked out of the back-door of the *duka* to find eight little camels browsing contentedly on straw from an old mattress. They were the reinforcements from Marsabit. I stared at them for several minutes and with more pleasure than I can easily describe; they were good animals by any reckoning but by comparison with our own string of cripples, they were fit to carry the wares of the Prophet who, I am told, knew a thing or two about camels.

At close quarters a camel is not a beautiful animal; it has been described as a racehorse put together by a committee. The giraffe-like neck terminates in the head of a giant tortoise. They are far more angular about the body than a mammal should be and there is a suggestion of a flightless bird, a chicken or an ostrich, in the way they strut about. But this is the impression of a camel reduced to its component parts. The animal is built to move easily on soft ground; its cushioned feet brush the ground with a scarcely perceptible thump and once it gets into the rhythm of a march it has the loose, sinuous motion of a wild animal. I am very fond of camels.

At Rodosoit we were joined by three new men: Aboud the syce who had driven the camels in and two game scouts called Lengama and Lenduroni. Both in character and features they were as unlike as two men could be. Lengama was tall, thin and distinctly dim: a Coptic Muslim from somewhere in the Borana country, he had strayed into the Game Department without any noticeable zest for his job. At first I thought he was merely an old soldier; he got out of the way when there was any work to be done and he came to attention quicker than any man I have seen outside the regular army. He was, moreover, a singularly inefficient slacker – he gave himself away; he hid behind trees where everyone could see him; he gave the impression that he was going out on patrol but before he was even out of sight he flopped down under a tree and curled up like a caterpillar. The men called him Sergeant Marduk. A *marduk*, I discovered, is the little bustard, a long-legged, harsh-voiced bird.

Lenduroni was the very opposite of the *marduk* in almost everything he did. Short and stocky, he had a studious manner; he alone of the company seemed to be aware of the world outside the desert; he asked me questions about Nairobi. He wanted to know if there was much game in my country and what he could expect to earn if he walked to England. He was a hard worker and he applied himself to a new problem by wrinkling up his forehead like a dachshund before suggesting what was usually an original solution. Although the two men were of the same rank, the big Lengama always took his orders from the little Lenduroni. Similarly, Goiti, our old camelman, quietly took over the job of chief camelman when Munta left. I noticed that he soon began to give orders to Aboud, the man who had driven the camels in from Marsabit. It was difficult to decide whether this was mere opportunism or the recognition of superior skills. I suspected the latter and decided not to interfere until I saw what they could do.

With a staff of seven I soon had a superb camp on the banks of a dried-up stream. We had almost everything we wanted: two pools of clear water, browse for the camels, an abundance of shade and a *duka* on the hilltop that might have passed for the village pub. The tent nestled under a tree where the bushes were cut back to make a screen for a field bathroom. Beyond the tent, conveniently shaded, the sprawling limbs of a fallen tree provided a gun rack, a hat stand and pegs for clothing. I lounged contentedly in the crook of its limbs with a ledge for books above and a place for tea things below. This was comfort on a scale I had rarely experienced before.

Groups of villagers visited us during the afternoon. The stream bed provided a high road between the *duka* and three communal homesteads or *manyattas* at the top of the valley. I had always wanted to visit a *manyatta* but apart from the embarrassment of staring and being stared at, it seemed an impertinence to walk into someone's private courtyard uninvited. I wondered how I should react if an African began to take photographs through the lower windows of my own house. Lelean suggested that I should accompany him on a tour of inspection. This was a regular part of his duties as a government game scout and one of the principal reasons why he had been allowed to accompany me; it enabled him to visit regions far beyond his normal circuit.

The local chief was not at home; nor were the majority of the elders and warriors. They had gone out to a sacred grove to arrange for a circumcision ceremony that night. When the moon rose sixteen boys would become sixteen young men. This was related to us by a very old man who shivered and pierced his sentences with a barking cough. Promising to give him medicine we walked round a miserable collection of mud huts.

The *manyatta* was roughly circular in shape and surrounded by a high barricade of thornbush. The individual huts resembled flat-topped igloos; they were about five feet in height with a floor space no larger than a double bed. Made out of a framework of branches plastered with mud and cattle dung, most of them were tenanted by families of up to five or six who kept their goats and sheep in an adjacent pen. Lelean poked about, looking for the remains of horns and skin; his job was to find evidence of illegally slaughtered game but finding none we walked back to the camp accompanied by the barking man. In the bright sunlight the *manyatta* was a depressing place. For an African a large animal represents a small fortune; whenever I saw Africans living in such poverty I marvelled that any game remained alive anywhere in the vicinity of the isolated tribes. What European would allow his family to starve while calves and sheep skipped around his front door? He might if the penalty for poaching were six months in gaol.

So many patients turned up for treatment that afternoon that I decided to open the surgery at five o'clock and close it at six. Lelean acted as receptionist and while I bandaged and doled out pills he questioned the next patient in Samburu and was usually able to tell me what was the matter with him in Swahili. In this way he dealt with about twenty cases of constipation, headaches and superficial cuts, three presumptive cases of dysentery ('much lavatory with blood') and a young man with a missing top joint to his index finger. He had sliced it off with a *panga* some days earlier. The wound seemed to be in excellent shape although I had the usual difficulty in deciding whether a skin which was not only naturally dark but unnaturally dirty was healthy or not. The man wanted something to make the finger grow. As he said he had treated the wound with cowdung I suggested he should continue the treatment.

Towards dusk the high road of the stream bed was used by little groups of red-daubed boys, striding out towards the grove for the circumcision ceremony. They took immense strides; they carried spears and they chanted in unison. The loud chorus was interrupted by individual solos of *Ah yah ikoto! Ah yah!* Whether in that final explosive, almost agonized *Ah yah!* there was sympathetic magic calculated to relieve the pain from the inexpertly used headman's knife, I cannot say. The boys were tense and purposive and Karo and Lelean teased them as they strode by. They took up the *Ah yah ikoto* and made a downward chopping gesture with their hands. The novitiates scarcely looked at their tormentors. There was no slackening in their exaggerated stride. They had an appointment with manhood. *Ah yah!*

During the early stages of the safari it was apparent that I was deeply concerned about game and gunnery. There is much to be said about the ethics of killing: I am not concerned with them here. As I saw it the problem was that we were moving towards deserts where we could neither buy goats nor carry enough tins to last us through the journey. A gun was a necessity but I was not much good at ranges of two and three hundred yards. In an effort not to lose too much face I used to invent reasons for not shooting but I'm pretty sure that the men saw through them. They knew I didn't want to shoot and they were determined that I should.

At six o'clock that night Karo shouted out something loud and incomprehensible from the far end of the camp. It sounded like 'Swara! Swara!' He began to run towards Lelean who was cleaning my rifle. Lelean looked up, threw down the ramrod and ran towards me. 'Swara!' he repeated pointing urgently towards the bush. Lengama called to Mezek; Lenduroni was already trotting along beside Karo. The situation was completely out of hand. I had the feeling that we were about to be attacked.

'Swara, it is what?' I said, panting behind Lelean. We were some fifty yards from the camp before I learnt that it was a *nyama*, that is some kind of animal.

'A fierce one?'

In imagination I saw a troupe of frenzied elephant, hysterical rhino, maybe a lion. But the word for elephant, I knew, was *n'dovu*; rhino was *faro*; lion *simba*. But what were *swara*?

Lelean was somewhat non-committal. After admitting that it was an animal 'for food', he held his arms over his head like horns. *Swara*, in fact, was none other than my old friend Grant's gazelle. At the far side of the *lugga* a sizeable male walked slowly towards the waterhole on our side of the stream bed. Not only was it walking slowly; it was walking towards us. The range was about four hundred yards.

Squatting behind a bush with three of the men, I was both excited and mildly annoyed that I had been beguiled out of the camp. Why had Lelean been cleaning my rifle? The weapon was not dirty. He had cleaned it earlier in the day.

The gazelle was about three hundred yards away and walking proudly, like an heraldic stag.

I tried to remember the target made out of four pages of a notebook on the night that I had decided that I could shoot better than Lelean. The first shot, as I remember it, had gone wildly astray, somewhere near two o'clock but far outside the outer circle. Nor' east by east. I had corrected towards eight o'clock but I had not corrected as much as I should have done. Even my best shots had been in the north-east sector of the target. I wondered what the correction would be in terms of a shoulder shot at the advancing gazelle.

It was about two hundred yards away.

The words of the instructor came back. 'Full ahead and *stay* with it.' I knew that when I squeezed I tended to flinch. I tightened by biceps, an action that lifted my right shoulder.

'Peega!' whispered Lelean.

Fire at two hundred yards? The range was still shortening. With any luck it looked as if I should be able to shoot with some confidence. A fly settled on the rifle barrel, brushed its back legs together and flew off again. I stiffened. A drop of sweat ran down my forehead. The animal had heard something. At a point about a hundred and fifty yards from us it stopped and lifted up its head.

I fired.

The thump seemed in no sense related to the explosion in the breech. I had no recollection of the physical recoil of the rifle. I was conscious only of a spasm almost sexual in its intensity. Even before I squeezed I felt as if the animal were already dead.

The gazelle collapsed, gently, like a coat that had slipped off a coat-hanger.

The boys shouted and rushed forward. They were led by Lengama, carrying a sheath knife. As a Muslim he was obliged to perform the grisly *hal-al*, the ritual cutting of the throat while the head was held in the direction of the east. He nearly decapitated the animal. Four men took a leg each and dragged it back to camp. They were excited and somewhat bloody when they got there, and in a different sense of the word so was I.

After a drum roll of thunder from the hills the sky cleared and the night began to burn with stars. The boys celebrated the occasion by lighting a fire which would have done credit to the coming-of-age of a duke. The centre of the blaze was the wreck of a tree. When the flames died down, the residue of white ash provided heat points of different intensity, like an old-fashioned kitchen stove. Mezek grilled a steak for me on a grid of green twigs; a pan of soup simmered on a cooler part of the ash and the men baked large hunks of meat by impaling them on sticks stuck in the ground at the edge of the fire.

Despite the splendour of the night and a somewhat ambivalent sense of achievement, it was impossible to sit down with my feet up before dinner. Hoards of flying beetles drove me into the smoke of the fire where I found to my annoyance that I had injudiciously sprayed a substantial shot of whisky with an oily fly-repellant containing DDT. The insects flew away before Mezek appeared with the steak and I was able to eat, quietly, and listen to the soft *ooo-ah-ooo* of the hyena.

At nine o'clock the moon rose above the topmost peak of Ol Doino Lengiyo. Against the velvet backcloth of the night it resembled a crescentic knife. I thought of the ritual mutilation and of the boys who sang as they strode out for their painful appointment with manhood. *Ah yah!*

The Red Elephants

We jogged along, comfortably, for several days, making our way north-west, back towards the mountains. The intention was to work round the edge of the N'dotos in an effort to keep the camels fresh for the lava fields at the south end of the lake. The first objective was the administrative post of South Horr, a little speck of a place between the parallel ranges of Nyiru and Ol Doino Mara. The long narrow gap between them ran due north. I anticipated no difficulty with the camels until we left the track and climbed over the escarpment by Kulal, the mountain of the winds. In London I had read all the old travel books I could find and memorized the Masai names and the position of most of the mountains such as Ol Doino Lengiyo, Lomolok, Losoi and Kulal. On Kulal over seventy years ago Arthur Neumann, one of the first men to explore the lake, had met gales that threw him to the ground.

At a place called Irrer which lies under a black rock we stopped at a miserable little *duka* for Pepsi-Cola and a long argument about money. The boys were paid monthly. At Wamba I had given each of them a small advance on their basic wage of sixty shillings. I handed it out on the understanding that they could expect no more until their wages were due. But Karo, the cunning, contriving Karo, had spun a wonderful tale that I owed him at least a hundred shillings for heaven knows what and on the strength of this quite fictitious insurance he not only borrowed freely from all the others but tied up the whole camp in a tangle of cross-debts.

Karo owed Goiti and Mezek ten shillings each and he had talked Lelean into parting with at least a pound. This was a feat in itself. When Lelean realized that Karo was dead broke he promptly laid off the debt by borrowing something from Lengama and Lenduroni and told them, afterwards, that Karo would

59

repay them. I got into the act when a harassed little man in charge of the *duka* said that Karo had ordered drinks all round and was unable to pay.

There were arguments, almost incomprehensible explanations. I tried to straighten out the situation but failed to distinguish between *kukopa* (to borrow) and *kukopesha* (to lend). This confused things even further and I finished up by losing my temper. We jogged along uncomfortably for the next hour or so. I walked ahead, peevishly, and tried to brush up my numerals by reciting the two times table aloud in Swahili. I never did like Pepsi-Cola.

A day, or maybe two days, later we swung into the broad dry stream bed of the Milgis only to find the *lugga* populated by a herd of most unusual-looking elephants; they were brick-red, the result of dusting themselves with dry earth. My instinct was to swing out again and leave them to it but the map showed clearly that somehow we had to cross that *lugga*. It ran at right angles to our course and it stood between us and the N'doto mountains. Lelean spotted the animals when they were no more than red blobs on top of the far bank. They were upwind of us; they stood in groups under the trees, munching and waving their enormous ears with the slow undulations of the fins of a fish. They seemed quite unaware of our presence. However, a slight shift in the direction of the wind would envelop us in the scent of elephant and that, as I had discovered, was enough to terrify the camels. We swung the team slightly off course and began a nervous game of hide-and-seek. The problem was to find a place where the steep banks of the *lugga* had collapsed so that we could lead the camels down into the stream bed. All the obvious crossing points had been recently used by elephant. Some of the animals were still standing in the shade of the trees on the opposite bank and it was not difficult to imagine they were standing there waiting for us.

After three unsuccessful attempts at crossing we decided to march west and then strike north where there seemed to be fewer trees and, we hoped, fewer elephants. The eight camels were divided up so that none of the boys was responsible for more than two. Everyone was ordered to keep close together except Lenduroni and Lelean who were sent ahead with orders to signal whenever the track seemed clear for more than a few hundred yards. As we moved west the *lugga* began to narrow in width but the banks became steeper and the crossing points fewer.

Lugga or dry watercourses are improbable features of landscape, even in deserts where the rainfall is meagre. It seems inconceivable that a torrent lasting no more than a few hours in each year can gouge out a rift as deep as a railway cutting and so wide that in places it is difficult to see what lies on the opposite bank. Most of the stream beds are littered with the stumps of trees and large boulders rolled in during the annual floods. On maps *luggas* are indicated by dotted lines and on some maps to the east of Rudolf they are the only features marked.

Lenduroni found a good place to cross. The bank had caved in; the slope was gentle and with the red earth up to their knees the camels lurched down into the stream bed. There were no elephant within sight but it soon appeared that it was no easier to get out of the stream bed than it had been to get in and we were obliged to trudge up the Milgis for several miles.

When we eventually ran into the trouble I had anticipated for hours I was at the end of the convoy, trying to take a photograph. The leading camel suddenly began to rear. Goiti tried to hold it down but it kicked and plunged so violently that it broke free and released the second camel. If fright is infectious there is a positively epidemic quality about panic. All the camels started to bellow and two bolted off faster than Lengama could run. I tried to stop an animal that bore down on me but it swerved, shed part of its load and raced off down the *lugga*. The leading camel attempted to mount the distant bank but became bogged down in the soft earth. Two others fled upstream. The cause of the trouble was an old bull elephant who rose above us with the dignity of a colossus hewn out of stone. At this distance from events I can remember only the plunging and dancing animals, the gear strewn across the stream bed and the imperturbability of the elephant on top of the bank.

It took us the better part of a day to reassemble the caravan. The stampede cost me two bottles of Scotch, a little petroleum stove and a lamp; my shaving mirror was cracked; the collapsible chair had collapsed but was effectively hammered back into shape; half a sack of maize meal and about thirty pounds of rice were scattered across the floor of the *lugga* and we never found a wooden box containing the water-purifying equipment and some collecting gear for biological specimens. I tried to be philosophical about the forcible removal of what I suppose were no more than inessential luxuries. At least it was of some comfort to know that the camels were uninjured although one had to be tracked back for two miles.

We pitched camp above the Milgis where I shot my second animal, a gerenuk, an extremely slender relative of the gazelle. I had gone for a stroll on my own, carrying the rifle for protection. There was a little bravado in this unaccompanied excursion. I felt that if the boys could walk around armed only with a spear at least I should feel safe with a high-speed rifle. I took the precaution of avoiding clumps of trees and bushes but was startled repeatedly by the harsh cries of birds and the sudden scurry of animals in the undergrowth. On the way back I was followed, doggedly, by a tall grave Samburu whom I remembered as one who had helped us to retrieve the camels. On a ridge above the stream bed where I was in some doubt about the direction, he walked up and pointed excitedly to a patch of scrub. Three gerenuk were standing on their rear legs, nibbling at the upper leaves of a bush.

Rapidly aiming at the nearest animal I fired and was disappointed to see it lower itself as if to resume feeding on the ground. The other two skewed round, startled, unsure where the crash of the shot had come from. As I pushed the bolt forward for a second shot, to my surprise the animal I had aimed at slumped to the ground. Although shot through the heart, it had remained standing for a few seconds.

That night we had about a dozen Samburu as guests for dinner. The only dissatisfied man was Lengama the Muslim who complained that as he could not eat an animal without first slitting its throat I owed him the cost of a meal. My impression is that he ate chunks of the unhallowed meat when he thought nobody was looking.

One indirect consequence of the stampede in the Milgis was that I polished up my knowledge of Swahili. I was obliged to; I had nothing else to do. To fill in the time between dusk and bedtime I usually dawdled over a drink and wrote up my diary. After the stampede, the routine had to be modified: my dining table was lit by two little oil lamps and in this pale religious glow I wrote for about half an hour, that is until my eyes began to ache. I drank whisky in small sips. Only one bottle remained, an emergency supply which, for protection, had been carefully laced up in two pairs of canvas shoes. By drawing lines on the bottle with a fanciful brush-pencil I reckoned it would last for about ten days. Searching round for something to do at night I chatted to Lelean about what we should do the following day and when we got to know each other better he told me about the difficulties of keeping his two wives apart: very instructive.

The next morning we made a short journey to the mountain village of N'gornit. It stood on a hump at the foot of a cliff where a patch of thick forest sheltered an extraordinarily large number of elephants. The villagers were terrified of them and reckoned the time of the day by the hours in which they could safely travel along the forest tracks. Nobody ventured out after dusk. As elephants are not normally aggressive, it looked as if the herd had been recently beaten up by the villagers but Lelean could find no evidence of poaching. He wandered about among the huts and guides took us up to the distant *manyattas*. In the N'doto mountains we were rarely without guides or hangers-on. This was a companionable state of affairs, although reciprocal hospitality began to develop into an apparently endless round of feasts.

The Samburu continued to give us goats. Their hospitality towards travelling tribesmen was such that we might well have journeyed from Wamba to the lake without buying an animal or shooting one. My game licence was strictly limited. I could shoot a certain number of specified animals but no more. I wanted to devote the bulk of my quota of twenty-eight buck, gazelle, zebra and bushpig to the desert where a gun was a necessity. In the mountains I shot animals because I had qualms about accepting goats without offering something in return. The result was that when guests turned up a gazelle was eaten in one sitting. I announced that I would shoot nothing more for at least a week but I would give medicine to those who wanted it. I very soon regretted this offer.

The number of patients increased from twelve at Rodosoit to eighteen at Irrer; some twenty or more were waiting for me on the Milgis while at N'gornit the better part of a tribe turned up for treatment and the majority of them were among the healthiest men I have seen. I had forgotten that the African *likes* medicine. Given *dawa* and *nyama*, medicine and meat, he regards wages as a subsidiary affair, something of a luxury in life.

I soon discovered that my patients knew very well whether they had a reasonable claim to attention or not. The malingerers tended to keep to the back of the queue. The genuine bellyaches went ahead of those who merely liked the taste of Epsom salts, and cuts, bruises and abrasions usually pushed in front of trivial forks in the head. One man said he wanted a lot of *dawa* – 'mingi mingi' – as he was very, very ill. Pressed for symptoms he first shrugged his shoulders and then slapped his belly with a re-sounding smack. It transpired that he had once had stomach ache after a marriage feast and he wanted to guard against the possibility in the future. Another man asked for medicine for a fever-ish child. Failing to make any sense in Swahili, I called in Lelean who found that although the child had spots on its face, it was the nephew of the man's previous wife whom he had last seen about three years ago. Yet among the malingerers and minor ailments there were cases of distress so acute that I wished I had more medicine and skill than I possessed.

One old man, the spokesmen for his tribe, asked me to visit a *manyatta* where he said 'all the people' were sick. I was some-what sceptical. I could make nothing of the symptoms – 'much coughing, fire in the chest and very sharp forks in the head' and as the *manyatta* was several miles away I gave him a handful of aspirins together with sulpha tablets for the bad cases. I heard later from a missionary that the fire in the chest was epidemical pneumonia. He knew the *manyatta*. Sixteen Samburu, most of them women and children, had died there in one week. I tried to console myself with the thought that it was unlikely that any-thing but powerful antibiotics could have saved them. All I possessed was penicillin powder and at N'gornit I used the last of it on a man who looked as if he had been thrashed with a length of barbed wire.

His face, shoulders and chest had been slashed by the spikes of a wait-a-bit thorn tree. The story as he told it through torn lips was that he had been walking back from the *duka* at dusk when he had been confronted by an angry elephant. As he fled down a

64

narrow path he had met a second animal and had escaped by plunging through the thorn bushes. What happened was apparent from his appearance. With the scepticism of a professional poacher-chaser Lelean was disinclined to believe the story and said that the man had either attacked the elephant or was up to no good in the bush at that time of the day. He was wrong. We examined the tracks and found that the man had given an exact account of what had happened. The elephants, as he described them, were 'big red ones'. I knew the kind only too well.

I dined that night on a fricassee of curried goat on a foundation of rice and tomato purée. Mezek made a success of it. He was a hygienic cook, which in Africa is a matter of some comfort, yet for all but the simplest preparations he needed instructions and there was not much I could tell him. I could make a number of fanciful dishes but it would have been an advantage if I had known how to make a decent stew or how much fat and maize flour went into a gravy.

During the night I managed to chase a hyena – not out of but into my tent. The only casualty was a canvas shoe. The animal bit off the toe-cap as cleanly as if it had been sliced off with a pair of shears. I don't know whether my foot would have been treated the same way had it been inside; I remember only my annoyance at being wakened up at midnight and the ridiculous scamper round the tent.

It had been erected in a gap between two large bushes. When the hyenas began to call with growing insistence I got up and saw two pairs of bright green eyes in the light of the torch. I threw a brick at them. When another animal started to yowl behind me I went round to the back of the tent to investigate. The hyena stood there – ashen grey in the bright light. It seemed so unabashed that I chased after it angrily. The animal swerved round the bush and disappeared. Walking round the bush to the front of the tent I saw it disappear through the back flap. It seems that I had chased it in. In the morning I found the chewed-up shoe and marvelled that it could have snatched at it so quickly. There is much to be said for leaving a tent open at both ends.

A white hunter told me that a lion once strolled into his tent at night to keep out of the rain. He had gone to bed early. He awoke about ten o'clock to find the lion with its rear quarters

towards him. He said he was terrified but, as he recalled it afterwards, the lion seemed to be only mildly annoyed that it had
been caught out in the open on a wet night. It peered out through
the tent flap, rumbling peevishly. As he couldn't reach his gun
without causing a disturbance, the hunter leaped up in bed and
shouted at the top of his voice. He said the lion seemed to become airborne; it rose vertically before it streaked out into the
night.

To reach South Horr on our last day in the N'dotos we had
to march for ten hours. Lelean woke me at three o'clock in the
morning. I rolled out of bed. Apparent confusion everywhere.
Camels roared, men shouted; in the light of the dying fires the
piles of gear looked bigger than ever before. I sat on a box,
drank a quart of thick tea and then wandered about among the
loading parties, trying to ensure that we left nothing behind.
At half-past four Lelean said, 'It is prepared'. I nodded. A fearful noise as the camels staggered to their feet. Then almost no
sound as we slid into the soft dust of the Korante Plain. We had
twenty-seven miles ahead of us.

In the saffron yellow of the dawn, wisps of cloud, like the tails
of egrets, flared pink, caught fire and burnt out in the blinding
light of the rising sun. The coats of the camels glowed. For half
an hour I marched behind eight golden camels. No hunting
prince went forth with greater splendour.

Karo sang. He had a harsh voice but on that occasion it had a
haunting quality. He sang of great meals of meat and of women
he had never had. I discovered afterwards that he also sang of
what an entertaining fellow the *effendi* was when he lost his temper over little matters, but even if I had known what he was singing about I should have forgiven him. It was a privilege to be
alive and to be there that morning.

I forget the name of the valley where we found the smallest
camel I have seen but it was on the edge of a lava plateau, a gap
into which we marched to cut a corner off the edge of the
N'dotos.

The calf had been born during the night; the stringy little
cord was still bright red and the animal had some difficulty in
standing up. The mother animal wore a seraphic expression.

When the men approached her she pranced in front of the new-born and licked it vigorously.

Karo looked at the animals and said something to Lelean which I couldn't make out. From the way he hunched his shoulders as if he were lifting a sack of coal, it looked as if he intended to strap the little one on to its mother's back in the manner of the Turkana herdsmen. My inclination was to leave the animals alone. They were no concern of ours.

After more talk among themselves the men cut some hefty cudgels from a tree and advanced on the mother animal. Lelean gave her a smart blow on the hindquarters; Karo poked at her muzzle with a stick and when she shied away from her calf, Aboud, the strongest man in the company, grabbed the little animal and hoisted it on to his shoulders, like a yoke. Holding the calf's spindly legs under his arms, he began to run. Everyone began to run including the anxious cow. I ran, too, although I didn't know why we were running or what we intended to do with the calf.

Aboud led the field. Even with the calf on his back he could hold his own. The distracted cow was hard on his heels. She bellowed and lunged at him with her jaws agape but whenever she seemed about to take a chunk out of his hindquarters, Karo or Lelean fended her off with their cudgels and Aboud gained a few extra yards.

By the time I managed to get among the first three runners, Karo had tripped the cow up twice and on one occasion had brought her crashing to the ground. This was really too much. Remembering the right word for once I bawled 'Simama!' and to my surprise everyone stopped. Aboud let the calf slide to the ground and the cow licked it, blabbering breathlessly.

The explanation was more simple than I could have imagined. Far from carrying off the calf, the men were trying to return both the calf and its mother to their rightful owners. From an earmark they had seen that the pair belonged to a nearby band of Samburu. As it would have been difficult to drive both animals, the men decided to carry the calf until they could leave it at the mouth of the valley, near the main track across the plain, where they knew it would soon be found. To move the calf, quickly, they had to separate it from its mother, but they were well aware that she would follow close behind. On this as on other occasions I was impressed by the Samburu's respect for one another's property.

By eleven o'clock we had done about fourteen miles. I felt pretty tired and suggested we should stop in the shadow of a gully for a brew of tea but the men pointed out that the camels were tired too; they needed browse and there was none in the vicinity. We came across some about midday and rested for two hours amid almost unbroken silence. A cricket squeaked; the desert shimmered; three vultures turned in the air as if suspended on the wires of a mobile and I felt giddy in the heat.

At half-past two Goiti went out to collect the camels which had been allowed to browse free, unhampered by the mats and sticks. Men and animals moved groggily; we crawled forward but managed to add another seven miles by five o'clock, when we left the plains and climbed up into the mountains. Ol Doino Mara lay to the east and the sun cast deep shadows in the South Horr valley. By six o'clock it was necessary to send scouts ahead: elephants had used the track earlier in the day.

The men were anxious to press on to the *dukas* down in the valley but I was worried about the possibility of a stampede in the fading light; I was also tired, irritably tired. 'How far now?' I repeatedly asked. 'Hapana m'bali sana,' replied Lelean. This, as I was to discover, was the most infuriating stock response of an African to almost any question about distance. 'It is not very far.' Nothing is ever very far.

Suddenly a commotion from the track above. Four gazelle raced along as if running in front of a bush fire. They were followed by two or three bushbuck and a small antelope, probably a duiker. All were apparently terrified. At points in their flight they dislodged little cascades of stones that tinkled down among us. With my mind on the possibility of lion I cocked the rifle. But the animals were not being chased by lion. The hunters were more fierce than any of the big cats. Through field-glasses I caught a glimpse of speckled shapes, fanning out to strike down a bushbuck some way behind the others. They were hunting dogs, the most formidable pursuers of game in the whole of Africa.

Like army ants, they have their home everywhere and nowhere, suddenly pouring into territory where they may not have been seen for years. We could only speculate on the outcome of the chase. The hunters and the hunted swept round a bluff and disappeared from sight. What seemed certain was that at least one bushbuck would be torn apart and devoured before dusk.

Hunting dogs never relent. In Ruanda on the borders of Tanzania some years earlier I had seen a pack chase an impala for about ten minutes. The antelope, utterly exhausted, had dogs on both flanks. From time to time one of the pack detached itself from the rest and sprang at the animal, tearing out a chunk of flesh from the quarters until the desperate antelope fell over and had its entrails ripped out. By the time we drove up to within fifty yards of the kill in a Land-Rover, the impala was not dead. One leg feebly rose and fell. But it had been eviscerated and as the dogs swung round at our approach they looked as if they had been bathed in blood.

The presence of hunting dogs can often be detected by an eerie, repetitive call which sounds like the last note in the call of the European cuckoo. It is usually heard about a dozen times and seems to be a rallying cry like the long-drawn *ooo-ah-ooo* of the hyena.

What impressed me most about the gruesome hunt I had seen in Ruanda was the discipline of the pack. When we first came across the dogs they were resting on the brow of a hill. They were in no sense put out by our presence but continued to gaze intently down on to the plain below. After a time we saw a solitary dog racing up the hill towards them and the pack rose to greet it. There was a great deal of tail-wagging and excited chatter and then all the animals ran off in the direction from which the scout had come. We followed the animals in the Land-Rover and, as I remember the occasion, there were about a dozen vultures flying overhead. I felt as if we were taking part in a mediaeval hunt with hawks and hounds.

When the chase was over and the impala dead, the pack leader took possession of the carcass, accompanied by two bitches. The rest of the animals stood aside, expectantly. The leader ate his fill and retired to the shelter of some bushes with a bone. As soon as he had turned his back on the remains, the other animals slunk forward in twos and threes in accordance with some obscure hierarchy of place. They ate until there was nothing left of the antelope except the horns and a little patch of blood-stained grass.

On the Korante Plain that night, shortly before we saw a pin-point of light from South Horr and realized the long day's march was nearly over, we heard a series of faint but melodic calls from the track behind us. It sounded like a succession of dashes in morse code. The hunting dogs were assembling before moving off somewhere else; obviously the bushbuck, as Lelean put it, was 'finished completely'.

The Wind and the Stars

Apart from the fact that the forestry station of South Horr clung to the side of a mountain, it had almost everything I associated with the word oasis. The air was fresh, water burbled and the trees rustled. I could recognize eucalyptus and the aromatic acacias but here also were olives, leathery-leafed evergreens and a sprinkling of flame trees a-quiver with sunbirds. The village stood in the gap between the towering walls of Nyiru and the Ol Doino Mara. It is the narrow gateway to Lake Rudolf and the highroad south for the tribes who live at the south end of the lake. With any luck we should reach Rudolf within two or three days. Above us were the cedar-clothed peaks of Pel, Tual and Kasapurai. They were reputed to be the home of unusually large numbers of elephant but, unlike the herds of the Milgis, I was assured that they kept themselves to themselves and if they strayed down among the villagers, they did so cautiously, as if conscious of trespass. An elephant is a dignified animal but it knows its place. When the Samburu went out at dusk they sang, loudly, to let the elephants know they were coming and for the most part the tribesmen respected their massive neighbours.

South Horr has been ravaged by raiding tribes (including the British) for a very long time. When the aboriginals, whoever they were, had been ousted by the handsome Samburu, the Arabs entered the valley for slaves and the Ethiopians for ivory. At the beginning of the present century, the rapid development of the more favoured parts of Kenya led a few far-sighted individuals to realize that wildlife would have the best long-term chance of survival in areas too poor or too remote to be required for development purposes. Two large reserves called the Sugata and Jubaland were created on either side of South Horr. Today, the game in most of the surrounding countryside has been wiped out by stark neglect and the valley is chiefly renowned for its timber, buffalo, elephant, cattle ticks and an extraordinary number of beautiful women.

A government *askari*, incongruously got up in a khaki cap, a red blanket and army boots, walked up with a visitors' book containing questions about where we had come from, where we were going and why. I shook my head. After resolutely tramping through the mountains this was too much. We were on safari. To hell with documentation. The *askari* looked worried. To keep him happy I wrote something facetious across the top of the page. He saluted and walked off. I wondered who was responsible for the book and when he last inspected it. Among the names of the more improbable visitors to South Horr during the months preceding our arrival were Julius Caesar, Nikita Khrushchev and Ella Wheeler Wilcox. In less time than it took to unpack the medicine chest we were surrounded by tall, red-painted men and their wives and girl friends.

One of the most endearing qualities of the Samburu is the affection they bestow on their womenfolk. Bantu usually treat a woman as a beast of burden. On the road up to Wamba I had seen young Kikuyu girls staggering along under immense loads of firewood, some with a baby peering out from among the sticks, like a nestling. Their husbands disdain to carry anything heavier than a spear or a stick and swagger alongside their overladen spouses in the manner of cattle drivers. This is never seen among the Samburu. They are proud of their aristocratic-looking wives. They brought them forward, hand on shoulder, for medical treatment. I listened to stories of how this woman had coughed for so long during the night that the moon had moved from here to there, and the man indicated the position in the sky. He had feared for her, he said; he had given her honey and had taken her to her mother's hut. What could be done for her? The simple answer was that I didn't know. I tried sulphathiazole. It probably worked but like a quack I had usually moved on before I could find out. However, we had a lot of trouble with the women of the South Horr. The men were far too fond of them.

Despite his years, Goiti disappeared with a saucy-looking piece on the first night and forgot to hobble two of the camels. The animals wandered off and had to be driven back, roaring loudly, at two o'clock in the morning. Perhaps they had a date of their own. Lelean, too, was rarely without a woman in his bower throughout the whole of the next day.

The men usually slept in the open, spreading their mosquito nets over their heads. As a fly-barrier the nets were almost useless. Sparks from the big fires had burnt holes in them within two days of leaving Wamba. But they were an insurance against a bite from hyena or any other kind of animal, and we rarely encountered mosquitoes. As a sign of class distinction, Lelean rarely slept among the men, but whenever he could he undercut a bush in such a way that he was as snug as a caterpillar in his own private cocoon. This was his bachelor apartment.

At South Horr, the last source of Pepsi-Cola before the desert, he went to considerable lengths to build a seraglio among the branches of a fallen tree. It had a front entrance overlooking the local equivalent of Main Street and a discreet approach from the rear. The interior was voluptuously furnished with mats laid over ammunition boxes; the bait was a continually boiling kettle of tea. Whenever he wanted company he stood at the entrance of his lair and, under the pretext of cleaning my rifle, he rattled the bolt. The sound carried a long way and as an indication of intent it could not have been bettered. Some women drifted into his bower from the sick parade. Lelean waited until they had been treated and then invited them in for tea. I was alarmed to find that cases of pleurisy and skin disease were using my crockery; I told him to use his own. I also noticed that he entertained two or three women at the same time. Quite a man.

The problem at South Horr was the old one of trying to keep troops up to scratch under luxury conditions. After the stampede on the Milgis, there was much to be done; torn sacks had to be stitched up, boxes mended and dented tinware hammered out. But instead of getting on with the work, the men quarrelled about whose turn it was to take the camels out to graze. I drew up a roster, made out a list of things to be done and said that nobody would get an advance on their pay until we were ready for the road. No strangers were allowed in the camp for tea, dalliance or gossip and I held an unsuccessful enquiry into the disappearance of about twenty pounds of dried camel meat.

I realized that the meat was being systematically filched when I saw a girl in the *duka* with a handful of the stringy-looking stuff tucked away in her bosom. She said the *askaris* had given it to her. Her companions, who had also been chewing vigorously, stopped, guiltily, when they heard me questioning her. Clearly the time had come for us to go.

I announced this, senatorially, at midday, from the verandah of my tent. It was received with a distinct lack of enthusiasm by the entire company. Karo, I was not surprised to learn, had hurt a bone in his foot but gave the game away by saying that he had hoped we would be staying in the valley for several days, Goiti claimed to be in the throes of recurrent malaria and was bought off with five tablets of paludrin. Mezek concocted some fanciful story about a shortage of rations: Lengama had a cough, Lenduroni was tired and Lelean said the camels were sick and could not be loaded until they recovered. This sounded untrue but I did not know enough about camels to disagree with any real feeling of conviction.

Of the eight beasts from Marsabit, five were as sprightly as fleas. Two had developed saddle sores which seemed to be responding to salt and water but one had an ominous, palpable abscess on what I took to be a lymph gland at the base of the neck. With some trepidation, I cut into it with a razor blade and squeezed out a considerable amount of thick pus. The camel was co-operative throughout and wore a dressing sprinkled with penicillin powder for about two hours. As the animal normally carried water I lightened the load and compromised over the time of departure by agreeing to leave at midday the following day. This, I was assured, would enable us to reach Anderi, the nearest permanent waterpoint, before nightfall.

As I stumped back into my tent wondering what to do next, a bird jeered at me and another one chuckled throatily. The noise came from a troupe of starlings gorgeously got up in metallic greens and golds.

These are Superb Starlings, the most colourful, cheerful companions one could wish for on safari. Half a dozen of them were making a nuisance of themselves, pulling things to pieces and expressing their delight in a series of pops, whistles and sneezing noises. It was just the encouragement I needed. South Horr was an important stage in the journey; there would be no more townships until we reached the outposts of the Ditsoli desert. As at Wamba, I was somewhat apprehensive about being to a great extent self-dependent. On similar occasions I have found that nothing puts the black dog of melancholy to flight more quickly than a conscientious bout of birdwatching, butterfly observing or spying on nature in general. Carrying the gun and a pair of field-glasses I strode off into the forest on my own.

A stream tumbled down through the trees between a series of flat-topped, highly polished boulders. Each little cascade tailed off into a clear-bright pool, fringed with fern and rush and curiously tenanted by fresh-water crabs and shoals of little turtles. It was as if a handful of small change had suddenly become alive. Copper discs of turtles paddled up to the surface, rolled over on to their backs and, catching the light, suddenly became silver. Farthing turtles played together in a kindergarten while the older coins hung about in the underwater shadows of great green rocks.

The stream made a tunnel through the forest. It was an artery of life in a dark, hostile world of trees. Away from the water one heard only the harsh cries of birds, the bark of a monkey or the crash of a falling nut or a fruit. From abundant droppings it was evident that there were buffalo about and elephant too, but I saw none. The evident drama of the forest was confined to the stream. It was visible in the cold poise of a leaf-green mantis or the diamond head of a water snake protruding above the surface of a pool.

For the most part the individual trees were indistinguishable. They had become intertwined and tied about with such a profusion of lianas, strangler vines and other forms of parasitic growth that the supporting trunks and limbs were lost in a tangle of living network. The whole forest was bound together by wires and cables of vegetation. Some were as thick as bell-ropes or the hawsers of a barge; other hung down limply, waving slightly in the breeze. I pulled one of them, cautiously, and was sprinkled with bright red ants. Another liana led to the upper storey of a colony of weaver birds which fluttered about, protesting harshly as they were shaken out of their coconut-shaped nests.

The belief that tropical forests are rich in birds and flowers may be justified in some parts of the world. In the Congo and certainly in East Africa, the high forests are disappointing places. There is nothing to be seen except the under-surfaces of tall trees and the ground is obscured by a riot of plants resembling rhodo and other dismal dendra, all of them without flowers.

On the banks of the Launit torrent under Nyiru, I saw relatively few spectacular birds although a scarlet-winged touraco fluttered up and down like a mediaeval painting of a comet. This is a relative of the more dowdy Go-away bird or plantain-eater, a creature which haunts huntsmen with a loud and derisive *ah-haaa*, effectively scaring away every animal within gunshot. Red-faced finches and cordon bleus skittered about searching for seeds and the bulbuls, especially the common species which wears a pair of canary-coloured underpants, sang 'What you too?' with such personal emphasis that I was tempted to throw a brick at it. The temptation resisted, I waved to the bird, gave up the task of trying to find a shrike with a ventriloquial call, collected a few insects, and sauntered back to camp feeling distinctly better.

During the talk round the fireside that night I heard the word *upepo* mentioned again and again. It meant wind, the great wind that roared west from beyond Kulal and thrashed the shores of the lake. As there was a light wind blowing at the time, I began to wonder what the morning would bring and whether we should be able to reach water by dusk, that is if we delayed our departure until midday as I had planned. But like most of my apprehensions, they disappeared overnight. The morning was hot, bright and scarcely breezy. At high noon, when we strode out of the shadow of the palms, the heights of Pel danced in the heat.

We walked for about four miles before I began to understand the curious topography of the gap. The symmetry was such that the mountain flanks on either side disappeared into the distance like railway lines or the perspective of a Dali landscape. The topmost tip of Kulal was just visible ahead, but with every step we took it seemed to rise a little from the floor of the lava below the crest of the escarpment.

The heat became intense. Apart from observing with monotonous regularity that there were 'forks in the sun' the men said very little. Goiti urged the camels forward with a throaty 'Hodai!', repeated at intervals. I never discovered what *hodai* meant if, indeed, it meant anything. And Goiti soon tired of saying it.

During the afternoon I discovered that Lelean could determine the sex of distant travellers by the way they sparkled in the sun. Samburu women positively glitter with reflected points of light. They wear polished necklaces and amulets on their arms and the majority of them are tightly encased in brass bangles from their knees to their ankles. It was somewhat more difficult to spot a man from a twinkle of light reflected from a spearhead but I checked the determination with field-glasses and Lelean was rarely wrong, even when the traveller was a dot on the horizon or partly hidden away in the bush. At one point our game was enlivened with a touch of drama when it looked as if we had located a poacher.

The flash came from the tip of a spear about a mile away. Lelean said 'a man' and then became tense at what he saw through the glasses. The man seemed to be crouching and instead of carrying his spear over his shoulder, like any respectable Samburu, the weapon was 'at the ready', point foremost in the manner of a lance.

Lelean loped after him; I followed, panting in the heat. It was not an ideal afternoon for a cross-country run. When we got close the spear-carrier turned out to be a very old man who could neither move quickly nor stand upright. His spear was rusty and blunt. It had not been used for years and, far from poaching, he explained in a quavering voice that he had lost one of his cows. He was looking for it. Had we seen it? I shook my head; Lelean said something uncomplimentary in Samburu and we hurried back to the camels with considerably less enthusiasm for our little game.

Shortly before sundown we marched over a ridge and looked down on to a lunar landscape of lava; it stretched out into infinity. Although the hot wind blew against us, gently, everything was deathly still; I had the impression that we alone were alive in a dead world. There was not even a drop of water in the Anderi *lugga*. This was not a serious matter; we carried an emergency supply of four gallons; there were said to be one or two permanent waterholes immediately ahead of us, and at worst we could march through the night to the lake which was marked on the map as 'brackish but drinkable'. What annoyed me was that although I had carefully consulted the map and sought local advice about the watering point, I had been completely misled by the men who wanted to stay in South Horr as long as they could. As there would be light for about another hour we decided to march on until we found a sheltered camping site.

It was hot, uphill work and the track had almost disappeared. The route was marked only by lumps of brown and black lava which were smaller in size than the big, jagged lumps on either side of us. Seen from a distance, the lava walls to the west and the north were apparently smooth and flat-topped, like railway embankments, but at close quarters they were seen to be composed of lumps of tightly packed slag and pumice stone, hot to the touch and riddled with holes like a Gruyère cheese.

Lake Rudolf, or the Jade Sea as some explorers have called it, was discovered on 6 March 1888 by the Austrian Count Teleki von Szek. He was an interesting man who had made an ambitious foot safari across almost the whole of East Africa accompanied by three Swahilis, six guides, eight Somalis, fifteen *askaris*, over 200 porters and his faithful, plodding, dull-witted biographer, Lt. Ludwig von Höhnel. What little we know of the count himself comes through the laborious and sycophantic prose of the lieutenant, poured out in two large volumes. When he was within a mile or two of where we were looking for a camping site, von Höhnel wrote:

The mountain district between us and the lake was, in fact, a veritable hell, consisting of a series of parallel heights, running from north to south which we had to cut across in a north-westerly fashion. The slopes of these mountains were steep precipices, most of them quite insurmountable, and those that were not were strewn with blackish-brown blocks of rock or of loose scoriae. The narrow valleys were encumbered with stones or debris, or with deep loose sand in which our feet sank, making progress difficult. And when the sun rose higher, its rays were reflected from the smooth brownish-black surface of the rock, causing an almost intolerable glare, whilst a burning wind from the south whirled the sand in our faces, and almost blew the loads off the heads of the men.

Far from blowing the loads off our camels, the wind for the most part was no more than a warm, sustained breeze. It neither rose nor fell for periods of about half an hour and then, quite unexpectedly, came a sound like a long-drawn-out moan from the direction of Kulal. After a few seconds, the increase in velocity was reflected in a scurry of dust devils, almost at our feet.

My floppy bush hat blew off once or twice and I had to pull it down over the side of my face. At the onset of the gusts the camels veered a little and had to be dragged back on to what passed for the track. Their gait became slower as they breasted the wind; they had to be hauled rather than led across the shattered rock. In this fashion we found shelter in a small depression in the lava which I shall always remember with distaste.

I used half of my water allocation that night on a brew of tea; there was not enough for a wash and I was not prepared to rinse my hands and face in camel urine as the boys did. Supper was a meagre affair of a little roasted bird on a plate of cold baked beans. I shot the bird, a dikkop or thick-knees, as it flapped off a slab of rock, crying mournfully. I don't know what it lived on. Nothing grew in the little valley except a few twisted thorn trees.

As I sat on my canvas chair, sipping tea, everything seemed to resolve itself into the absence of water. I had made a bad mistake in not setting out with more than an emergency supply. It would not have happened if I had paid more attention to the map and less to gossip. The water in the Anderi was up in the hills and not at the point where we crossed the *lugga*. It would have been better had we camped in the stream bed and sent out a party to look for the well.

Mezek came up to ask whether he should erect the tent; the alternative was that I should sleep in the open. I agreed that the tent might be blown away but remembering the hyena that bit off the end of my gym shoe, I told him to put the mosquito net over my bed. Mezek pouted and reminded me of the *upepo*. Thinking this an excuse to avoid work, I told him to get on with the job without further argument. I regretted this later in the evening when a gust picked the net up like a handkerchief and threw it into one of the twisted trees. It took us about half an hour to unhook it, badly torn, from the claw-like thorns.

Despite the wind there was a vast assemblage of stars and once, when I awoke, I tried to work out the time from the position of the pointers in the constellations of the Great Bear. Due, I suppose, to our position within two degrees of the equator, the Bear was lying with its feet in the air and its tail almost brushing the horizon.

I remembered that in Arabia they speak of the north-east wind as the Na'ashi and say that it blows from the very centre of

79

the constellation. 'Can'st thou guide the Bear with her train?' asked the Lord of Job when he spoke from a whirlwind. As I gazed at the pointers I wondered whether the pattern of stars was a finger beckoning us on or a fist with the thumb pointing ominously down.

To the Jade Sea

The wind began to rise at dawn until at times it had some of the skull-wrinkling intensity of a scream. The hot blast of air might have come from a furnace. When the thorn trees shrilled and sand began to pile up against my pillow I had no desire to do anything except stay precisely where I was, curled up under a dirty brown sheet on the ground. It seemed as if the expedition had come to a dead stop before we had even reached the lake. In fact, if the men had not been so cheerful about the wind I might have ordered a smart counter-march back to the South Horr valley. Yet, Mezek seemed to think it funny when a gush of precious tea was carried away like spume before it reached the cup; Lelean conceded that the *upepo* was very bad but he thought it would soon die down and Karo laughed uproariously when my sheet blew away. He bounded after it, whooping and cheering. This did me a lot of good. Our affairs, as I saw it might have been much worse. I got up, ate a mouthful of moistened porridge oats and dates, and went off on my own to see what the landscape looked like from the top of a nearby hill.

It looked bad. No tracks were visible in any direction. The foot of Mount Kulal and the Longippi Hills were hidden in orange-coloured streamers of wind-driven sand. The foreground was entirely covered by lava boulders and clusters of polished rock which had either collapsed like bombed houses or seemed to be on the point of collapsing. I walked back to the camp, leaning against the wind. My impression was that it was less violent than it had been at dawn. When we began to lumber forward at nine o'clock I got some comfort from the fact that if we could put up with the hard going until the midday halt it was unlikely we should find conditions much worse anywhere else.

At this point in the journey I want to say plainly that I felt both apprehensive and jubilant – apprehensive for obvious reasons: jubilant because I felt physically competent to walk as far as the camels would take us. My feet were tougher than they had ever been before. This was largely due to Thesiger's advice about wearing canvas shoes; it was the best I could have had. The men wore their variation of Somali sandals made out of pieces of discarded tyres. Among the lava the straps broke and they pulled out the tacks with their teeth, hammering the strips together with a stone. The canvas shoes were more adaptable. When the going was easy I pulled out the laces and slouched along, sometimes taking the shoes off altogether for short periods, walking barefoot in the dust, a delightful sensation. But during the rock-hopping stages I put them on again and laced them up lightly.

After about an hour I realized we had gained more height than I had imagined during the latter part of the previous stage. Mountains which had appeared insignificant suddenly rose to an impressive height, yet because of some optical illusion I was never sure whether I was looking at a pile of rocks in the immediate foreground or a range on the horizon.

Lelean was concerned about the haze ahead of us. He said it was a very bad sandstorm and indicated that we should avoid it if we could. To this I readily agreed even if it meant spending a night with no more than half a gallon of water among us. Although it streamed along some two or three miles to our left, the corridor of blown sand looked dense and suffocating. Dust devils scurried towards us and I was relieved when the haze veered away.

Lelean led the column but after shouting questions at him above the noise of the wind I could not be sure whether we had reached the famous Sirima track which led direct to the lake. It looked as if he intended to seek shelter behind the Longippi Hills. To avoid the sandstorm we took a northerly course. Despite my good intentions about using the map and compass I had made a singularly bad attempt at taking a cross bearing on two distant peaks. Far from being the mountain I thought it was, one turned out to be a little pimple of rock on a distant mound of lava and the other slowly disappeared like the Cheshire Cat until only the fragments remained suspended in the sky. It looked as if it had exploded; it was, in fact, a mirage.

Hopping along, dodging the boulders and trying to keep my mind off a cool, clear lake of drinkable water, I thought of Teleki and von Höhnel who had marched that way without the certain knowledge that there was a lake ahead of them. In their diary they wrote: 'No living creature shared the solitude with us, and as far as our glass could reach there was nothing to be seen but desert, desert everywhere. To all this was added the scorching heat and the ceaseless buffeting of the sand-laden wind against which we were powerless to protect ourselves.'

Stern stuff this. Had I been on the trail half a century earlier I should have preferred the company of Arthur Neumann, the elephant hunter who thought that the local formation was a 'marvellous jumble of different kinds of rocks, chucked about in chaotic confusion'. When he was within a few miles of the lake he said, 'We got among still more terribly rugged hills, full of kloofs and chasms, the tops flanked by red precipices and the valleys full of boulders from top to bottom.' But he added that he felt 'confident' of reaching Reshiat, the country at the top end of the lake. And in my more optimistic moments so did I.

The midday halt brought us to a place where the lava had been ground down to powder by the rare floods of the Balessa Kulal, a *lugga* which rose in the Chalbi desert and ran for eighty or ninety miles roughly parallel to the east shore of the lake, behind Mount Kulal.

Asleep under a bush in the *lugga* was a naked Turkana fisherman, one of the tallest and one of the thinnest men I have ever seen. He put me in mind of a black sand-eel. His name was either Ekali or Ekairu; I have forgotten which. I remember him as the Indolent Ikky and, although I have almost no sense of smell, it was apparent that Ikky, his camel and almost everything about him stank like a box of ferrets. He had been fishing in the lake; his catch, which looked like long ribbons of haddock, was hung about the bush to dry. It was covered in flies and so was Ikky. But he was fast asleep, lost in whatever the Turkana dream about.

We stood round him for a moment without speaking and then Lelean greeted him in Swahili. No response. Mezek repeated the salutation, in Turkana. Ikky continued to snore. At this, Karo, with a delicacy which did him credit, put a little pinch of dust into the sleeper's broad nostrils. Ikky awoke, explosively, and reached for his spear.

Assuring him that we were peacefully inclined and merely wanted to share the *lugga* with him ('we friends'), Mezek, who spoke Turkana, elicited that he was on his way to a nearby *manyatta* with a load of fish and fresh water from a nearby spring.

At the word water I brightened up considerably. Ikky carried about twelve gallons in the goatskin *baromels* slung over his camel. No doubt he would be prepared to make a second journey to the well. Would he accept five shillings for the water?

'Shilingi tano kwa maji,' I said to Mezek but before it could be translated into Turkana, Lelean rounded on me with a furious 'No! No!' My inability to bargain with people and the ease with which they get the better of me inspired him with an angry compassion. He was as close-fisted with my money as he was with his own. In Swahili he gave me to understand that the man was only a damned nigger (*Mshenzi meusi*) and would probably part with whatever he had for a handful of tobacco.

In this he was mistaken for neither money, tobacco, nor tea appeared to be of the slightest interest to the self-sufficient Ikky. What he wanted, he said, was *argri* and *argri*, I knew, was meat. We offered him dried camel meat. After chewing at the end of a fatty-looking piece he nodded, reluctantly, as if implying that it was, indeed, edible – something I was inclined to doubt – but what he really wanted, he said, was fresh meat and he leered, smacking his lips and pointing to my rifle.

Depressing suggestion. I had hoped there would be no more shooting until we reached the lake. Moreover we had not seen a gazelle since we left Anderi. I shook my head. Mezek said 'No meat here' and Lelean turned his back on the man in feigned disgust.

'Mom?' said Ikky, incredulously. 'Mom? What! No meat?' He sprang to his feet with surprising agility and began to speak rapidly to Mezek. It seemed that even as the man had slept he had heard the explosive whistle of a nearby duiker. He thought the little antelope was somewhere among the bushes on the far bank of the *lugga*. No doubt it was still there and if it was, he could find it and I could shoot it. *Mom?*

Cursing the need for both food and water I followed the naked Turkana into the bush with Lengama and Lelean following along behind. As a tracker, Ikky could have out-tracked a pack of police dogs. He never hurried. He kept his eyes on the ground and gave the impression of a dull but diligent child, slowly reading aloud from a primer.

After a leisurely stroll up and down the *lugga* we (that is to say Ikky) picked up the little hoofprints of the duiker in a bed of sand scarcely a hundred yards from where he had slept. He showed us where the animal had paused, turned round and defaecated. We followed it up one bank of a gully and back down the other side. The spoor was plain enough in the sand but how Ikky kept on its track when it moved over stony ground was beyond my comprehension. I suspect that, given the general direction from points in the sand, he anticipated where it was likely to go and kept on moving backwards and forwards until he picked up the trail again.

We found the duiker on a knoll among a troupe of baboons which began to bark and run away. The duiker ran, too. It was like a bouncing ball. After four or five strides it bounded into the air so high that it staggered a little as it landed and ran on again. During a brief pause in its flight, it slewed round to have a look at us. I took a chance on a snap shot and fired the moment I got it in the foresight. When something like a leather glove was flung into the air I realized that I had blown the antelope's head off as surely as if it had been hit on the back of the head with an axe. It was not just dead and done for; it had disintegrated.

At that time the ambivalence of my attitude towards shooting was still unresolved for, describing the incident afterwards, I find that I wrote in my notebook:

Got it slap in the head first shot. Head disappeared. Damn all shooting. Why damn? Who ate the animal? We all ate a bit of it – all except that clown Lengama who complained he couldn't cut the throat of something without a head and asked for a tin of bully. Gave him dried meat. Scarcely anything left of the duiker. The 'Turk' ran the guts through his fingers before wolfing something which looked like undigested grass in the stomach. Seems to be a local delicacy. Looked horrible.

When Mezek walked up with a large pot of tea I discovered that either Lelean was in league with the 'Turk' or I had completely misunderstood the long-winded argument about exchanging meat for water. There was a waterhole in the *lugga*. During our absence the boys had filled up four jerricans with a clear but slightly salty liquid. This came as such a surprise that I spluttered indignantly when I tried to find out why it had been necessary to shoot the duiker. Post-mortems were always difficult. In up-country Swahili the past tense is indicated by the word *nakwisha*, literally 'I finish'; this seemed to make nonsense of most verbs, especially those used in the negative. To make matters worse, there is no Swahili word for the verb 'to have'. One is 'with something' or, negatively, 'not with it'.

When he grasped what I was talking about, Lelean said that of course he knew about the water. What did I imagine had brought the duiker and the baboons to the *lugga*? Everyone knew about the water in Balessa Kulal. As for the duiker, we had shot it because the Turkana had not eaten meat for a long time. As everyone needed meat it was necessary for us to give him some.

I looked hard for signs of deceit in his dark brown eyes but, finding none, I concluded that on this, as on other occasions, there was no more than a little self-interest in the remarkable hospitality of one African to another. I was reminded of one of Thesiger's stories about a Bedu sheikh who was known as the Host of the Wolves because whenever he heard a wolf howl around his tent at night, he ordered his son to take a goat into the desert, saying that he would have no one call on him for dinner in vain.

The clouds of blown sand began to disappear during the afternoon and hoping the worst was over for the day, I ordered the camels to be loaded. I wanted to be at least within sight of the lake before nightfall. The order was received with marked apathy. Both Lelean and Karo went to some lengths to explain that where there had been one duiker there was likely to be another and we would be advised to stay. However, with the indolent Ikky as a guide, we left the shelter of the *lugga* only to discover that the wind was still blowing like an express train.

As we marched towards the Longippi Hills, Kulal, away to the north, began to rise to a formidable height. The map showed that the two halves of the long, narrow mountain were divided by the steep walls of the El Gijata gorge but our course was such that the south flank was like the bows of an approaching liner seen head on. It seemed to be bearing down on us, an illusion heightened by the pressure of a warm, unwavering stream of wind. From the top of a pile of dirty brown rocks, honeycombed with bubbles like the fossilized foam of a sewer,

I searched the landscape with field-glasses for a long-anticipated glimpse of the lake. Beyond Longippi were hills of a smoky violet colour which, Lelean assured me, were 'among the homes of the Turkana'. This meant that they rose from the western shore of Rudolf and that the lake, although still invisible, was somewhere in the hollow immediately ahead of us. At any moment I expected to catch the flash of bright water.

What did catch my eye was a row of cairns ahead, each about twelve feet in diameter at the base and so regular in shape that they alone seemed real among the unrealities of the landscape. Neumann had seen the stone circles seventy years earlier and thought they 'must have formed the ground plan of some sort of rude huts'. But, as he said, 'who made them or what they should have been doing in the desert and why they should camp, even if travelling, where there is no water is a puzzle.'

The cairns, I had been told in Wamba, are memorials to the dead. Some had been erected by past generations of Turkana but the majority were built by the Elmolo people who still live along the shores of the lake. Lelean had no respect for the shrines and clambered up one of them to get a better view but neither Mezek nor Ikky would go near them.

During the afternoon I discovered that the going was far easier than it had been during the morning although the conditions were much the same. This was because, without being aware of it, I had slipped into an easy stride which was rather like wading through water or stepping slowly and deliberately across a field of tall grass. Instead of wasting energy by pushing against the wind, I found it was possible to lean against it and by lifting my knees a little higher than usual I could roll one foot over the other, easily, without much strain.

The warm wind dried the skin and evaporated perspiration to such an extent that my arms and legs felt slightly cold. I remember thinking that if this was the worst we could expect, I had nothing to fear except apprehension. What I did not know at the time was that the effects of sustained heat and the down-pouring of powerful sunlight are slow and insidious and it was possible to go far without realizing that much was wrong.

I became very irritable. I had a strong suspicion that Ikky had lost his way. Instead of making for the hills as we had done, he cut across what appeared to be one of the worst patches of broken lava and then paused, uncertainly, before waving us on to higher ground. I began to think that the man was just as much of a rogue as I had been a dupe in accepting his services as a guide. It looked as if he had got us into a bigger mess than we should have got ourselves into if I had not taken him on.

As if he had read my thoughts, Ikky suddenly stopped and said something to Mezek, Mezek nodded and turned to me. 'The Turkana,' he said, 'wants to find the barra-barra m'zuri.' The *good* road! Feeling thoroughly ill-tempered, I said if he could find any sort of track, good, bad or indifferent I should be obliged to him. From east to west I could see nothing but lumps of chocolate-coloured lava. It was a landscape for a night-mare and we were unquestionably lost. With irony which was lost on everyone concerned, I asked *how* the Turkana proposed to find the good road.

They told me we should rest for a little while and while we rested the 'Turk' would reconnoitre from the top of a hill. I watched him walk away with an easy, open stride, his sandals plopping as he skipped from one piece of sharp-edged rock to another. He seemed to have a lot of confidence; I had very little. Our route lay to the north. The hills were still due ahead of us but as far as I could see it was not possible to walk much farther across the intervening country. The lava was getting worse. To add to my misgivings, two of the camels flopped down on to their bellies as soon as the head ropes were released. The others stood motionless. This was a bad sign. Ordinarily they would have wandered off at once to look for food.

Squatting with my back against a rock as hot as a radiator, I watched Ikky carefully picking his way towards the higher ground. Possibly I had misjudged him but I felt excessively bad-tempered – not apprehensive, merely bad-tempered. On long marches I found that irritability invariably rose and fell with the sun. In the early hours of the morning I could make plans, chat to the men, think beautiful thoughts and take a reasonably intelligent interest in what we saw. But after about half-past ten, especially in desolate places or when we had made an early morn-ing start, I tended to become morbidly introspective. This I took to be the 'acidie or white melancholy', described by John Cassian, a fifth-century monk. It seems to be related to 'the destruction' that wasteth at noonday.

For this interpretation of the processes of melancholia I am deeply indebted to Helen Waddel whose *Desert Fathers* I read when I became bored with maps, dictionaries, paper-backs and a biography of the Crown Prince Rudolf after whom the lake had been named. According to Waddell's translation of Cassian, the white melancholy is 'akin to dejection' and is 'especially felt by monks or wandering solitaries, a persistent and obnoxious enemy to such as dwell in the desert, disturbing . . . especially about midday, like a fever mounting at a regular time'.

Ikky by this time had shrunk to the size of an ant on a grey rock. Through glasses I watched him scan the horizon without shading his eyes. He looked round once and then walked back as nonchalantly as he had walked away. As I might have guessed he told Mezek that the 'good road' was 'not very far'. The camels were dragged to their feet, blabbering and blowing out blood-stained froth. We marched on. I began to wonder whether it was anything more than a coincidence that a lake in a violent landscape had been named after a suicidal prince.

Count Teleki reached the lake in 1888 the year in which his royal master, the Crown Prince Rudolf of Austria, met the girl with whom he entered into a death pact in the famous affair at the castle of Mayerling. It seems now that the seventeen-year-old Marie Vetsera was not the innocent young girl that romantic literature makes her out to be. Various young men in Viennese society were mentioned as enjoying her favours. She had an especial weakness for cavalry officers at a time when her mother, the widow of a Turkish dragoman 'preferred elderly gentlemen of sound financial standing'. But it is reasonably certain that Marie realized her royal lover needed peace and gave him warmth – 'like a little animal' as one of her biographers puts it.

Rudolf, the man who gave his name to the Jade Sea, was a virtual prisoner of the Austrian court. His father, the Emperor Franz Josef, suspected him of conspiracy with the Hungarian separatists; like his father he was haunted by the ever-present spectre of a war with Russia. His mother, the Empress Elizabeth, one of the most beautiful women in Europe, continued to regard him as a child while his wife, the Princess Stephanie, a loud-voiced woman 'with the daintiness of a dragoon' simply ignored him.

Rudolf was subject to bouts of acute depression; he must have been aware that many of his relatives were unmistakably mad. He had tried to enter into a death pact with various courtiers and Uhlan officers so that when the end came at Mayerling in the early hours of Wednesday, 30 January 1889, it was not a surprise to those who knew him well.

Rudolf spent the night in the hunting lodge with Marie Vetsera. By the light of candles, the girl wrote her farewell letters. 'Dear Mother: forgive me for what I have done. I could not resist my love . . . I would like to be buried beside him at Alland.'

After some talk about whether they should die by poison or revolver, Rudolf courteously left the decision to Marie. 'Rather a revolver,' she wrote. 'A revolver is safer.' She stretched herself out on the bed and her lover shot her through the forehead. Why he did not follow her, immediately, and what his thoughts were, alone in the room with the dead girl, for several hours, none can ever know. After contemplating death for so many years it may be that when he was actually obliged to make the ultimate decision, Rudolf lacked the courage to kill himself. It was not until dawn that he called his valet Loschek and told him to prepare breakfast. The last respite was over. Rudolf picked up a hand mirror and a small revolver and pulled the trigger.

He died so quickly that when they carried the body to the family grave of the Hapsburgs his right forefinger remained in its crooked position. As the top of his skull was missing the Emperor had some difficulty in convincing the papal authorities that the Crown Prince had died suddenly of heart failure. There was the added complication that the dead body of a young woman had been found on his bed.

The Mayerling affair was high drama that ended on the authentic note of anticlimax. The Baroness Vetsera was not buried beside her royal lover. The unwashed naked body, dressed only in a fur coat and a hat to hide the gaping wound in the temple, was smuggled out of the hunting lodge at night by the police. On the orders of the Emperor, Marie's relatives were compelled to sign a document saying that the young woman had committed suicide. If she had died for love, the emotion was not wholly reciprocated. Before he left for Mayerling, Rudolf had spent several hours with another mistress, Mitzi Kaspar, to whom he left 60,000 gulden and a letter 'overflowing with love'.

The reaction of his wife Stephanie was one of pious indignation. 'My whole personality,' she wrote 'rose in revolt against the impiety, the wicked frivolity with which a life has been thrown away.' What she was incapable of appreciating was that Rudolf had died of a not uncommon disease called despair. The lasting memorial to the melancholic prince is the Jade Sea.

I was surprised to find that none of our company had ever heard of the name of Rudolf. To the Samburu, the Big Water beyond Nyiru is *Basso*; the Turkana knew it as *Aman* and the northern tribes as *Gallop*. To me the lake was a will-o'-the-wisp, and I wondered if we should ever reach it.

Slow as it was, our progress showed that, far from justifying my suspicions, Ikky was a thoroughly competent guide. The *barra-barra* he sought was not what I would have called a road. It was a long rib of rock that rose from the crusty surface of the lava. Once we got on top of it, the going was slithery but less arduous than the way through the boulders on either side. The rock led to the mouth of a deep gorge, the Sirima, which had nothing to commend it except that at the far end I thought I saw an occasional flicker which might have come from the surface of a large sheet of water.

Before I could ask any questions, Ikky indicated that his duties as a guide were over. He said the lake was at the end of the gorge and he was anxious to get back to his own people. He left us, apparently satisfied, with three fish hooks, a length of monofilament line and a few sticks of dried camel meat. When I looked down the gorge again I could not see the flash and Lelean irritated me beyond measure by saying that he *knew* that *Basso* was not very far.

The wind had sunk to a mere breath but on the floor of the Sirima it was the hot breath of a boiler-room. It was as if the once-molten basalts that towered above us had retained the heat of the volcanoes from which they had been spewed out.

The light flickered again. I wondered at first if it were lightning or the reflection of sun on distant rocks. But I said nothing to the boys. Lelean, I knew, would tell me that the lake was not very far away and that we should soon be able to prepare a good camp where there was plenty of water. I had heard this many, many times before.

The sun had almost set by the time we came within full view of Rudolf. It was a satin sunset of amber and oyster blue with the distant hills of Turkanaland painted in bold brush-strokes of purple water-colour. I had thought about the Jade Sea so often that I cannot remember my first impressions except that the lake was olive-green and more vast than I had imagined, certainly more beautiful than I could have foreseen. A spiral of birds turned like tea leaves in the sky. They were wood ibises and pelicans which sank down from a great height, slowly until they became lost in a host of unidentifiable birds on the surface of the water.

It was a romantic sight. I felt romantic. With a crumbling stucco of dust and sweat on our faces, I think we probably looked somewhat romantic and we kept up this appearance until we were within a few hundred yards of the water. Then we behaved quite normally.

Karo broke the spell with an exultant yell and started to run down the slope, pulling off his pants on the way. Lelean and Mezek pounded after him, shedding their shirts as they ran. I jumped into the water before I remembered I was wearing a non-waterproof watch. But it was of no great importance. For ten minutes the orderly, reserved relationship between master and men was thrown aside as if it had never existed. We behaved like children.

Karo and Mezek churned up the water in a mock fight while Lelean stood on his hands on the bottom so that only his wildly thrashing legs were visible. I rolled about in the shallows, floated on my back and duck-dived, head backwards, until I realized that I had drunk a great deal of the water. It tasted and felt as if it were slightly soapy, but, despite all I had been told about its soda content, it was cool and refreshing and during our days by the lake I never suffered from anything more serious than a slight loosening of the bowels.

The camels lumbered up to the water with their lower lips quivering, tremulously. They knelt down, extended their snake-like necks and drank and drank until they had to be hauled off into the dusk.

We slept that night in a crack between two walls of pock-marked lava. Lelean assured me that it was safe to sleep in the open, that is without the protection of the mosquito net. But I remember very little of the night except that I soon slipped into an intensely satisfying sleep, perhaps the most profound of the whole safari. Whatever the outcome we had at least reached the Jade Sea.

Lolita of Loiyangalani

We got away from our first lakeside camp at eight o'clock in the morning and marched along the water-line in high spirits. Karo threw back his head like an operatic tenor and sang from his heart; the camels, marvellously refreshed by a bellyful of thorn, belched contentedly and even the lugubrious Goiti conceded that their droppings were in better shape than they had been for days. I felt pretty good myself. Overnight the lake had turned from an opaque piece of jade into an enormous sunflashing sapphire.

After a few days I began to understand something of the intimate relationship between the colour of the water and the state of the prevailing wind. When the wind began to blow hard from the east, as it usually did from dawn until about eleven o'clock in the morning, the colour of the water became indistinguishable from the blue of the sky. White-capped wavelets grew bigger and bigger until long lines of white maned horses raced out towards the Turkana shore. But when the wind began to drop, all the vitality drained out of the water: it took on the colour of a plate of pea soup. There is a fairly simple explanation for this change in complexion. The water contains a vast amount of green algae. These little plants have a rhythm of their own, rising and falling under the influence of light. When they are close to the surface at calm periods of the day or when they are piled up under Kulal by a westerly wind, the lake seems to be covered in a viridescent skin. This, as far as I understand it, is the scientific explanation. I prefer to think of Rudolf in terms of sapphire and jade.

We had the choice of two tracks. One of them, a serpentine affair, followed the ins and outs of the shoreline; the other ran about a quarter of a mile inland, high up on the lava scarp. It was situated on what I took to be an ancient beach, a relic of bygone times when the lake was much higher than it is today. Lelean wanted to take the high road and I the low. I didn't like the look of the lava although I suspected that the upper track was more direct than the shoreline since it cut across the neck of a disconcerting number of promontories. As three recognizable peaks stood out like church steeples, I tried to get a fix on them.

Every good traveller can use a compass as readily as his razor. I am an exception. I have always had some difficulty with the instrument, simple as it is. To my intense surprise on this occasion, instead of pointing due north, away from me, as it should have done, the little red tip of the needle swung round as if my navel was intensely ferromagnetic. I stood to one side. The needle followed me. Thinking that the basalt and lava beneath us might be magnetic, I put the compass on the dead stump of a tree. The needle tip pointed towards Turkanaland at the other side of the lake, which I knew to be west. I sighed, put the compass away and said we would take the low road. I have since discovered that other travellers have experienced similar difficulties among the magnetic rocks of the shore-line.

Another set-back had to do with my chronic inability to shoot straight. We had been marching for about half an hour when a wedge of Egyptian geese bore down on us, flying low and fast and veering only slightly as they passed overhead. We were just inside a shooting zone but they caught me unprepared. I let them go but kept the gun cocked and walked towards a headland where a few birds were preening themselves among the rocks. Three geese promptly took off, skeetering up into a gust of wind and presenting the sort of target that wildfowlers dream about. My first shot was a clean miss. Worse still, I got nothing more than a puff of rusty-coloured feathers with my second; by the time I had reloaded the birds in the air were far away. In desperation I took a snap shot at a sitting bird which appeared undecided what to do. I hit it full charge but instead of falling back on to some rocks where it could have been retrieved, it was blown into the water. It floated for a second or two, wings outspread. Then there was an immense swirl and it disappeared as if the lake had licked it from its lips.

'Mamba,' said Lelean.

'Mamba?'

'Cockydee,' he said, using one of the very few words of English he knew. It was a very large crocodile and had much to do with my reluctance to bathe during the rest of the day. I had been told that it was safe to venture only into very shallow water and to make double sure the boys threw in a volley of rocks before we waded in up to our thighs.

Lelean was a happy man because, as he explained at great length, his father's *manyatta* was somewhere on the slopes of Kulal and he hoped that I would give him a few days' leave. He said he had not been home for two or three years. After a somewhat grudging assurance that he could have a couple of days on his own, he asked if he could borrow my ammunition belt and hunting knife for the occasion. As he put it, nicely, he wanted to appear *maridadi*, an elastic expression that means, among other things, a dandy. I agreed and volunteered to throw in my spare watch and a pair of long khaki stockings which he had had his eye on for a long time.

Our next objective, as the travel books say, was Loiyangalani, a luxurious fishing camp said to be equipped with a bar, a bathing pool and an atmosphere distinctly at variance with my ideas about the austerities of the Jade Sea. Sportsmen are flown from Nairobi to the camp where they can catch massive Nile perch from a launch hired at the rate of £5 an hour. In my zest for solitude I should have preferred to turn my back on the sophistication of Loiyangalani. This could have been done by marching behind Kulal and rejoining the lake about a third of the way up the eastern shore, but I had good reasons for getting to the camp as soon as I could. I had arranged to pick up a supply of rations there; they included half a dozen bottles of Scotch and a fishing rod. Moreover, I was under an obligation to meet a game warden and, what seemed most ludicrous of all, the armed escort. We had arranged to meet at a place called Ballo *lugga*, some fifteen miles north of the camp. As it would take us the better part of the day to reach Loiyangalani we decided to march without the usual halt at midday.

Rudolf is a long narrow lake, about a hundred and eighty miles in length and thirty-five miles across the widest point. Most of what I had learnt about it comes from the account of an expedition in 1935, led by Dr, now Sir Vyvyan, Fuchs, the

to the Matthews

2 The smallest camel I have seen

e Elmolo seemed happy enough

4 Lolita of Loiyangalani

lean inspects an Elmolo palm-wood raft

6 Samburu chief

home of Karo's father

8 Lakeside days

Antarctic explorer. It ended in tragedy. Two of his companions, Dyson and Martin, tried to reach the large island at the south end of the lake in a collapsible boat and were never seen again. Fuchs said the wind that swept over the Serima scarp was 'tremendous'. Remembering what we had gone through the previous day, I was inclined to think that we had been very lucky.

South Island lay ahead of us. In the light of the morning sun, the extinct volcanoes on the island seemed to be no more inhospitable than the rest of the lava fields around us, but through field-glasses it was clear that even a light wind threw a curtain of spray over the black rocks. Lelean surprised me by saying that he had flown over the island in a big bird. This seemed so improbable that I questioned him closely. I found that during his service with the King's African Rifles, he and fifty other members of his company had been flown in from Nairobi to Lodwar to settle a local war among the Turkana. Asked what he thought of travel in the belly of a big bird, he said it was horrible. He had vomited for two hours.

From the shoreline I looked up towards the heights of Mount Kulal. After being blown about by winds which always seemed to come from the direction of the mountain, I had come to think of the old monster as Aeolus, a violent fellow who was determined to blow us into the lake. He belched violently on one or two occasions during the morning. One puff was followed by such a spectacular darkening of the sky that I changed direction so that, if necessary, we could shelter in the lee of some overhanging rocks.

After an uneasy silence, the leaden clouds turned slightly yellow and we heard the familiar moan from the heights. There was a flicker or two of lightning and a veil of dust slowly crossed our track some distance ahead. When the squall reached the lake, it made the water boil as violently as if a flotilla of speedboats had raced out towards the island. If Dyson and Martin had run into a gust of this kind it is unlikely that they could have remained afloat for more than a few minutes. The track of the gust was about three hundred yards in width and, due to the mountain, somewhat contrary to the direction of the prevailing wind.

At midday we reached the drab huts of the Elmolo, a race of lakeside fisherfolk whose funeral cairns we had seen on the other side of the escarpment. They are a people who possess almost nothing. They live in huts like untidy birds' nests, made of grass and bits of driftwood. Rotting fish remains littered the ground; naked babies snatched at the flies; a few sticks upheld tattered nets. The impression was Neolithic. I felt as if we had stumbled on a race that had survived simply because Time had forgotten to finish them off. Lelean put on his cap and official expression and strode into one of the huts to look for skins, hippo teeth or other signs of poaching. To the delight of everyone he got chased out by a very old woman with a fish spear. In an attempt to retain his dignity he tried to reason with her at a respectful distance but she threw stones at him and screeched like a parrot.

From the amused expression of the rest of the community, I gathered that we had upset nobody except the old woman. As the great-grandmother of the colony, she had a privileged position and Lelean had disturbed her midday sleep. She accepted a gift of tobacco without grace and threatened me with the spear when I refused to give her any more.

The Elmolo or 'Impoverished Ones' are said to be degenerate Samburu or Rendille who got tired of the endless search for water and grazing and took to a new way of life by the side of the lake where at least they had an abundant supply of water and fish. Fuchs and other explorers have commented at length on their emaciated appearance and strangely bowed legs due, they thought, to some dietary deficiency. Perhaps there has been a change for the better in recent years when the government has taken some interest in the tribe and supplied them with maize meal. At one time or another I met the whole tribe of a hundred and twenty-eight individuals. Although they are poor they are an extremely healthy-looking people; some are unusually good-looking and as plump as pigeons. They pole about in the shallows of the lake on simple rafts of palm wood, either netting or spearing fish.

A missionary told me that the Elmolo spoke a language containing at least a hundred basic words unknown elsewhere. Listening to them chattering I thought I could detect the rapidly rolled consonants of the Samburu but Lelean said he could understand only a little of what they said. I asked one old man what he feared most, expecting him to say the wind or the droughts which threaten to dry out the lake. Instead, he said 'the bad ones from the north' – the Marille from Ethiopia who both kill and castrate their victims. They are obliged to collect human testicles before they can undergo their own initiation ceremonies. It was for protection against the Marille that I was obliged to accept an escort from the Ballo *lugga* onwards and after hearing how many Elmolo had died, mutilated, I felt rather better about the escort.

Looking back on a curious series of events at Loiyangalani I can see now that I was almost entirely to blame for not getting out of the place earlier than I did or resigning myself to luxury life as I waited for a 'plane that was delayed for days on end. Instead, I pitched camp on the periphery of luxury and dodged between a chromium-plated bar and the task of keeping my own camp in order.

The fishing camp has been built among palms around a warm, clear spring. The manager, an efficient little Malagassy, had to be everything to everybody including diesel mechanic, launch master, fisherman in chief, hotel manager, barman and the scourge of a motley collection of Elmolo and Somali 'boys'. I slept under a palm tree and wrote up my diary on a bar stool. My rations arrived in a truck but the whisky and the fishing rod were still at the airport in Nairobi. Each morning between half-past eight and ten o'clock a belt of static from somewhere in the general direction of Kulal effectively insulated the short-wave transmitter from all reception points south. A miserable situation, as I recall it.

Lelean provided a little light relief. He wanted to impress his family and everyone did their best to dress him up. On the day before Christmas, when the temperature was 107 degrees in the shade, we put him on a donkey and watched him ride up the mountain track towards the family *manyatta*.

His khaki shirt and shorts had been scrubbed and ironed until they glistened. He polished the leather brim of his *kepi*; he wore my belt and hunting knife. He carried the rifle on a sling that had been liberally daubed with blanco and, to crown all, his donkey had a bow of scarlet ribbon on each of its ragged ears. Looking like a lieutenant in the Foreign Legion, Lelean Linewe-muru rode off into the hills.

Christmas Eve was uneventful but shortly before dawn on the following day we got the full blast of an impressive squall. With some hesitation I had accepted the assurance of the camp manager that a patch of ground between a group of palm trees was reasonably wind-proof. The boys put up a tent which had not been used for a week and I went to bed at midnight in the hope that the 'plane would soon arrive and that I could get away from incongruous luxury.

I awoke under the impression that I had heard the ominous moan from the hills, but I couldn't be sure. Perhaps I had been dreaming. Before I could make up my mind, there was a crack of thunder like a gun shot. A palm tree at the back of the compound had been struck and before I had the wit to get out of the flapping tent, we were beset by a wind of quite extraordinary violence.

In far less time than it took to record the incidents later, two panels of the canvas were torn apart, the tent pegs were wrenched out of the ground and I was bowled over in a confusion of guns, bedding and clothing as the tent was blown away.

It blew against a bush where it stuck. I crawled out to find it was almost impossible to stand up against the wind. The palm trees roared. I was concerned lest they were torn out of the ground and flung down among us. Not until I saw the boys striving to cover up the sacks of food did I realize there was rain in the wind, and when the squall subsided it drenched us. The warm spring became a cold muddy river and the hobbled camels knelt in six inches of water. The deluge was over in about half an hour but with everything soaked and part of the camp literally under water, the dawn was one of the most unpleasant I can remember.

When all our blankets and clothing were hung out to dry on the camel ropes we had cause to be grateful for the fierce heat from the sun. Although the aluminium poles were twisted and the outer fly badly torn, to my surprise the tent was not a complete wreck. We cut up some of the canvas and used it as a ground sheet. I folded up the inner walls, determined not to use them again until we got away from the lake. What disturbed me most was the condition of a new two-hundred-pound sack of *posho*. It represented a month's supply of maize meal. The bottom of the sack was soggy and it was too windy to open it and dry the meal in the sun.

Taking stock of the damage I noticed that the sugar sack had split open and I told Karo, the best handyman of them all, to ew it up. I knew that somewhere in the ammunition boxes were needles and a ball of twine. Before I had time to find the key I was surprised to see Karo busily at work. Assuming that he had to provide his own tools, he had cut a wooden needle from a long sliver of acacia wood. By scraping one end of the needle flat and boring a hole in it he had made an 'eye' for the strips of bark he used as twine. As I frequently discovered, Karo was a very good man to have about the place in an emergency.

Tuesday, 25 December, is summed up in my diary as an 'eventful day'. The words '(i) tent wrecked', are followed by '(ii) touching gift of bugs and beetles; (iii) thief in the camp; (iv) Karo unpopular; (v) erotic dance by the Elmolo' and, finally, 'Still no 'plane, dammit'.

At breakfast time Mezek reminded me that it was the Chief Day. In a little speech, he said that he was a Christian (*Mimi Mkristo*) and that on the Chief Day (*Siku kuu*) it was the habit of Christians to give presents to one another. Suspecting that he wanted something for himself, I nodded, dispassionately, and waited to hear what it was. But Mezek didn't want anything, he had a present for me.

Holding his head down, shyly, and keeping one hand behind his back, he said that he knew I liked *dudus*. This was true. *Dudus* are insects. Mezek often stopped on the march and pointed them out to me. With his big toes he would turn a beetle over on its back or bring me a praying mantis, perched angrily on the tip of his forefinger. Mezek put an old tobacco tin down on the table and invited me to open it.

Inside was a remarkable collection of partly squashed beetles, grasshoppers, bush crickets, a decapitated butterfly and a large dead scorpion from which the sting had been carefully removed. The gift was so unexpected and so wholly appropriate that for a second or two I was unable to speak. As so often happened I was both surprised and ashamed of my surprise at the zeal and kindliness of men cheaply hired. After a belated, reciprocal gift of a bar of almost liquid chocolate I looked for a place to hang up some Christmas decorations given to me in London by affectionate daughters. I found a convenient bough over my bed for a slowly revolving bell of coloured paper and sat with my feet up, sorting out the insects.

Nostalgic thoughts were cut short by an uproar from the direction of the cookhouse. Aboud and Goiti were chasing a little nipper who had stolen a tin of dried milk. I was unable to discover who he was. Nobody would accept any responsibility for a pock-marked child who threw stones at the elders and pilfered his food. The previous night he had scattered a herd of goats.

On this occasion he had sneaked into the back of the cook-house while Mezek was serving breakfast and run off with the tin. Aboud got hold of him but promptly let go when he was bitten on the thumb. Goiti closed in but had to duck when the tin was hurled in his face. After a vigorous chase, Mezek grabbed the naked child and began to give him some hard smacks on his backside. But to the amusement of everyone except Mezek, the little blighter defaecated, violently, and managed to slip away into the bushes. We never saw him again.

As Karo had worked harder than anyone else to put the camp to rights after the storm, I was sorry to find that he, too, was in trouble at Loiyangalani. It was the old story. He had borrowed money which he was unable to repay. He had also fallen into the fundamental error of trying to pull off a series of confidence tricks on a tribal group who remembered only too well what had happened the last time he had turned up.

Karo came from a little *manyatta* to the north of Loiyangalani. After various jobs in the neighbourhood of Marsabit, he had persuaded either the Game or the Forestry Department to appoint him as a part-time scout on the slopes of Mount Kulal. I was told that he was a very efficient scout; he had brought in a number of convictions for poaching and he might have become quite an important local official had he not been entrusted with the task of paying his fellow game scouts. Inevitably, Karo 'borrowed' heavily from the cash he carried from Marsabit and when one of his colleagues complained to headquarters that he had not been paid for six months, Karo went to gaol for a similar length of time. In gaol they discovered that he had abandoned at least three wives and as a result of various sums borrowed on the strength of his government position, he was heavily in debt.

By the time I had learnt something of his history from Mezek, Karo was squatting imperturbably on his heels in the centre of a circle of villagers who were conducting an unofficial court of enquiry into his affairs. From what I could gather he was faced with debts incurred over a period of three or four years. But instead of keeping out of the way, he had borrowed money as soon as we arrived on the curious grounds that the local headman owed him a considerable sum for seducing one of his wives. As the third Mrs Karo had left Loiyangalani, destitute, some weeks earlier, presumably in search of her errant spouse, Karo put up a spirited defence based on the fact that no one could produce the missing witness.

'Where is the woman?' he asked. 'Find her and she will tell you the truth. Why is she not here? I will tell you why. The headman has hidden her away. He is scared. He knows that he owes me ten cows for the bride price.'

Karo's misdeeds were discussed for about two hours. Apart from a witness who was struck across the face for alleged perjury, it was a most orderly enquiry. The old headman sat on an empty paraffin tin, drew figures in the dust with his stick and paused for several seconds before weighing up some of the arguments put to him.

Karo was a disarming defendant. He denied nothing and seemed to be gaining the support of everyone except the plaintiffs. He admitted that in addition to the old debts he had borrowed about thirty shillings the previous day. Some of it had been spent on soft drinks for himself and his friends. Was it not the custom for a man to treat his friends? As for the rest, he said he had given it back to those from whom he had borrowed money on previous occasions.

The case became extremely complicated and I refused to arbitrate on the grounds that it was *shauri yao* – their affair. Had I agreed to meet even one of the minor debts it looked as if I should be responsible for the maintenance of three abandoned wives. There was also talk of putative fatherhood. 'Whose child is the little pock-marked one, the one who steals?' An aggrieved villager suggested that the brat was the unrecognized son of Karo and if he was the father of the child it was his duty to look after him.

Karo was completely unmoved by this, to me, quite unexpected accusation. He shrugged his shoulders and fell back to his old defence: 'Where is the child? Ask him who his father is.' If this was a bluff it was superbly handled and I was not entirely convinced that it was a bluff. The headman looked somewhat abashed. He dug his stick in the ground and from the way he brought the enquiry to an unresolved conclusion, I began to wonder whether his interest in the third Mrs Karo was entirely charitable. When it was all over I did what I could to maintain good public relations by distributing aspirin tablets and a capful of raisins.

At midday, when the lake began to shimmer, hazily, and take on the colour of bile, we were encircled by a frenzied horde of Elmolo dancers. I hesitate to describe the performance as entertainment. At the height of the ecstasy they grunted like animals and flung themselves about wildly, erotically, until the weakest collapsed in a cataleptic trance. In the dance there may have been the elements of bygone Masai or Samburu ceremonies. I have not been able to find anything about the vocabulary of the movements in the literature. Nor could I learn anything from the missionaries, who were not in favour of the rituals of the lake. The dancers hoped for reward. They ran up to us and held out their hands, but receiving nothing they continued to grunt and dance as if we had not existed. It was an incongruous, disturbing performance, wholly in accord with the torrid, incongruous atmosphere of Loiyangalani.

About eighty dancers made their way up from the lake. They were not a professional élite: among them were elderly women who jerked and grimaced in the train of their grand-daughters while little *totos* tripped up their elders. Everyone seemed to be there. It is likely that I was present at a gathering of most of the Elmolo from Sirima to Ballo.

They assembled under a palm tree in a mob and began to drone and stamp their feet in a movement which at first had no discernible rhythm. But, gradually, I detected a concerted and explosive 'Ah!' followed by a pause until the effect of the 'Ah!' (pause) 'Ah!' (pause) 'Ah!' (pause) sounded like a local train pulling out of a rural station.

The mob divided and reassembled in a ragged line. The rhythm became faster as the exhaled 'Ah!' was punctuated by stamping movements. 'Ah!' (stamp, stamp), 'Ah!' (stamp, stamp), 'Ah!' (stamp, stamp). It was hypnotic. I found that I was nodding my head and beating my knees with my fists. Karo promptly joined in the dance. The other boys stood up and stamped their feet hesitantly, uncertain whether to follow him.

At the height of the rhythm, a young brave closed his eyes and collapsed, taut as a bow string. He lay on the ground, making a nasal noise, like a wasp in a bottle. An old woman forced a piece of wood between his teeth to stop him biting his tongue. The others ignored him. Before the rhythm began to subside, two others fell down as if they had been hit with a club, one of them drooling a reddish-brown nut-stained froth.

The climax of the dance was a contest of a frankly erotic nature between six young girls and any of the braves who cared to take them on. The rest of the tribe formed a loose circle around them. They still grunted and stamped their feet but with less fervour than before. It seemed as if all the emotion generated by the preliminaries had been transferred to the ecstatic contestants who bounced up and down with such vigour that a patch of sharp-edged lava cinders was soon pounded to an ashen-grey powder.

On the Serengeti plains of Tanzania, I have seen the Masai leaping high, their hands held down as if they were standing to attention in mid-air. They remained on the same spot, rising and falling in an effortless, elastic manner. Among the Masai the leaping seems to be confined to the males. But among the Elmolo the women leapt into the air. The young men left the circle of outsiders and hopped towards them, grotesquely, with their legs apart, jerking their thighs forward in a piston-like pantomime of the sexual act. When they were within a few inches of a selected woman, the braves thrust themselves forward with knees bent and their backs arched. It looked as if the object was to touch, perhaps to seize hold of the women who rose and fell like marionettes but I never saw the object accomplished.

At the anticipated point of impact, the women thrust out a hand and pushed their suitors away. It was a vigorous push. If the men lost their balance and fell backwards by as much as a few paces they were obliged to retire amid the giggles of the rest of the tribe.

Of the six girls who resisted these satyric attacks, five barely managed to hold their own. But the sixth who seemed to be the Lolita of Loiyangalani was a consummate destroyer of virile intent. She was beautifully made and very young. Unlike the other girls who wore only a grass skirt behind and a fringe of discarded fish netting in front, Lolita flaunted her sex with a narrow V of bright white stuff that hung from her thighs to her knees.

Karo was pushed over within a few minutes. After an hour of apparently effortless dancing under a vertical sun, Lolita had discomfited all the others and when at last there were no other males to match her, she looked round disdainfully and strode from the dance floor like a queen.

Out of the Depths

Three days elapsed before the 'plane droned high over Longippi, like a tired bee. As there was nothing I liked about Loiyangalani more than the prospect of getting away from it, the sound was more than welcome; it was the prospect of deliverance. We hastened down to the airstrip and waited, impatiently, as the bird, the *N'dege* as the men called it, slid under a patch of cloud and thundered over us, twice, before the pilot considered it safe to settle down among the lava dust and the indolent pelicans on the edge of the runway. The pilot was a cheerful fellow who said it was like landing in a bloody oven with the gas turned on. Knowing something about the local winds, he lashed his 'plane down with steel cables before he would accept a drink. An hour later it was loaded up with three hundred pounds of perch fillets for the most expensive hotels in Nairobi and took off again; we held the camels' heads until the dust and the uproar subsided.

I remember a smoke ring in the sky as the 'plane disappeared from sight. It had been blown from the guts of one of the active volcanoes at the south end of the lake. It was an improbable sight, a visible hiccup from one of the safety valves in the rocks. Yet over Rudolf it was far less improbable than the roaring machine from a distant city. I was pleased to find that the men were eager to get away and we walked about seven miles to Elmolo Bay before I felt we were on our own again.

The Bay was a wholly unexpected haven of sunlight and tawny sand. Instead of the usual midday translation from sapphire to jade, the breeze-wrinkled water took on the colour of cornflowers. It was the soft blue of northern latitudes. I was entranced by the change in atmosphere and set up camp under what appeared to be the only tree on the eastern shore. Looking back on those pleasurable days, I think I was utterly relieved that we had got away from the winds of Kulal, the more so because the old monster did his best to catch us out before we got very far. During the afternoon he blew a squall in our direction but, remembering what he was capable of, I thought it a feeble affair; the scurrying dust devils faltered and collapsed before they got within a mile of us and, through glasses, I had the uncharitable satisfaction of seeing that it was ominously dark over Loiyangalani.

That evening I started to fish. The usual feeling of expectancy was heightened by all I had heard about the great Nile perch in the lake. Some of them were said to turn the scales at a shade under three hundred pounds. They were reputed to fight like bull terriers and there was a tale of a man who had been dragged into the water and drowned when a monster had stripped the last foot of line from his reel. This is the sort of cheerful story that warms a fisherman's heart. I wanted to get to grips with the big stuff, but clearly Elmolo Bay was not the best place to make a start. Big perch are found in deep water, especially in the vicinity of rocks or at the foot of an underwater shelf. Here were neither rocks nor shelves. The tawny beach slipped imperceptibly into shallow, weed-laden water, the haunt of a curiously silent host of pelicans, spoonbills, ibises, long-legged stilts and little mousy-coloured waders. The beach might have been one for the birds but I wondered where I should find a patch of open water into which I could flick a spinner.

Lelean obligingly scared off the animals we met on the way. Solicitous as ever, he insisted on walking ahead of me and while I was looking at a little herd of hippo far out in the lake, he flushed a surprisingly large-looking crocodile from beneath a bush. Instead of slithering into the water on its belly, as I had expected, it hissed like a pressure-cooker, arched its back and galloped down the slope on the extremities of its squat legs. We dislodged two others, small ones, before I found a promising patch of open water.

As far as the eye could see the shallow water was blotched with purple-coloured patches of up to a hundred yards in length. They were shoals of fish, moving slowly beneath the surface. From what I could see of a patch near the shore, they were squat fish, each about the size of a soup plate. There must have been many thousands of them in some of the larger shoals. The sight was spectacular but not wholly encouraging to one accustomed to an occasional glimpse of a solitary trout in a clear stream. I had the feeling that I was about to fish in an over-stocked aquarium.

After casting into the thick of the shoals for half an hour, the feeling of over-abundance was exchanged for one of acute frustration. I couldn't catch anything. I tried little spoons and big spoons; I tried to tempt them with fidgety plugs and a variety of artificial minnows. The fish were not only uninterested; some of them were positively scared by what I had to offer. When the lures splashed into the water, the purple patches disintegrated and then disappeared as the fish dived deep to get out of the way. To say the least, it was not what I had expected. In the light of a flamboyant sunset I strode out towards a spit of sand in the hope of finding deeper water.

The little spoon flashed as it fell; the pick-up clacked and I began to reel in. Almost at once I felt as if I had received a powerful electric shock. The bite was so vigorous and so totally unexpected that for a moment I thought I had hooked one of the giant perch. But instead of the downward surge of a big fish, a silver boomerang, no more than a foot in length, bounced out of the water, fell back and seemed to go mad under the surface. I hauled in a galvanized two pounds of tiger fish with its protuberant teeth agape. It was of no size to boast about but I felt that if it had been much bigger it would have bitten off my thumb.

When it was almost too dark to see where the spinner fell, I began to catch the fish that left a purple shadow on the water. They were fringe-finned tilapia, one of a group of fish that have invaded and conquered many of the African waterways with the resolution of the Roman legions. The tilapia of the Rift Valley have split up and changed to such an extent that zoologists who have studied them can get a foreshortened view of the normally long processes of evolution. They are pre-eminently adaptable. Lake Rudolf is one of the great kingdoms of tilapia; it was an added pleasure, indeed a privilege, to know that the fish that came kicking to the shore in the dusk were probably the same as those that broke the Apostles' nets in the Sea of Galilee nearly two thousand years ago. The fish fought hard and we took three brace back to our camp under the solitary tree. The biggest weighed six pounds.

Mezek grilled the best fillets of two in an empty petrol tin from which he had hacked out a side with a *panga*. When the ashes of the fire were piled around the tin it also served as an oven for making bread. The mustard sauce I made that night was not an entire success. Maize meal proved to be a poor substitute for flour and the fat had a distinctly fishy flavour. But with a plate of fried potatoes, the rubbery relics of those we had bought before Christmas at South Horr, the tilapia tasted excellent. To my surprise, however, no one else would touch them. Karo thought that as food fish were fit only for the Elmolo or me.

When the plates had been cleared away and I had nothing but the mosquitoes to contend with, I stretched out, luxuriously, with my feet on an ammunition box and let my thoughts run into what I believe the psychologists call free association. There was not much else one could do. It was about eight o'clock. Although I should be awake at dawn, it was far too early for bed. I had written up my notes. The light from the little oil lamp was not of the best; it was certainly not strong enough to read by for more than a quarter of an hour. I had no other recourse but to play at a variety of thought associations which, if not intellectual, were at least soporific, a process in which a glass of whisky was of assistance. On innumerable occasions such as this, I found that it was necessary either to focus on some evocative object from which a pattern of thoughts would gradually emerge or to strive to unravel the subconscious links between two successive and apparently disconnected ideas. The exercise would have been even more trivial than it was if I had had anyone to talk to or anything better to do in the loneliness of the long evenings.

After gazing at the camp fire for a few moments, I became dimly aware of the first sombre chords of *Francesca da Rimini*. The association was not particularly complex. The bright tongues of flame from the burning acacia wood resembled the illustration on the sleeve of one of the most popular recordings of the music. The memory dissolved and gave way to others when I soon discovered that I could not remember more than a few disconnected bars.

The chain of thought association was somewhat more pronounced when Mezek came up to say goodnight and put down four jerricans in front of my table. The water containers were made of coloured plastic through which the flames of the fire flickered green and blue. Instantly, the eerie colours put me in mind of a dreadful little place called Andorra in the Pyrenees. It was a walking tour of years ago ... I had been trying to get from Aero and the Pic d'Estats to Puigcerda and the railway that would get me into Spain. For some reason, probably no more than idle curiosity, I left the keen air and the hospitality of the mountain villages for a principality that appeared to exist almost entirely on the sale of exotic stamps and duty-free cameras, watches and other expensive articles. The main street was blocked by unnecessarily long Cadillacs and Mercedes, each owned by loot-hunting tourists, intent on ridding themselves of surplus cash.

At dusk I leaned out of a little hotel window and watched the sun sink behind the peaks. The noise from the town below was appalling. Almost everyone carried a portable radio which was loudly but inexactly tuned in to a variety of dance bands from Madrid to Paris. After dusk I was astonished to find that a flock of brightly coloured bats were flitting in and out of the eaves of the main street. Most of them a hideous green colour although some were orange and others blue. I discovered that the bats acquired their satanic hues as they skimmed through the glow of the neon signs above the shops. It shone through the membranes of their wings ... the colour was almost precisely that of the plastic jerricans in front of my bed at Elmolo Bay.

The memories of three days beside the lake are so pleasant that I tend to forget the mosquitoes, the snakes and a brush with an irritable hippopotamus. In the long view, these things were of far less consequence than the abiding peace of the camp, the absence of wind and the spectacular sunsets. And yet at the time the animals were an irritation or a point at which I knew I was afraid.

The mosquitoes would have been more tolerable had we had anything to spray them with after the first night, but as far as I could discover, Mezek had emptied the tin of insecticide. He liked the noise of the aerosol and thought the contents were inexhaustible. I could have boxed his ears and the next night, when we were attacked in force, I wished I had.

Although I had been warned about snakes and carried an expensive armoury of anti-venines, it was not until I walked through a sparse patch of grass near the lake that I realized that this was indeed the home of the saw-scaled viper, one of the most poisonous snakes in the world. At the time Lelean was some distance behind me, carrying the fishing rod.

The first snake I saw was coiled round a tuft of grass in such an intimate manner that it resembled a flower pot. In colour an undistinguished sandy-brown, it had a spangle of diamond markings on its back. Almost before I had registered the fact that it was potentially dangerous, the lithe body had arched into a figure-of-eight and disappeared. I discovered another, similarly marked, near by and a third stretched out on the open sand within ten yards of its fellows. It was mildly aggressive. Instead of gliding away at once, as the others had done, it lunged at me – ineffectively, since I was some distance away from it and ready to leap out of the way. But it was by no means a peaceful snake. As it lunged it made a peculiar rasping noise that might be written down as *zizz-zizz-zizz*. Saw-scales sound like kettles of boiling water. Why there should have been nests of them on this particular hillock when we had not met them elsewhere, I cannot say. Lelean made a careful detour around the grass. Asked why he had not come straight towards me when I called, he said that thinly covered dunes were 'bad places for *nyoka*' and he blandly pointed to places on my bare ankles where I was liable to be bitten.

For some inexplicable reason Elmolo Bay turned out to be the most snake-ridden place we stopped at. For all their prudence, the boys occasionally ran into trouble; Mezek, for instance, usually carried my camera, compass and a pair of field-glasses in an old army haversack. At first I had no objection to his using it for his private possessions but when I found a piece of stinking meat in one of the pockets, I told him he could put anything into the bag except food. The result was that the haversack was usually empty and in camp it hung on a bush. Putting his hand inside it one day, Mezek yelled and threw it up in the air. Another snake.

The haversack landed upside down. Goiti grabbed a stick and hit it so hard that the stick quivered and leaped out of his hand. But the snake was far from dead. About a foot of it emerged from a fold in the canvas before Goiti pulped its head with a second blow. It was a young black mamba. We met a number of snakes during our months together in the desert; one of them nearly put an end to me before the journey was done. Looking back on events, I think the instructions written on the large phial of anti-venine from the *Institut Pasteur* were only slightly less ominous than the prospect of being bitten.

Every morning after breakfast I used to look for a bush at an adequate distance from the camp. Apart from the urgency of the operation it helped to fill in the time between reveille and departure; it also meant that for a quarter of an hour I was insulated from the frightful roar of the camels, a sound that reached crescendo when the girths were tightened.

Looking for a place one morning, I carefully avoided all the uneven patches of grass and followed a little path that led to some stunted bushes. They were tenanted, I discovered, by a hippopotamus who was apparently asleep. I say apparently because in less than three seconds the animal had rolled to its feet and was close on my heels. Ignoring the path and all the tle patches of grass, I pounded off at a tangent. The hippopotamus went straight on. He ploughed through the bushes like a bulldozer out of control. Without swerving or changing speed he ran through the camp and didn't stop until he had splashed into the lake. Lelean was as solicitous as ever when I limped in but, as he pointed out, it was 'not good to walk on the little road of the hippo'. Remembering how I had tried to exercise my fieldcraft in the first place I had a feeling that somehow I couldn't win.

Karo came from Elmolo Bay and I was curious to know where his family lived, but the circumstances in which he pointed out his home were so pathetic that I wished I had been less curious. The two of us were walking towards the lake on a fishing expedition. I noticed four or five huts on a rise of ground; as there was nobody about and the huts were in such a dilapidated condition, I assumed it was an abandoned encampment of the Elmolo. 'Ghost' *manyatta* are quite common between the hills and the lake. Most of them are relics of a Marille raid. We were almost level with the first of the huts when I said: 'Your home, it is where?'

'*Yuko!*' said Karo, pointing to a sorry heap of sticks and grass. It had been plastered with dung but the daub had dried and cracked until most of the ribs of the hovel were exposed like the carcass of a beast. I asked him where his people were. The place looked completely deserted. He said the men were up in the hills, tending their goats because the grazing in the Bay was not good. But his father, he said, had been left behind because he was too old to walk.

He shouted something in Samburu and an emaciated old man crawled to the entrance of the hut. He was wrinkled with age and disease. He had lost one eye. The socket was closed under a fold of skin. The other was watery and ringed with pus. 'It is my father,' said Karo.

I tried to tell the old man that we would send him tobacco and medicine for his eye but he couldn't understand a word. Karo put it into Samburu. He had to shout. The old man nodded and mumbled something but I doubt whether he even recognized his son.

As we walked down to the lake I could think of nothing to say about the old man. As if guessing my thoughts, Karo said, 'Karibu amekwisha kufa.' He was, indeed, 'nearly quite dead'.

A few days later we were off again at dawn. I was eager to cast a line among the giant perch and from all I had been told I was unlikely to encounter the leviathans until we reached the rocky shores of the Ballo *lugga* where I was due to meet the game warden from Marsabit. I was also suffering from eye-strain. From the day we had entered the desert, I had worn a pair of dark glasses. They were adequate for most purposes but whenever I took them off to use the gun or the camera the glare from the sand and the polished slabs of lava was as painful as a magnesium flare. Elmolo was a beautiful place, but as the sand reflected too much of the sun, it was in no sense a sight for sore eyes.

I am not among those who gaze with any satisfaction on the face they see in the shaving mirror each morning. A candid friend once told me that I looked bashed about a bit. This may be a fair description; I am, to say the least, rugged, but I was a little surprised by what I saw in the mirror at the Bay. After a few days in the desert my normally small and close-set eyes were tightly puckered with crows' feet and the irises had receded to little black dots. I looked peculiarly aggressive. This is what the residents of the Northern Frontier District call the Wajir Stare. I shaved quickly and put the mirror away.

Ballo is not the sort of place I should have chosen for my retirement. An outcrop of basalt had become thickly dusted with grey sand and lava dust. A few trees struggled out of the dry bed of the stream but they had become so gnarled and twisted by the wind that at times I found myself listening for the ominous moan up in the hills. Nevertheless, we found two pools of sweet water and the boys were quick to point out that the cloven prints around them had been made by gazelle.

Lake Rudolf is long and narrow. We had reached a point where the eastern shoreline takes a sharp turn towards the west. As far as I could judge from the colour of the water, the lake is shallow on both sides here; it may be that in years to come Rudolf will become two lakes, a large one and a smaller one, divided by a neck of sand across the present constriction at Ballo.

After walking for about nine miles, we camped, early, at the foot of a little hill. I brought off a couple of long shots at a brace of Egyptian geese and, unwarrantably encouraged by my prowess, I used up more cartridges than I care to mention in pulling down three more. Their flesh had a plastic texture which no amount of marinating and boiling in a concentrated solution of curry powder could disguise. However, there was food for all of us; I ate my portion, over-hastily, with my thoughts on the lake and, burning with enthusiasm and dyspepsia, I went off to do battle with the Nile perch.

In terms of the weight of the catch it was an almost entirely successful afternoon. This is something that so rarely can be said of a fishing expedition that I record it as a statement of fact. Without moving more than a hundred yards between two points of projecting rock I caught about five hundred pounds of fish in less than three hours of casting with a light rod. As a weight-lifting exercise it was a novel experience, but as a sporting fish the perch has no more cut and dash than a wounded cow and I am surprised that it has gained a reputation as a fighter.

I caught an immature fish with my first cast. By Lake Rudolf standards it was a shrimp, probably weighing no more than five or six pounds. Moreover, I fluffed the cast. Lelean, squatting on a rock behind me, stood up as the big plug bait swung backwards and had to duck. I tried to correct the cast in mid-air; the hooks picked up a loop of the wire leader and when I reeled in the plug got caught up in the line. As it bounced towards me on the surface, two or three large fish made an ineffectual snatch at it. One of them must have unravelled the leader because the plug began to twist and dive again and ten yards from my feet it was seized by the little fellow who was soon hauled out.

I had caught a curious-looking fish, much like the European perch but a dull slate-grey in colour with a disproportionately small head that looked as if it had been squeezed out of its humpy shoulders. The smaller, darker fish are the males; the females are as bright as herrings and they grow to a prodigious size. Some are nine feet long and heavy as a sack of coal.

Once when the plug landed far out in the deep water, it was held, immovably beneath the surface, as if a giant hand had come up from the bottom of the lake and grasped it. I tightened the clutch on the monofilament line and held the rod vertical. The line quivered, slightly. There was none of the usual agitation of a hooked fish. My impression was of a fine wire attached to an electric motor running at full speed.

After a few seconds, an immense perch rolled up to the surface of the water and thrashed about, idly, like a friendly porpoise. Angling literature is rich in stories of fish that escaped. It would be futile to guess how big this one was. I shall content myself by saying, modestly, that it was probably the biggest fish in the world. When it sank down again and began to swim away, there was nothing I could do to stop it. It pulled about two hundred and fifty yards of line off the reel. When I put on all the pressure I could, it seemed to pause, momentarily, and, for the first time, I felt the full weight of the creature. But it slipped away and the line went slack. Hauling it in, I found that the perch had straightened the hooks as effectively as if they had been wrenched backwards with pliers.

After catching several fish, including a sixty-pounder, I began to think of ways of returning them to the lake alive. Lelean had been hauling them out by slipping his hand under their heavy gill plates. Once he got them ashore, he bashed their heads in, horribly, and cut the hooks out with a hunting knife. He was splashed with blood; the fish continued to shiver and gulp in air long after they had been thumped repeatedly and I could not be sure they were dead until their large luminous eyes changed from gold to green and finally hardened under a gelatinous skin.

I told Lelean to wade into the lake where, with a knife between his teeth, he contrived to hold the fish steady with one hand while he snipped out the hooks with the other. If the fish had seized the tail end of the plug bait, a cut or two usually sufficed to release them, apparently unharmed. But if, as sometimes happened, the gill plates or the eyes had been pierced by the barbs, the surgical operation was, to say the least, messy.

During one brisk fight with a stubborn little black creature that seemed more reluctant to leave the lake than its fellows, I was surprised to see that it was accompanied by another perch, a vast fish, so much larger that, at first, I thought it was a crocodile. The fish swam underneath its companion and nudged it so vigorously that I wondered if it was trying to help it escape. Both fish milled backwards and forwards in diminishing arcs until Lelean waded out, brandishing his knife. By the time he had cut the black fish free its mate had sunk down into the depths where I hope that the little male and the enormous, importunate female were united.

Towards dusk we were joined by three naked Elmolo who greeted the capture of every fish with such a vocabulary of exultant grunts that to land anything, large or small, became a pleasure. I weighed the sixty-pounder by chopping off the tail, dividing the body into three pieces and weighing the bits separately. During the operation, the guts sprawled out in a mess of coils and were left on the rocks. When we turned to go, the Elmolo pounced on them, avidly, and carried them off in a pannier of palm leaves.

In the softness of the evening, the men told me that seven camels and several men were trudging towards us up the Kibrot Pass from the Balessa Kulal. They were our reinforcements, the little army that was to protect us against the Marille. I was mildly irritated to think that solitude so newly gained was so soon to be lost, if only temporarily.

The quiet of the night was emphasized by a soft piping from the men's lines. It was a poignant variation of two or three notes, unsubtle yet melodic. It was as if a satyr had come among us. I had not heard the sound before, and imagined it came from some ancient instrument of the Samburu, perhaps unknown elsewhere. But after a time I began to tire of the sound and asked Mezek to show me the flute. He brought me a piece of aluminium tubing, a section of one of the twisted tent poles, in which Karo had bored holes with a tin-opener.

Marille Country

Most travel books give the impression that encounters between one Englishman and another in the bush are invariably chummy and usually remain that way. During my days in the bush I met only one Englishman for a period of more than a few hours, and that was the Warden who came to meet me at Ballo. At times my relationship with him was, frankly, not too good.

I had considerable misgivings about his arrival. Would he be aloof or convivial? I had no very clear preconceived picture of a safari under the command of two individualists. In the event he turned up like a god in a golden cloud. It proved to be a dust cloud which soon dispersed to reveal a big black truck to which I took an instant and quite irrational dislike. Standing there with its engine overheated and surrounded by a host of men I had never seen before, it seemed to relegate me to tourist class and destroy the independence I had enjoyed since the day I set off.

Perhaps the truck stood between the Warden and myself at a point where we should have grasped each other like brothers, drunk half a bottle of Scotch and said what splendid fellows we were, each in our own way. But it didn't work out like that. Highly efficient, conscientious and reserved, the Warden saw only too clearly that I was singularly inefficient, imprudent and doggedly determined to do my fifteen miles a day, Marille and mountains notwithstanding. He pointed out that he was my escort. I agreed. He said he would be in charge of the safari; I agreed again. He said that if I persisted in wearing nothing but a pair of shorts, a bush hat and sand shoes I should probably get sunstroke. Looking at his big brown boots, puttees and heavy khaki drill, I silently disagreed. During our two weeks together, the Warden and I never openly disagreed about anything. We merely agreed to differ. Thus it was that from Ballo *lugga* we set forth to affright the Marille (whom we never saw) with fifteen camels and twenty-three men, eight of them armed: he at one end of a long-drawn-out caravan and I at the other. Substantially, I was still on my own.

As we walked along the edge of the lake for miles and miles, it occurred to me that although a lake is not such a good conversationalist as, say, a brook or a river, it had eloquent silences which were wholly to my liking. On some days when the sun stood high and harsh, the Jade Sea looked as tranquil as a pond. Yet even without wavelets, the water slowly dribbled up the beach and then fell back, gently but regularly, as if responding to some heart-like pulsation in the depths. On other days, when a breeze pewtered the surface, the water gurgled and plashed on the shingle; pebbles produced a high-pitched but almost inaudible hiss, like steam escaping from a diminutive kettle. On the whole Rudolf and I got on well together.

When the sun began to bite I walked into the lake and sat with the lightly soapy water up to my arm-pits. Lelean assured me that there was not danger from crocodiles in the shallows, although he always stood on guard with his gun cocked. He affected an enormous disdain towards the reptiles which I only half-shared and I waded in only when I thought the Warden wasn't looking.

Our first camp in the company of the escort lay beside an isolated peak that resembled a pyramid. It was called Porr. Unlike Kulal, which was invariably ominous in outline, I regarded Porr as a friendly milestone. By that time I could not remember when I had been out of sight of at least one dominant mountain: Waraguess stood over us at Wamba; Nyiru had guided us to the South Horr gate to the lake; Kulal was in the centre of the wind belt and now Porr marked the beginning of the unknown portion of the east shore. We had seen it from the top of the Serima. From a distance of thirty miles it looked ridiculously small but there it was, in front of us, and I decided to climb it. God knows what the Warden would have said had he known.

As this is a strictly truthful account of relationships between the Warden and myself, I have to admit that Porr put me in an extremely difficult position. I don't mean that I was in much danger that afternoon. I do mean that I climbed up to a point from which I had considerable difficulty in climbing down and, dreadful thought, for some time it looked as if I might have to bawl for help. As the Warden and his merry men were two miles away, they might not have heard me. Lelean at least could have tracked me but the fact is I felt a bit of a fool, not least because I faced ignominious rescue. This is how it happened:

Seen from a distance, the southern face of Porr made an almost perfect equilateral triangle. At close quarters it was composed of rusty-red rocks, interlocked so rigidly that I had the impression that a once-solid mountain had been shaken to pieces by an earthquake. Perhaps it had.

It took me an hour to reach the base of the rocks. At half-past three I sat on a boulder about half-way to the summit and looked at the view. Apart from the sun, there was nothing particularly difficult or even arduous about the climb. I might have been scrambling over a dilapidated pyramid. I am not a mountaineer and Porr, for that matter, is not much of a mountain. It is probably no more than three or four thousand feet from the top to the bottom. But I discovered that sun-shattered rocks are painfully hot and I tried to keep in the shadow of the southern face.

Porr is said to be sacred to the Elmolo. I had heard of rock carvings and graves at the summit which is normally reached from a long sloping shoulder on the north flank. I found some erotic scribbles on a flat rock: genital organs, big fish and little men, but nothing suggested they were of great antiquity. As the summit seemed to be inaccessible from where I hung on, I decided to climb down. During the descent I dislodged a large rock which started a minor landslide and left me isolated at the top of a steep pile of rubble with nothing to hold on to. I began to climb down in another direction. More trouble from more rubble. On both sides I was hemmed in by screes which began to move as soon as I stood on them. Wondering what on earth to do next, I sat on the only stable rock I could find and gazed down at the camp out on the plain far below. Through field-glasses it looked very peaceful and the Warden, I felt sure, was enjoying his afternoon sleep. He told me it was unwise to move far during the afternoon.

The Porr episode ended precipitously. Trusting that the seat of my pants would hold out, I sat down, nervously, on the brink of a high scree composed of small stones and pushed off.

My recollection is that I slid down several hundred feet in several seconds. Badly scratched, slightly bruised and covered in dust I limped back to camp and washed and changed before I told the Warden I had been out for a stroll.

That night we mounted a guard for the first time. The six *askaris* brought in from Marsabit were under the command of the formidable Sergeant Ibra'm who gave them ten minutes of butt-crashing arms drill before he sent them out into the dusk. They had orders to watch out for the Marille whom they called the *Galubba*.

Feeling stiff and in need of exercise before I turned in, I walked to the edge of the camp where the guard stood, staring into the darkness. Karo joined us and talked fearfully of the *Galubba* and how they usually attacked in the early hours of the morning, crawling up as their victims slept. He said his own *manyatta* had been raided twice. On one occasion he had been awakened by screams. Everyone had fled and when they crept back next morning a youth had disappeared. They found him by the edge of the lake, still alive, but mutilated. A young Marille must produce physical evidence of a successful raid before he can select a bride. Most of these emasculators live near the delta of the Omo river which flows into the north end of the lake. From what I learnt later they worship a supreme being, a bull-god called Wak, and during centuries of raiding they have built up elaborate rituals around the bull and the use of fire. Bulls are always speared before a raid and the warriors smeared with the stomach contents. They are also painted with white clay. During an epidemic, or before a prolonged campaign, all fires are extinguished and ceremonially re-lit by the tribal soothsayers who incite the young to bring back their tokens of manhood. They usually prey on the Turkana and the Elmolo. I asked Karo whether his people ever fought back but he shook his head. They always ran away from the white-painted ones.

For three days we followed the lake as far as the Longondoti Hills. With fifteen camels and twenty-three men stretched out along the shoreline for at least a quarter of a mile we must have presented an impressive sight to marauding Marille or anyone else but, as it turned out, we saw nobody. During one false alarm we hurried after an armed man, alone and darkly loitering. A smart pursuit and much staring through field-glasses showed that we had tracked down one of the Warden's own *askaris* who had got lost, looking for water. I said nothing and the Warden said nothing.

At the beginning of the Longondoti Hills the shoreline became more rugged; steep cliffs rose high in the air and I wondered whether we should be able to get through without making a long detour inland. The Warden sent scouts ahead who reported the way clear for about another twenty miles; after that it looked as if the lakeside walk had come to an end. We were advancing towards the flank of a cliff. I wanted to press on, hard, and then stop for a day or two where I had a chance of catching at least one of the really big perch but the Warden wouldn't hurry. He couldn't hurry; his camels were lame. I certainly had no complaint on this score since the beasts I had driven up from Rodosoit were his own property. He had lent them to me and I was grateful to him. To reach Ballo he had hired some more from an old scoundrel who thought he was getting his own back on the government by handing over some abject cripples. We tried to coax them to life by stopping for two days under a whaleback of a wall called Moiti where I caught more fish than we could eat.

On the first day the wind blew hard and made the long monofilament line groan like a 'cello. When I hooked a big fish, the increased tension raised the note. It rose and fell as the fish plunged about; the effect was dramatic if not musical and the men thought it vastly entertaining. My rod became 'the music stick'. I had no shortage of gillies. They all wanted the job.

Mezek was better at hauling out fish than Lelean but the sight of the struggling captive brought out something primitive in the Turkana and he bashed the creatures unmercifully when he got them ashore. I explained, laboriously, that perch would swim away quicker if they were put back into the water uninjured but it was clear that he could not understand why I took the trouble to catch what I didn't intend to keep.

On the morning of the second day the wind dropped to a breath; the lake turned from blue to green and the fishing fell off. On green days the plankton probably provided more food than the fish needed but I might have done better if I hadn't fished in a pool that held an extraordinarily large crocodile.

After trying various baits I cast a heavily weighted spinner far out into the deep water, hoping to catch something near the bottom. Nothing happened until the spinner twirled up to the surface. Then something that looked like a porpoise wallowed up from the depths, engulfed the bait and sank down again. The rod arched, the reel screeched and I imagined I had hooked the Rudolf record for all time. Mezek hopped up and down and shouted something I could not understand. He seemed frightened. I told him to be quiet and applied myself to the task of shifting the apparently unshiftable. By dint of sheer donkey work I managed to gain a few feet of line but it felt as if I were hauling a corpse up to the top. Bubbles came up with it – not a few leisurely bubbles but a gush. Slowly and without any struggling I lifted about ten feet of crocodile to the surface, yellow belly uppermost. It rolled over, opened its jaws and the spinner catapulted out of the water. I told the Warden about it that night but I don't think he altogether believed me.

One the fourth day the scouts came back to report that the track between the hills and the lake was completely blocked. A big disappointment this, since after spending a long time negotiating a tricky corner the previous day we assumed the worst was over and that we should get to our next objective, Allia Bay, without leaving the lake. As the Warden saw it there were three possibilities: either we should be able to wade through the water around the rocks, or find a track above them, or we should have to strike inland and work our way around the back of the hills. We left the camp to Sergeant Ibra'm and inspected the situation together.

It proved worse than we thought. In prehistoric times, when Rudolf was connected to the Nile, the Longondoti Hills were probably islands in a lake twice as large as it is today. Wave-polished rocks high up on the cliffs marked the height of the ancient shoreline. At the point where we had hoped to squeeze our way through, the cliffs dropped almost sheer into deep water. Obviously there had once been a track at the foot of the rocks but it had been submerged when the lake rose during the great floods of 1962. A platform hundreds of feet above might have provided an alternative route but the sight of eagles soaring among the crags suggested that the Longondotis were more precipitous than they appeared from formal contours on an inaccurate map.

We decided to countermarch south for a few miles and make for a visible gap in the hills where the Warden thought we would find water and a camel track that would take us round the back of the Longondotis. I wanted to get to the north end of the lake. My original plan was to walk right round the lake. Nobody, as far as I knew, had done it before. I had dropped the plan when I had learnt that it was very difficult to cross the Omo river without going many miles up into Ethiopia, through Marille country. I might have taken a chance with the tribes had I not got a permit from the local District Commissioner on the strict understanding that I stuck to my escort. When did the escort propose to leave me? I thought I might go north with my own men. The Warden said We Were Going to Allia Bay and then We Should Strike Due East Across the Ditsoli. This, he said, would bring us to a trading post called North Horr where I could restock with food and he could go about his own business. North Horr was about seventy-five miles from the lake. I walked back to the camp feeling somewhat cast down. I had not thought of tackling the deserts to the east. When I left the Warden (or, more precisely, when that conscientious man released me) I should have to decide where to go on my own. To the east of North Horr lay the Chalbi which, when the wind picked up the sand, was reputed to be almost impassable on foot.

We turned our backs on Rudolf soon after sunrise the next day. Had I caught a big perch the previous night I might have turned my back on it for ever, but after an hour of romantic but unprofitable casting into the light of the setting sun, I had caught nothing. I had a feeling that I was not putting the rods away for the last time. The next morning we breakfasted apart. As the Warden seemed gloomy and little inclined to conversation I walked immediately behind the scouts at the head of the column.

Towards midday we reached a deep slice in the hills that appeared to be buttressed with petrified organ pipes. Some of the black columns of basalt were ten or twelve feet in diameter, but so high and so regular in contiguity that the impression was of perpendicular architecture. Abhebad, one of the Somali scouts, said it was indeed the work of God and when he saw the shattered columns sprawling across our path at the far end of the cleft, he added 'God's will be done'.

The following day we met lions in such ludicrous circumstances that I forgot some of the fearful stories I had heard about them from Wilfred Thesiger. About eleven o'clock in the morning, I was ahead of the column in the company of Lelean and Mezek. We had been walking since dawn and I felt tired, excessively thirsty, and irritated beyond rational explanation by all the trivialities that invariably arose shortly before the midday halt. Lelean was leading us between the unusually green bushes of a dry *lugga*. I hoped we should find water and I didn't want to stop until we did.

The lion had its head in the remains of a zebra. Lelean shouted 'Simba!' and swung the rifle off his shoulder but before he could even cock the weapon the beast bounded away, scattering a ring of vultures like a dog among chickens. As the lion had run in the general direction of the oncoming camels, I told Lelean to head them off and Mezek to stay where he was. I followed Lelean.

Mezek gave a horrified yell. We turned round to see him pounding towards us with the lioness running about ten yards to his right, but far from chasing him the frightened animal was merely staging a parallel escape. When Mezek recovered his breath he told us that when he had walked behind a bush to relieve himself he had almost trodden on the lioness crouching there, alert, with a hunk of zebra between her paws.

That night when I told the Warden about the encounter he said, as Thesiger had done, that the smell of camels often attracted several lions to a camp. He thought that lions knew when the camels were bunched together in the vicinity of men; they either put themselves upwind or roared loudly at close quarters in the hope of starting a stampede to a point where the waiting lioness would knock one down.

About eight o'clock that night, while we were waiting for Mezek to serve dinner under the branches of an immense tree, an unearthly commotion arose from the cookhouse. It sounded as if the camels had broken loose. They bellowed and reared.

Some plunged among the pots and pans. The men shouted and tried to grab them as they hopped about grotesquely with one hobbled leg held high in the air. The incident occurred so soon after the talk about stampedes that I thought we had been invaded by lions but the explanation was far more prosaic. A camel had nibbled at a branch of a tree behind us and disturbed a large flock of roosting guinea-fowl. The birds squawked and fluttered their wings like a round of applause. This terrified the camels and before the men quietened them down, one of them kicked over a *sufuria* containing our dinner.

As we drew near to the windy flats of Allia Bay a sad-faced Gabbra youth approached us; he had been savaged by a lion. Since there was suspicion of poaching the Warden cross-examined him through Sergeant Ibra'm. The youth said he had been seized by the shoulder and dragged along the ground during a hunting expedition. He related these facts, doggedly, as he squatted on the ground with a blanket thrown loosely over his shoulders. He said he wanted medicine. I looked at a black crusted area of skin from which a portion the size of a fist had been torn out below the shoulder blade. He had deep lacerations on his chest and at the base of the neck but none of them was obviously septic. I asked him when he had been attacked. He said half a month ago. What had he put on the wound? He had rubbed in some antelope fat. I asked him why he had not walked to the dispensary of North Horr but he said 'Who will look after my goats?' When asked to raise the injured arm he admitted it hurt 'a little' but he managed to lift it up. Marvelling that he was not already dead, I sprinkled penicillin powder on the raw-looking patches but I doubted whether it would do as much for him as the fat.

Until I saw the opalescent haze over the great Bay I little thought that Rudolf was capable of any change of moods beyond violent turquoise and tranquil green, yet what could be seen of the water here was as misty as an autumn morning in England. However, like so many vistas in the Northern Frontier District, the spectacle contained much illusion. From north to south the immense horizon lay partly hidden in a mirage; above the ribbon of light writhed ever-dissolving witch-shapes of blown dust, rusty-red, smoke-grey and yellow. From where we stood on a rise of ground, the wilderness of water and sand dunes seemed to be an arena for conflicting winds.

It began to blow, fitfully, as soon as we rounded the northern-most flank of the Longondotis; by the time we had dropped down to the plain to the east of the lake, where the Warden announced he intended to pitch camp, we were hit by a gale as bad as any I experienced. I was unwilling to leave the lake without seeing it at close quarters, possibly for the last time. The Warden insisted that it should not wander about in Marille country without an escort, so with two scouts for protection I allowed myself to be blown down towards the animals on the shoreline.

Allia Bay holds a peculiar position in the melancholy story of wildlife protection in East Africa. Although the big parks and reserves to the south, such as the Amboseli and the Tsavo, shelter large numbers of wild animals, the protection covers little more than sixty per cent of the known species in Kenya. Some animals which used to be quite common now have no home of their own. Not long ago a chocolate-coloured antelope called the topi was described as 'very adaptable and widely distributed'. It is now confined to three remote regions including the land to the north of Allia Bay. Grevy's zebra, a large, hand-some animal with narrow stripes and prominent rounded ears, used to be 'seen in thousands at the various waterholes'. It is now found only in the Northern Frontier District and is especi-ally common at the north end of the lake.

The list could be extended to include several other en-dangered species. Major Grimwood, the Chief Game Warden of Kenya, tried to create a lakeside reserve extending from the bay to the Ethiopian border. He considered that a remote area where there was no conflict with human interests would remain perpetually inviolate from depredation by man, but the Somali secession problem intervened and at the present time the future of the Northern Frontier District remains uncertain.

The hot wind was charged with a fine spray of dust that stuck to our sweat. I felt tired after the early morning walk through the hills but for once the destination stood out clear and the prospect of a bathe in the lake appealed to me. As usual, the

Africans got excited by the sight of animals and began to name beasts so far away that they resembled a sprinkling of dust on the bottom of a soup plate. They pointed out a large herd of oryx which to me was scarcely distinguishable, even through field-glasses. Grant's gazelle and topi were even more numerous. As we approached they disappeared in a cloud of dust, running hard with a few ostrich striding alongside, like the outriders of a troop of cavalry.

A lagoon at the edge of the lake proved to be so shallow and so muddy that we could not even wade in among the spoonbills and flamingoes; nor could we drink the salty water. We splashed off some of the adhesive sand, wriggled our toes in the mud and turned round to face the full force of the wind. I estimated that it would take us about an hour to walk back to the camp. I trod in the footprints of the scouts ahead. To look up for more than a few seconds hurt the eyes.

One incident alone remains in my memory. Labouring up a succession of step-like plateaux, I noticed that a frolicsome young animal, like a very young bull, persisted in following us. With its reddish-brown coat, stumpy face and short ears, it reminded me of one of the Oxo advertisements. The scouts said it was a young *shuroa* – an oryx – and they tried to catch it. It ran away but never very far and when we marched on again it plodded along behind us, as if seeking protection. I was puzzled by the animal's behaviour and touched by its appealing expression. I learnt afterwards that female oryx sometimes abandon their offspring behind bushes or in the shelter of a *lugga* where the young ones play together in a crèche or nursery school. This was one of the strays. I cannot imagine how they manage to survive in lion country and it is perhaps significant that the beast quickly ran away when we got within sight of the palm trees and the shelter of the camp.

The Warden seemed surprised that we had not seen a more impressive display of game; I also had the feeling that he expected me to make a meticulous count of what were mostly indistinguishable antelope in a blur of dust. In a subsequent aerial survey of the coastal strip, the Warden and another member of the Game Department recorded over two thousand topi, thirteen hundred oryx, over a thousand Grant's gazelle, nearly five hundred zebra, ninety giraffe, seventy ostrich and nearly thirty gerenuk. Conscientious work, this, but I'm glad I saw Allia Bay on foot.

We covered the seventy-five miles between Allia Bay and North Horr in four stages; there is not very much I care to say about any of them.

For the greater part of the first day we walked head-down into a rip-roaring, shirt-rattling wind that made conversation below the level of a shout impossible and sight-seeing a discomfort. I jammed the floppy brim of my bush hat over my sunglasses and plodded along in the shadow of Lelean. Even platitudinous thoughts about the importance of keeping going were difficult to maintain for more than a few minutes. The Ditsoli did not stimulate much thought. An empty world in which hummocks of lava without shape were cut by dry gullies thinly clothed with grey bushes. No water and no game. On the second day the wind slackened and the landscape to the south was dominated by an ugly volcanic cone called Suga. Behind rose the no more inviting shoulder of Kulal. I viewed Suga from all points between south-east and west and liked it no better when we got close.

The Warden took repeated fixes on our position at midday and corrected his maps with minute crosses and pencilled-in bearings. Sometimes he stared at a map for an hour. I stared at him in admiration. Neither of us spoke.

On two occasions I tried and failed to get within striking distance of a lumbering line of oryx and had to buy two very old and expensive sheep instead. Goiti slashed his calf on a spike of wait-a-bit thorn and Mezek worried me by spitting blood. He said he had a cold; Lelean said he smoked too much and the Warden said Africans often spat blood when they had colds. I tried to forget the matter, especially when Mezek was preparing food. On the third day we had momentary views over the immensity of the deserts to the east. Sheltering in a *lugga* at midday we heard the groan of a truck as unexpected as a dinosaur in the hills. A squad of the King's African Rifles was being shipped north to sort out some trouble on the border. The Warden went to bed at eight o'clock that night. I tried to read something weighty and gave it up after ten minutes – too many flying ants.

On the fourth day we coasted down the banks of a seemingly endless series of slag heaps. The salt flats of the Chalbi gleamed ahead and the men brightened up. At midday the Dom palms of North Horr appeared in a momentary mirage. Our objective was in sight; even the camels seemed to sense something attractive ahead and the men began to talk of the women they would have that night.

Into the Desert

I shall remember North Horr for its pool of sweet water, for the leaves of the Dom palms that clattered like a toy windmill and for the fact that I could wander about and do what I liked. I was on my own again. After a few days of gadding about in a Land-Rover with the Warden on a ration-buying expedition, we said goodbye and went about our own affairs. He had an appointment near the Ethiopian border; his *askaris* were ordered back to Marsabit and he disappeared as he had arrived, in a cloud of dust. North Horr was emptying. The police swept out of their barracks on riding camels; there were reports of distant riots between the Gabbra and the Boran over the Somali secession question. On the day we arrived an engaging little priest called Father Tablino got ready for his self-appointed task of converting the Rendille from the worship of cows to the worship of the Christian God and then he went. Everyone seemed to be going out into the desert. After poring over a large bleak map I realized that I alone had nowhere to go but everywhere.

Since I had been abroad for nearly five months I was inclined to travel in a southerly direction and get back to Wamba in a foreseeable period of time. To return to Allia Bay, direct and without an escort, would be to court trouble with the District Commissioner. Yet I wanted to see something more of the lake. During our relatively short journey from the Serima track to the Bay I had been intimidated by conditions on the east shore; I felt that I had by no means reached conclusions with that turbulent country. If I got as far as the volcanoes on the southern shore of the lake I knew that I should encounter the wind at its worst. Thesiger had told me how he had nearly come to grief in crossing that particular piece of country on his way into Turkanaland.

I decided to return to the lake. But how? I could strike due east across the Chalbi desert until we met the lava wall on the edge of the Huri Hills and then edge south. Alternatively, we could amble south-east in a more leisurely and direct fashion towards the Balessa Kulal. This was the great *lugga* in Rendille country, behind Mount Kulal. I reckoned that it would take us four or five days to cross what was laconically described on the map as 'open bush'. The men tried to persuade me to take a different route but I realized they were not thinking so much about the physical hardship of the desert as the meat and *man-yattas* they would miss if we went due east.

The view across the Chalbi from the radio-room of the police post was far from encouraging. For the most part it stretched our into a blur of sand and sky bounded only by a milky ribbon of mirage on the horizon. At close quarters the surface was dark-brown and perfectly even, like an English field that had been ploughed and harrowed in the spring. Here and there patches of bright green salt bush relieved the sense of desolation but the vegetation was confined to the foreground. Farther out the faint outline of the Huri Hills shook in the heat and the sand had a metallic sheen. I could see immediately visible landmarks to the south, that is towards the wells of Woroma and the source of the Balessa Kulal, but without overmuch conviction I decided against that route as something which had been trampled over many times before.

The camels worried me. The Warden had tried to dissuade me from returning to the south end of the lake. He said it was unlikely that we should be able to get the camels over the lava fields. As the camels which we had brought up from Rodosoit were his own it would have been neither easy nor gracious to take the best of them. I said that if we got as far as the lake I was prepared to leave the animals at a base camp and see how far we could get into Turkanaland on foot, that is carrying our own gear. I did not say that I had thought of trying to cross the Chalbi. This put me in a difficult position. Assuming that we were going back the easy way, he asked me to take the seven worn-out beasts which he had hired from a Rendille chief some-where near the Balessa Kulal. There, he said, we could hire some more animals for the remainder of our journey. I had to agree. To my intense regret the honey-coloured beasts which had served us so well were marched off and we were left with another string of cripples. I was able to keep two other animals including my favourite, the little white one. Although this made a total of nine camels at least three were incapable of carrying full loads.

The night before we left I sat on the verandah of the block-house and watched the colour slowly drain out of the desert. When it grew too dark to see I called for lamps but found they attracted such a host of insects that I sat in the shadows and plaited the loose ends of frayed rope, relying on the bats to keep the insects down.

We started very early the next morning and marched for six hours. It was like walking on puff pastry. The sand was covered in a thin crust into which the feet sank and slipped back, not far enough to put a strain on the calves.

With some experience of lava, thorn scrub and the fine shingle of the lake I had thought that walking would present no further problems but in the Chalbi I had to adopt a shuffling gait. The men literally dragged their feet along without much effort; they were also far better than I at finding patches of light-coloured sand where the going was comparatively firm.

Lelean took the lead, striding ahead with a fine air of assurance. He was followed at an interval of about fifty yards by Goiti who led the first three camels. Karo was close behind him with the second three. They were the best beasts we had and were loaded with basic food supplies, thirty gallons of water and my chair and table carefully wrapped up in sacking. Mezek and a young Somali called Sidi who had come along as a guide brought up the rear with two unloaded camels and the little white one who carried very little. The unloaded animals had not recovered from the journey from Allia Bay and for a few days at least I wanted to keep them in reserve. One of them had a large open sore on the crest of its hump. It was an ugly place that failed to respond, as other injuries had done, to an eye ointment that contained an antibiotic. The other camel was both lame and tired.

Sidi turned out to be a useless fellow. He knew almost nothing of the desert apart from the track between North Horr and Marsabit and for a Somali he was not even good at handling the camels. I made an order that if anyone thrashed the animals they would have to look after them during the midday rest. This was an unpopular duty. It was technically one of Goiti's responsibilities but as he worked as hard as anyone during the day, I put the job of shepherding the animals on a rota basis. The maltreatment of camels seems to be a characteristic of the Samburu and Rendille and it was surprising to find that the Somali was as bad as the others. Three of our beasts were equipped with head halters, that is the head rope encircled their jaws in a slack loop attached to the neck band. This enabled the camels to chew contentedly. Animals with head halters were far more contented than those with a noose slipped over their tongue and lower jaw, but they were not so easy to control. Camels fitted with the diabolical lip bits could be couched with a light tug on the head rope; the halter bit into their lips; their tongues were frequently lacerated and it was a sickening sight to see the headropes daubed with blood-stained froth. I tried the experiment of putting a head halter on to them but they were unused to persuasion; they had been trained to respect only brutality and the men were amused at my unsuccessful efforts at trying to make the animals kneel down to a repeated 'Toa! Toa!' All I could do was to ensure that the noose was not so tight that it cut into their lips and I spent some time in trying to jam the slippery wet loops with a knot at a point about two inches under their chins.

The wind began to rise fitfully the following afternoon and I noticed with some apprehension that the sand was beginning to rise too. The ribbon of mirage on the horizon turned from misty white to orange red but as the cloud neither approached us nor increased in size I assumed that the dust was being thrown north by a cross-wind. At times we were buffeted by irregular gusts from either the east or the south. As most of the Chalbi seems to have been worn smooth by the easterlies that sweep in from the heart of the Northern Frontier District, the less frequent southerly gusts raised little dust devils of loose sand. Sometimes they whirled away from the feet of the camels. There was always a critical size at which the vortex collapsed or increased in size. It depended on whether it had been generated on a loose or a crusted surface. I found that my sunglasses accentuated the sight of the clouds, making the normally nebulous outlines all too visible and apparently more dense in content than they actually were. During one particularly violent gust it seemed as if a legion of ghosts had arisen around us. The sky darkened and the pale clouds became leaden grey. Goiti un-hitched the camels and when the leading animal began to shy he couched them. Half an hour passed before we resumed our way. I remember that as I knelt on the hot sand with my back towards the force of the wind a big Tenebrionid beetle struggled up through the dust as if aware that it might be buried for ever. I felt much the same myself.

A walk of three hours brought us into the shelter of a lava wall at dusk. It was an austere refuge but infinitely preferable to the open desert where I was conscious only of a feeling of utter nakedness. While the men searched for wood I scrambled up through a crack in the wall and found that, as far as I could see in the gloom, the brown sand had given way to closely packed boulders of lava. We had evidently crossed a narrow neck of the Chalbi and further progress east would be unwise if not im-possible with ailing beasts. I walked back to the fire, ate a little rice and bully beef, and reflected that it was no place to be in for any length of time. Two days' easy march along the foot of the lava wall would probably bring us to the Kalacha wells about twenty-five or thirty miles to the south-east where there would be grazing and water. If the going was hard I intended to turn back and retrace our steps until we met the junction that led to the Balessa Kulal. I now began to understand the surprise of those who said we were setting out on a journey that led nowhere. I slept that night in the sand. Mezek had a stomach-ache; he had eaten too much meat in North Horr and I was too tired to fit my bed together.

A crack like a rifle shot awakened me twice. Remembering, hazily, something the Warden had told me about Hamarkoke raiders from the hills to the west of Lake Stefanie, I jumped up wondering whether we should extinguish the fire. Lelean was already on his feet. He stared into the dusk for a time and then said it was 'the big stones'. When lava cools and contracts it sometimes splits. The second bang was followed by a little avalanche of rocks that clinked around us as they came to rest. We were too far away from the wall to be in any danger but only a fortuitous decision had led us to camp in the open. I curled up again and slept until four o'clock when Goiti got up and led the camels in. He began to belabour them as he usually did and I argued with him as I usually did. But it was no use. He could not conceive that the camels would stand up without first receiving a hefty thwack on their backsides. They usually broke wind at this point but they also stood up which is more than they would do when I tried to coax them to their feet. In half an hour they were all roaring and belching and another day had begun.

It was not a good day. When the wind became charged with sand we tried to avoid the worst of it or else we squatted until it blew over. There was nothing else we could do. I doubt if we were in any dire danger but I began to doubt whether we should reach the wells without having to abandon some of the loads.

From dawn until about ten o'clock I felt fine. The wind rose with the sun but we had some protection from the wall and only an occasional gust raked us with sand. The full force was spent on the desert to the west where a veil of orange-coloured gauze rose and fell with curious regularity. After ten o'clock I began to be irritated by the usual trivialities. I began to imagine that the camels were spread too far apart in their groups of three. Sometimes I had to wait until Mezek caught up with us and it was impossible to see whether all was well from a quick glance backwards. I told Lelean to slow down so that we could march along together. At this he began to dawdle to such an extent that the camels were bunched under each other's tails and a frisky movement from the leader rippled through the whole string. I told him to get a move on again and felt that he should have known what I meant the first time. In giving orders in Swahili I found it extremely difficult to express niceties of action and irritation arose only too often through a splutter of words. This caused even more confusion.

For hour after hour we trudged south in a long-drawn-out line that, from afar, must have borne some resemblance to a trail of ants. Lelean was heading for a distant mound which he took to be a hill on the north side of the Kalacha and the rest of us followed in his footsteps. After vainly trying to get a fix on our position in the dawn light I put the compass away convinced that the louring mass of Kulal away to the right was the only land mass I could recognize with any certainty. The Huri Hills swam hazily through the mirage. Sidamticha, the Rageh and half a dozen other little hills might have been outliers of the

Andes for all the navigational help they afforded. They appeared as if they were beginning to melt.

On one occasion I pointed out a possible route on the map to Lelean, but Mezek had to hold the sheet down in the wind and I doubt whether Lelean had much idea what he was looking at. Even when I orientated the map and showed him where the sun rose and where his home, Mount Kulal, was ('Manyatta yako eh?') he said 'Yes' (*n'dio, n'dio*), but he could not understand the conceptual relationship between symbols and reality. To him it must have been a rather dull line-drawing in pink and black.

'Is this Kalacha?' I asked, pointing to the minute blue circle of the water-point.

'N'dio.'

'Do you *know* Kalacha?'

'N'dio.'

'So we go *this* way?'

'N'dio.'

'So tonight' – this triumphantly – 'we shall be *there*!' And I stabbed the smudgy-brown symbol of lava at a point where it was intersected by the interrupted line of a *lugga*.

'No, no!' he said. 'Hapana! We shall be *there*!' He stood up and pointed roughly in the same direction. Clearly, Lelean was no cartographer and I, for that matter, was unlikely to gain many prizes in a navigation school. The marvel is that we got anywhere.

More trudging. Nothing to look at. Only sand and the wraiths on the horizon. A waste land. Nothing to think about except whether the camels would last out and whether we should find a shelter at dusk. Nothing to listen to except the high-pitched whine of the wind, the flat-footed *thoomp thoomp* of the camels' hooves and the plash of water in the jerricans. When the animals faltered or tossed their heads and splashed froth, Mezek grunted 'Hodai!' but he said it rarely and with no especial conviction. We were all of us very tired.

In the absence of shade and with no prospect of any lessening in the intensity of the heat before nightfall we plodded on through a series of irregular stages broken only by brief halts to rest the camels. On these occasions we stopped in what appeared to be the exact centre of an enormous bowl of sand. On the horizon we could see the flanks of Kulal but, due to our southerly progress, the long narrow mountain resembled a range of hills. Somewhere to the south I hoped we should again strike the lava wall and find shelter there but, after following it closely for several hours that morning, we parted company when it swung east in what I took to be an extensive bay. I wanted to get as far south as I could by nightfall.

During these brief halts I sat with my back to a camel, pulled my hat over my eyes and tried to think of something to think about. The important thing was not to think about tea; we had no wood for a fire. I also tried to keep my thoughts off the unprofitable subjects of navigation and how long the camels would last out. The name of Cassian, one of the Desert Fathers, came to mind. What had he said about the white melancholy and the demons of noontide? That they 'mounted at a regular time, like a fever, bringing their highest tide of inflammation at definite accustomed hours'? I dismissed Cassian and tried another tack.

What were the names of the Muses? Through some almost forgotten association with a girl in a pantomime chorus I remembered Terpsichore; Clio became mixed up with asps and Egypt and I was unsure about Erato's association with sacred hymns. It seemed improbable. I dismissed the Muses.

How far had we walked? I remembered that a man can outwalk a horse – I had this evocative but useless piece of information from an old copy of the *New Yorker*. I also remembered that Roman soldiers used to average twenty miles a day with a pack, and that a man called Barclay once walked a thousand miles in a thousand hours.* What was the medical term for exceptionally fast walking? Festination! Was it a symptom of good health or neurosis? Probably the latter. Sitting there with my back pressed up against the rumbling chest wall of a camel I reflected that nobody but a fool would walk in the desert.

The sand continued to blow. For the most part it drifted past without touching us, like a veil of rain across a lakeland valley. In the distance the streamers appeared to be motionless; they had the feathery appearance of wind clouds and I wondered whether they foreshadowed wind.

* Allowing for counter-marches and digressions, including daily hunting expeditions, we covered more than a thousand miles, but not in a thousand hours. It took us about three months.

The camel which had provided me with a back rest refused to get up. It was kicked and thrashed. Goiti poured water into a skin and tried to make it drink but it refused until he squeezed its nostrils and forced some down its throat. Then it began to groan, rhythmically and miserably. I thought it was dying. Lelean looked at the liquid green dung on its back legs and said it had been browsing on salt bush. The plant is nutritious but it makes the camels thirsty and it gives them colic. All the animals were given a drink before they were loaded. By this time the sick beast could stand although unsteadily and the little white one had to be pushed to its feet.

When Lelean came up to say that all was prepared for the start the sky became a sickly colour and we were stung by another squall. Hoping that it would soon blow over, I told him to wait for a few minutes and we stood with our backs turned to the wind. After about a quarter of an hour we were obliged to couch the animals and unload them again. The sand was thrown against us with unusual violence. Unlike the winds of the lake shore, the gusts rose and fell at unpredictable intervals. Sometimes, during a rising inflection, the light faded and I imagined that the whole of the Chalbi was being blown towards the lake, but it was never long before the squall reached its peak and the sky brightened again. Kneeling there, during another moment of unreality, I was aware that I was being sheltered. Mezek had come up behind me and arranged the sacks in the form of a windbreak. It was one of the many voluntary acts of kindness which endeared him to me.

Looking back on that afternoon I realize now that we should have camped in the sands and moved on the next day but I was obsessed, irrationally, by the idea of shelter. We had always stopped for the night in the shade of rocks or vegetation and I could not imagine doing anything else. Thus it was that during the lull we hauled the camels to their feet and pressed on.

The move cost us more than half of our remaining water. We carried eight four-gallon jerricans. Some of them were only half-full. With the object of balancing the loads I told Karo to put all the water into four containers. For some perverse reason he opened all the cans at the same time and left them within a few inches of a camel. While he was looking for a funnel the camel struggled to its feet and knocked over three of the cans.

After using all the Swahili invective I could remember I turned to find that Lelean was jabbing his stick into the anus of one of the sick animals in an effort to make it stand up. This made me so angry that I walked off in the wrong direction. Nobody said a word. By the time a recognizable peak reappeared I was about ninety degrees off course. Keeping the compass in my hand I headed south-east by east.

From time to time I glanced back to see how the camels were faring. Three of the heavily laden beasts were bearing up reasonably well and they acted as pace-makers for the rest. I was very thirsty and, like a schoolboy who counts off the days to the holidays, I kept saying to myself that in half an hour I should be able to say that it's nearly dark; the wind would drop and I should be able to have a long, long drink. Lelean and I were soon on good terms again. He came up for a piece of sticking plaster. Like the rest of the men he wore sandals cut out of a piece of motor tyre and they continually cut into his feet. Karo too, was anxious to make the peace. He borrowed my knife, stropped it on a sprinkling of dust in his palm and began to hack off a piece of his own tattered sandals. He grinned hugely when I asked him whether he was not yet dead.

'Eh Karo, bado kufa?'

'Not yet,' he replied.

Shortly before sundown a long low table of rock loomed out of the murk ahead. For some minutes I had an uneasy feeling that it was not the wall but a mirage and would disappear from sight. Through field-glasses I saw to my relief that we were within a mile of shelter and that come what may we had at least crossed another sector of the Chalbi.

Camp was a makeshift affair. The staff sick parade that night was the longest I can remember. All my diffidence about medical matters had long since been pushed aside in the certain knowledge that medicine was the key to contentment. Apart from the camels for which I could do little, Goiti was the only case that caused me any concern. The others needed aspirin and iodine. Goiti had cut his calf on the way to North Horr. Although he said the wound was not painful the flap of muscle was encrusted with sand and should have been stitched. He had put some dung on the wound the previous day. After removing the dung with carbolic soap and an old toothbrush I tied him up with a sprinkling of sulfa and a crepe bandage. He wore the bandage like a puttee long after the wound had healed.

Karo had something on his mind. The symptoms were unmistakable. Whenever he hung about and enquired solicitously whether I was comfortable I metaphorically buttoned my wallet and asked him outright what he wanted. This time he was unusually evasive. At first I thought he was going to tell me that the men had seen three gazelle among the rocks. Lelean had already pointed them out to me and I had agreed to go out with the gun. Karo wanted to know whether he could accompany us. Ten minutes later when I was peering anxiously at three shadowy animals and wondering whether to risk a long shot he began an involved story about how he had unloaded his camels many, many times during the heat of the day.

'Something is lost?'

He nodded. He had lost a bag of rations. They were my rations. The bag contained flour, rice and much of the tinned stuff I had bought at North Horr. He said he had divided his load with Sidi and perhaps the missing bag would be found on one of the other camels. I said we should go back to the camp and find out.

'Wait!' said Lelean. 'Look! A big male.'

The gazelle appeared on a shelf of rock above us. They were in silhouette. The buck half-turned in our direction, scenting the wind. He presented a perfect target – perfect, that is for me. The animal was not more than fifty yards away. It seemed to collapse before I felt the thump of the rifle. As Karo ran forward, Lelean blew his whistle for help in carrying the animal back to the camp.

The first man to appear was Sidi who of course knew nothing about the missing rations. For most of the day he had walked at the end of the caravan. I regarded the loss at that particular moment as a not very serious one and this Karo had foreseen.

The Balessa Kulal

In the dawn light the wall turned out to be far less extensive than I had imagined. The flat blocks of weathered rock had cracked and broken under the violence of the sun. Earth movements, perhaps a quake or a subsidence deep in the desert, had forced the biggest of them ends up towards the sky. They rested against each other, poised so perilously that it seemed as if a slight tremor would bring them crashing down among their fellows on the sand. The wall tailed off towards the south. The height of the unfractured parapet became progressively lower until only a few resistant blocks remained above the dust. Behind the parapet a hummocky waste of lava boulders stretched east to the Huri Hills for many miles.

Nothing more was seen of the missing rations and we were in no state to go back and look for them. Two camels were so weak that it might have been a humane act to shoot them. One shivered incessantly; the other leaned forward with its chin on the ground and scarcely stirred when Goiti threw the *herios* over its flanks. I gave orders that the loads were again to be distributed among the five sound animals. I did my best to ensure that they were coaxed and not thrashed to their feet. Water was not yet a problem. We had about five gallons and would have had more if I had doled it out more prudently, but it was obvious that we should need more, urgently, within twenty-four hours. After an unrewarding reconnoitre from the top of the wall I resolved to march due south to Kalacha, even if it meant a stage into the night. A curious band of dark-coloured sand appeared to lead to a smudge of a hill. Lelean said it was a track but I could not imagine who would cross the desert at such a point.

We marched for several hours. Mezek came up to the head of the column and questioned me about the mysterious wet country called *Breeton* from whence all white men came. As he had once been hired as a cook by Thesiger he thought that all Englishmen walked about with a bag of money, two guns, four pairs of shorts and a dozen pairs of tennis shoes. We discussed several matters from food to air travel but it usually came down to what it cost in terms o f an *n'gombi*, a cow. An *n'gombi* unit was approximately five pounds. Thus a shotgun was worth twenty cows or half the cost of a wife, or nearly three years' wages.

My *manyatta*, I tried to explain, stood on the hills above London. It was in a reserve called Hampstead. A big river flowed in the valley below. No, the hunting was not good. Bad, in fact, *m'baya sana*. Nor was my father a chief. This seemed to disappoint him and he turned to the question of circumcision. Was it so that I could carry a gun? I explained that we had quite a different ceremony and as far as I could remember it was not painful.

Some questions about the cost of travel showed that Mezek knew nothing whatever about geography. Wamba was the centre of his universe and other places were simply 'very far'. He said he had once been to Nairobi and he wanted to know more about Mombasa. Was that where the *meli* made the long safari to England? (A *meli* is a mail boat. Other ships are *man-owaris*.) He asked how much it would cost to travel to England. I suggested fifty cows for a berth on a big *meli*. From Mombasa? I nodded. Were there many boats in Mombasa? I nodded again. Then why had we not seen them on the lake? This puzzled me until I realized that Mezek thought that Rudolf (*Basso*) was Mombasa.

The curious band of dark-coloured sand proved to be not a permanent track but the footprints of a large number of camels and men. From the quantity of blown sand in the base of the prints Lelean reckoned that at least fifty Borana had passed that way two or three days earlier. He said that the rains were coming and the pastoralists were moving south. As the track was as well-marked as a high road we turned west and trudged along it until late in the afternoon.

It was hard going. The leading camels still strode out with some vigour if not enthusiasm; the others had an inebriated stagger. The last animal in the line was in such bad shape that I had to exchange it for one of the three led by Karo. During the course of the safari, especially when we were accompanied by a lot of hangers-on, I noted that the last animal in the line in-variably received more than its fair share of thwacks about the hindquarters. The tail end of the caravan is always the place for the unemployed. The men walked there in pairs, gossiping. From time to time they urged the beasts forward with a shout and, as if justifying their own inactivity, they regularly hit the last camel with their sticks. Definitely no place for a sick animal.

On one occasion I thought I was beset by serious hallucina-tions. I was used to mirages and was never unduly surprised when Kulal seemed to shiver at the base and slowly dissolve into the air. During the afternoon the blurred outline of an enormous beast, somewhat like a cow, loomed above the horizon and remained improbably suspended there for several minutes. It was a most unusual mirage, a projection, possibly, of one of the animals that had gone ahead of us. At least I hoped so. I had a suspicion, now and again, that we were alone in a desert that covered the whole world. I saw my shadow rising to meet me. I saw fear in a handful of dust. A puff of wind and a dust devil no bigger than a soup plate arose with a clattering noise and scurried, crab-wise, across the sand. The base of the vortex was sharply defined, like a screw. At the top it appeared to smoke. I was a little alarmed as we had met few dust storms that day and dust I feared more than anything else. The vortex waltzed away to an almost imperceptible ridge where it collapsed.

The sand got harder. Immediately ahead the ridge became fringed with the stag-headed tops of dead trees where, to my almost inexpressible delight, a shallow valley lay hidden in a gully. Fleshy-leaved aloes and immense tufts of brown grass stuck out of the sand, completely isolated, like stooks of corn in a new-mown field. As we drew nearer, hastening all the time, we saw dilapidated huts among the trees. From them emerged a tall hawk-faced man who stood with his hands on his hips until we were within ten yards of him. Then he held them above his head in a patriarchal greeting.

Conrad, as I called the chief of the Boran, was unusually tall, perhaps fifty years old and superbly self-possessed. No situation that I could imagine appeared likely to disturb his air of leisured composure. With his narrow, sensitive features and fringe of black beard, he bore a striking resemblance to Conrad Veidt in the part of *Jew Suss*. Indeed, Conrad was the only word that passed directly between us. He accepted the nickname with a momentary broadening of his dark eyes and then a smile of comprehension. The rest of what we had to say to each other had to go through Swahili and sometimes Rendille *via* Karo before Sidi, who also knew Rendille, could put it into Borana. For most of the time it was not necessary to do more than acknowledge what he indicated with histrionic sweeps of his hands. Old Conrad had a fine command of gesture. Most of it had to do with the care of camels about which he knew a great deal. We relied on the unctuous Sidi to interpret the rest.

Conrad's people had come down from the frontier several days earlier and were making for the Balessa Kulal where, Lelean told me privately, they had no right to be. They were in Rendille country. They had 'many camels' although I could not discover how many. Their tracks had led us to the depression. The majority of the tribesmen had pushed on south the previous morning. Conrad, his wife and an equally grave young fellow-tribesman with a withered arm had stayed behind with two sick children. One had malaria; it was bathed in sweat and shook violently; the other was weak with dysentery. They responded so quickly to large doses of paludrine and sulfaguanidine that Conrad's gratitude was an embarrassment. The children, a young girl and a boy of about ten, lay on clean, neatly stitched goatskins in an abandoned Rendille hut of which the Boran was manifestly ashamed. The walls were lousy and the floor carpeted in two inches of goat droppings as hard as cherry stones.

Before we set up camp on the edge of a clearing, away from the gaunt, cattle-rubbed trees and verminous huts, I asked Conrad to look at our invalid camels. He made them stand up and stagger forward a pace or two before he couched them again. He ran his hands over their flanks and necks, sniffed deeply into their mouths and said that one might be used after a day or two's rest but the other would not be fit until half a month, perhaps more, had passed. Its skin was tight and cold and insensitive to a host of flies. From its sibilant cough I suspected that it had something akin to pleurisy or pneumonia. Conrad indicated that if it could not be used it could at least be eaten and pointed to my hunting knife. I agreed to the murder. By the following morning the animal had been dressed and the flesh hung in long ribbons on bushes to dry in the sun.

That evening I shot coldly and methodically at every guinea-fowl I could find within maximum radius of the camp. When Karo was laden with enough speckled birds to feed the whole company, I returned to my chair determined to think no more of the welfare of camels until I had learnt a little more about how to keep them alive. Yet despite the food, the shelter and the knowledge that the Borana had water to spare, it was a disturbing night.

Mezek crouched over a fire laid in a circle of stones. As I watched him burying the aluminium *sufrias* in the hot ash, I was startled by a violent explosion and a cascade of sparks from the periphery of the fire. I rose from my chair, wondering whether he had been hurt. By good fortune he was not even singed; I was even luckier not to be hit on the head by a red-hot piece of rock. It crashed through the branches above me, struck the chair and burnt a hole through the plastic webbing. A piece of lava had disintegrated in the heat of the fire.

During the evening I knocked a spoon and a mug of water off the table. When Mezek brought coffee I fumbled for the spoon in the dark but couldn't put my hand on it. In the feeble light of the oil lamp I found it lying by the side of a little pool of water on the ground sheet at my feet and around the pool, drinking, were two pallid scorpions.

At midnight we were awakened by several hyenas who chuckled as they tried to dig up the guts of the camel. Above all sailed a salmon-coloured moon, the only familiar object in an alien world. On the whole a very disturbing night.

I had intended to reconnoitre the surrounding country the following morning but on Conrad's insistence that we could follow the tracks of the Borana until we reached the Balessa Kulal, I stayed in camp and learnt something about the welfare of camels from an expert. Conrad's wife followed us round the camp and while he talked about ropes and harness, she ran her fingers between the ears of the sick beasts and stroked the soft mounds of flesh below their nostrils until their grunts and roars subsided to a contented throaty blabber. Goiti stood by, doggedly, absorbing what he could. Lelean affected indifference; although he was a competent loader and driver he gave the impression that as a game scout he regarded the care of beasts of burden as fit only for lesser breeds without a khaki jacket.

The best pack camels, I learnt, are the big Somalis with the Gabbras a good second; the small Rendilles, the commonest animals between Allia Bay and Marsabit are by far the worst of all. They are usually ill-treated and their only advantage seems to be that they are accustomed to the hard-going of lava country and can withstand long periods of drought. A good pack animal has a compact frame, a small head and well-developed hump. Apparently the skewed humps so frequently seen in the N.F.D. are not necessarily a disadvantage if the flesh is firm. The forelegs have to be straight. All our animals had out-turned toes; their legs brushed against each other at the elbows, forming large callouses which impaired their normal swinging gait.

Because the local tribes are obliged to provide pack animals at reasonable rates they tend to unload their oldest animals on to the unwary. We had been palmed off with a string of senile cripples, dilapidated by time and worsened by ignorance and neglect. Unlike a horse where the teeth project with age, the older the camel the more upright the incisors. They are reckoned to be mature at the age of five or six when they develop their complement of thirty-four teeth. Some live to the age of forty. Conrad could not say how old our beasts were. He shook his head slowly and said something which Sidi translated as *wazee sana*. They were very old men. Strangely enough, the oldest were the best we had; they were geldings.

When the camels had been hand-fed with an invalid diet of a grass called *darema* and sprouts of young mimosa acacia, Conrad daubed their sores with a transparent liquid which I took to be salt and water. The treatment was accompanied by a simply spoken incantation. I could be certain that the chief was doing his best for us. When his son began to stroll about, he shepherded him towards me and with one hand on the boy's shoulders he grasped mine. The contrast with the Samburu, who often begged insistently for tobacco when they had been given medicine, was marked.

Conrad, I should guess, was a pagan. Several of the Hamitic religions spring direct from pre-Christian and pre-Mohammedan times. I was neither willing nor able to ask him any questions about what he believed in or why but he seemed to show an unusual reverence for fire, water and, of all things, an owl. He gave us water from his own goat-skins with a great air of ceremony and that night he presented me with a glowing brand from his own fire. Later in the evening he returned to stand beside the blaze, not speaking but gazing into the tree above my head. When an owl rolled a melancholy call into the night he became animated and repeatedly pointed towards it. Mezek said it was 'his bird' but Mezek viewed the Boran with a certain amount of suspicion. He said he was a witch doctor.

We left the next morning with eight camels, a hideous sackful of meat and enough water for a two-day march. The transition from the shade of the depression to the blinding glare of the Chalbi was disturbing. It was like venturing out of a vault into a sunlit courtyard. Within an hour the familiar streamers of sand were whirling round us; the mirage had settled down over the horizon and the trees and dilapidated huts of the ghost *manyatta* had disappeared below the crest as if they had never been. The boys were in high spirits. They sang songs, teased Goiti, who never knew when his leg was being pulled and told me until I was heartily tired of hearing it that the Balessa was not very far away.

Both Lelean and Karo were skilled at interpreting the tracks of the Borana. They showed me how families with camels or donkeys were divided up into groups with this man lame or that man carrying a load. The children tripped along, dodging in and out of the way of the animals while the young girls walked behind the vigorous purposive *morans*, always in threes or fours. To me it was a confusion of impressions, few of which were clear. I could recognize the animals on the extreme flanks, but to decipher the centre of the track was like trying to interpret what had been drawn on, and then partly wiped off, a school blackboard at the end of a day.

We were heading south-west towards Orloma and another massive scarp that stood between us and the eastern shore of the lake. The cones of a dozen dead volcanoes were spread out ahead of us. They ranged from the rusty brown vent of Asie to the sprawling backside view of the ever-visible Kulal. On the first night we spent a vigorous half-hour in re-excavating some water-holes dug by the Borana but the product was both meagre and salty. Karo did better by thrusting his spear deep into likely depressions and examining the blade for any sign of moisture. At the foot of a rock he shouted excitedly and began to dig like a fox terrier. He found sweet water at a depth of five feet. I distributed the week's rations with some formality; each man got a handful of chewing tobacco and what with the roast camel, which I did not eat, and a bath before supper, which I thoroughly enjoyed, we had a good time of it that night.

Beyond the somewhat dingy-looking oasis of Orloma with its wind-tattered palms and impoverished herdsmen we strode down on to the firm sands of the great *lugga* of Balessa. This stream bed, which is dry for the greater part of the year, rises on the edge of the Chalbi and winds south for eighty miles, intersecting another desert, the Karoli, before it sinks, apparently exhausted, into the cracked lava at the lower end of the lake. Although the Borana were far ahead of us we were by no means alone. A long procession of Rendille with their cattle, sheep and goats were winding down the western wall of the lava. At the mouth of the Sandaslo Pass, the rift between Asie and Kulal, they were joined by yet another file of tribesmen. The two streams merged and continued on their way together. We became part of a river of migrating animals and men. Oryx and gazelle were also on the move; we could see them winding through the hills while overhead at dawn and dusk the sky was freckled with sandgrouse.

The magnet that drew the migrants south was rain. Bales of woolly-looking clouds were beginning to pile up over the distant mountains. In the dry season the movement of animals is to a great extent unpredictable; they wander here and there, looking for dribbles of water. But at the onset of the rains their movements become dramatically purposive. Perhaps they are guided by scent or a change in humidity; they may even get a visual fix on a storm from a distant flicker of lightning. All strove to be the first to reach the fresh-green grass.

The drawback about the Balessa was that for the past week it had been used as a high road by every man, woman, child and captive beast in the neighbourhood. The wells were foul with droppings; the vegetation had been nibbled down to the sand and the game had fled. Had we been ahead of the procession I might have enjoyed the pace and the competition for food and water, but we were far behind and the race was nearly over. It was like occupying a bathing beach on Bank Holiday Monday. However, the men liked the company they met; they tended to disappear at night and after two temporary desertions I laid it down firmly that if anyone else had to be fished out of a neighbouring *manyatta* at dawn he would lose a week's pay.

After a tick-tormented night on such a camping sight as I hope never to see again I decided to leave the squalor of the *lugga* and cut a trail of our own. The news was badly received. Chorus of objections. Where could we go? How dare we part company with camelmen when our own beasts were in poor condition. These were cogent objections. I looked at the map long and hard and decided that with any luck we could march along the ridge that skirted the desert we had just left. As for the camels I was resolved to buy some more. The Warden had said we should be able to hire another string at the Balessa Kulal, a famous water-point farther down the *lugga*. If I could replace one or two of our cripples I reckoned the remainder would hold out for at least another week. Six good camels would see us through. With Lelean as interpreter and business manager I walked into a Rendille *manyatta* one evening and indicated that I wanted to see someone about a camel.

There were endless formalities. I had completely forgotten that among fortunate, leisure-loving people it is neither customary nor polite to get down to the object of a visit at once. We told the story of our safari, sketched maps in the dust and in return we heard about the welfare of the old Rendille chief, his wives, his worries and all the rest. He offered me a big bowl of cool camel milk but remembering something about undulant fever I patted my stomach and said I had a touch of *kuhara*. This brought us round to the treatment of forks in the head, the breast and the bowels and thus by easy stages to the welfare and value of camels.

The actual bargaining was over and done with in about five minutes. Surrounded by a ring of red-robed *morans* I made a pretence of examining the back teeth of two young cows and a bull. They seemed excellent. Uncertain what to do next I lifted up their tails and peered, knowingly, into their fundaments. They seemed excellent too. Lelean muttered something about 'no females' so I concentrated on the bull. It looked fit enough;

moreover it could be persuaded to stand up and walk without being kicked in the backside. We eventually acquired it for two hundred shillings, three pounds of tea and a hand-mirror tastefully backed with a coloured portrait of the Prime Minister of Uganda. I thought we did rather well.

We did less well on the way back to camp. Lelean was leading the beast; I walked behind him. In the half-light I was vaguely aware that we were among dense vegetation. Suddenly there was a prodigious crash. The camel reared. Lelean shouted 'Faro!' and I had about a second's reflection on what to do about a rhinoceros at close quarters. The problem was a purely theoretical one because the rhino ran away. To my surprise and annoyance the camel promptly followed it. But for the curious stamping noise made by the rhino's feet it is doubtful whether we should have re-acquired our bargain before dawn but we eventually caught up with it on the far side of the *lugga*. Lelean explained afterwards that the stamping noise was due to the rhino's habit of putting forefeet and hindfeet down together. He demonstrated the action on all fours. Big *faro*, he said, went 'Bang! Bang!' I nodded; I was getting rather *blasé* about rhinos and I was glad to get the camel back.

The route over the ridge was more comfortable than I had expected. We had a panoramic view of the mountains on one side and we could watch the dust storms in the Chalbi on the other. We got peppered with the dust before the day was out and it was uncomfortably hot, but the only incident worth recalling is that shortly after midday I was confronted with a mild outbreak of mutiny.

It arose, as such things do, from a series of trivial mishaps. Goiti flogged the new camel for no good reason and I ticked him off. I then discovered that Karo had lashed the load on another animal so tightly that one of the ropes sawed a hole in a fourgallon *debe* of paraffin. We lost a lot of paraffin and I lost my temper.

Shortly afterwards I found three or four white ants in my tea. I traced them back to source and found that my last canister of dried milk had been left open all night. It swarmed with the creatures. I had a row with Mezek. He blustered. He said someone else must have opened the tin. As he had been in trouble the previous day for losing a *panga*, he was touchy and he thought he was being persecuted unnecessarily. He said he wished to resign then and there. *Sasa!*

There was worse to come. Goiti said he would join him. The old man, usually so patient and self-effacing, had been more upset than I realized by Conrad's gentle criticism of the treatment of the camels. Although I had an uneasy feeling that the whole staff was going to walk out in the middle of the Balessa Kulal, I said that the resignations were accepted and that when they had thought a little more about it I would discuss paying them off at sundown. This left me about six hours to think it out for myself. I stretched out under a bush and dozed until about half-past one.

The sound of a rifle shot brought me to my feet. Lelean, who had been cleaning my rifle, had seen a gazelle on the hillside. He had crawled up to it and fired. This was not only in defiance of orders and Game Department regulations: he had also missed the animal. This was too much. I told him that if he took a pot shot at another animal he would lose his *bakshishi* and I should report him to the *B'wana m'kubwa*, literally the big white chief. To my dismay, Lelean handed back the uncleaned rifle and said that he too wanted to go back to Wamba *sasa*. It looked as if I had lost three men in one afternoon.

We held a meeting then and there. Grievances were aired; the men went over all the points in meticulous detail. I remember that the situation began to brighten when Lelean scratched his head and eventually shook a couple of ants out of the lining of his khaki cap. Karo giggled and even Goiti smiled. In what I fervently hoped was a convincing speech I said that of course all the resignations were accepted but sometimes when the sun was high men got little forks in their heads and used angry words. We would discuss the situation again at six o'clock. Did they wish to leave that night or the following morning? Dreadful silence followed the bluff. To my relief, Lelean admitted that he had got a headache and he wanted an aspirin. He hoped the safari would go on for a long time because we had a lot of medicine and a lot of meat. Nothing more was said about resignations and afterwards, whenever minor arguments arose between mid-morning and late afternoon, I could usually clear the air by pointing at the sun.

For three days we ambled along the ridge, nursing the camels and putting the heaviest loads on the shaggy beast I had bought from the Rendille. It was by far the strongest of the string and from a fancied resemblance to Tolstoi in his peasant costume, I called it Leo. Apart from the little white one, distinguishing between beasts that were very much alike in all but temperament and physical fitness was not easy. Two of them had a tendency to panic and throw off their loads. With an ink brush I put a large B on their necks. B for bad. An earlier attempt at labelling them M for *M'baya* (bad) led to some confusion with M for *M'zuri* (good). In time the bad ones became known as *beefs*.

Whenever the Chalbi threw a shower of dust over us we went to ground in a gully, sometimes spending the night there. Dodging the storms became a tedious form of sport. They were usually very localized, and when, as sometimes happened, they raced across our path, blotting out the landscape for a few hundred yards ahead, we waited, camels couched, until the commotion subsided. It was rather like standing beside the closed gates of a level crossing, watching the trains go by.

In the evening I shot spurfowl and sandgrouse. The indigestibility of the latter can be relieved by almost nothing except bismuth powder, but when the sack of camel meat was empty they were appreciated by the men. The company had been augmented by an unaccountable number of camp followers. Among them were little boys who collected wood and three of the Warden's ever-hungry *askaris* who were making their way to the wells of the Balessa Kulal. At night we were still haunted by hyenas who dug up bones wherever they were buried. Awakened in the dark by a cracking noise, I saw a dirty grey-coloured beast scarcely ten yards from my bed. Poking the shotgun through the mosquito net I fired both barrels from beneath my arm but succeeded only in skinning two fingers on the unchecked recoil.

Wrapped up in three cotton vests at the bottom of my medicine chest I kept a little wireless set, made in Japan and extraordinarily efficient at picking up three, and almost only three, types of music. Europe and North America seemed to transmit almost nothing but rock-and-roll, augmented by peculiarly British Early Morning and Workers' Playtime type of bands. Whatever the repertoire the *dumpty dumpty* ditties were delivered at exactly the same tempo, *encore et encore*, *ad nauseam*. A twist of the dial brought in the wail of Islam, costive and insistent in North Africa but enriched in the Sudan by full-throated recitations from the *Qu'ran*. From Nairobi, the coast, and all points east came the cheerful, irregular songs of India in Gujuratic and Hindi, to me the most attractive oriental sounds of all.

One night, high above the Chalbi, I went to bed early, intent on hearing a retransmission of a Festival Hall concert in London, due to begin at half-past nine. I tuned in to the short wave and turned the volume down to a mere breath of sound to dampen either a quiz programme or a spelling bee. The radio twittered on the floor about a yard from my ear and I fell asleep.

Shortly before midnight I awoke to find the blades of four spears outlined against the sky. The shafts were held by four young Samburu who were kneeling with their heads bent down over the radio. They were listening to the whine of a late-night dance band. Softly, I asked them if they liked it. They ran away. Calling them back I repeated the question. Was it good? Did they like the noise? In a phrase which I treasure, one of them said it was *asali kabissa*; the very essence of treacle.

On the fifth day we left the ridge for the trampled sands of the Balessa Kulal. The *lugga* there was two hundred yards wide, densely fringed with trees and dug up in a score of places where the caravans ahead of us had watered their stock and passed on. Normally the Balessa has a resident population of Rendille and provides dry season grazing for a few families of nomadic Samburu. The stream drains the eastern flanks of Mount Kulal. We were told of *manyattas* high up in the hills but they were said to be almost deserted. The tribes had gone south and with them had gone the flockmaster from whom we hoped to hire an entirely new string of camels. This was a disconcerting state of affairs.

Lelean went off to learn what he could from a local forest guard and I strolled among the dismal covering of droppings, the shreds of ropes and mats and the burnt-out fires on the *lugga* floor. The waterholes looked like bomb craters. To keep out wild animals the tribesmen had ringed the rims of the pits with a barricade of thorn as impenetrable as barbed wire. The barricades were densely populated with colonies of scarlet finches into which goshawks dived and carried off screaming birds. Man had gone: the place was being cleaned up. Vultures soared high over the remains of a cow. Hyenas would soon carry off the bones. The *lugga* would soon be scoured out by a torrent and left immaculate until the nomads returned.

The flockmaster, we learnt, had left for a *manyatta* that was at least forty miles away. It was thought to be under Kurior Dele, not far from the southern end of the South Horr Gap. Lelean suggested that two of us should march there and return with the camels later in the week. I shook my head. I was unwilling to split up the caravan and from what I had heard of the elusive chief he was unlikely to stop anywhere for any length of time. He was not only a professional trader but a favoured vassal of Lago of Marsabit, the paramount chief of the Rendille. Kenya was on the verge of independence. For most of the desert chiefs the prospect of enlarging their power by hanging round the towns was of far greater importance than the sale of a few camels to an unimportant traveller. Lelean said we might be able to hire a string of donkeys from the Turkana at Laisamis on the edge of the lake. This was not a pleasing prospect. The camels were sick. At least three of them would have to be left in charge of the *askaris* from Marsabit who were still hanging about the camp. But they were camels and for me their patient character and generous rolling gait was infinitely preferable to the twitchy feet and narrow deceitful eyes of donkeys. After resting for a couple of days, we set off for the lake with Leo, the little white one and the best of the rest. As we hoped to pick up reinforcements on the way, the *beefs* were left behind.

Beyond the Balessa Kulal the country opened out; the ridge that had protected us from the blown sand of the Chalbi fell away and we were soon heading into another bluster. It was the wind we had encountered on our journey up to the lake some months earlier. I recognized the insistence, the absence of gustiness and once again we heard the ominous moan in the hills.

As the wind blew from the east and we had by this time almost entirely encircled Mount Kulal – which lay to the north – I realized that the old monster was not directly responsible for our discomfort. A meteorologist eventually explained that the monsoons from the northern part of the Indian Ocean are sucked into the equatorial low pressure area over East Africa. This means that a vast front of westward-moving air is forced into the relatively narrow gap between the highlands of Kenya and Ethiopia. As Lake Rudolf lies in the mouth of this natural wind tunnel it is probably not only one of the hottest but also one of the windiest places in the world.

We spent a night at Longerin within a quarter of a mile of our old camping site. The next day, when I was beginning to wonder, as I so often did, whether the camels would last out until nightfall, Lelean procured another beast for us, by a masterful stroke of fieldcraft.

We had been marching over country that looked like a Victorian print of the biblical wilderness. Almost entirely devoid of vegetation, the flat-topped boulders seemed to be lying on a waste of lava dust and shingle in sheer despair. In a gully at right angles to our route, Lelean discovered a line of tracks. From the angle of a crushed wisp of thorn he said that a man with a laden camel had passed that way earlier in the day and he proposed to follow him. While we waited Lelean set off and returned two hours later with a big Gabbra camel and an old Turkana who made it plain that if we hired his beast we should have to hire him. We promptly took him on and I gave him a week's rations. He ate a lot of it at lunch time and belched for the rest of the day.

That night we reached the home of the hyenas. On the map the *lugga* is called Laisamis. Like the Serima a few miles to the north it is a deep cleft in the high escarpment around the southern end of the lake. One of the animals began to call as we walked into the shadow of the rocks. It was the usual insistent *ooo-ah-ooo*, haunting and strangely beautiful. The hyena is a hideous-looking animal but it is also one of the most useful and its call is the keynote of night life in the bush. 'Fisi,' said Lelean. During his army days a *fisi* had carried off his highly polished belt. He was not well-disposed towards them. Another animal started to moan. It was echoed by two more. Before we halted for the night under the face of a cliff the canyon rang with a chorus of calls. 'Manyatta ya fisi,' said Karo.

Some districts are infested with hyenas. On my way down to Wamba I heard a strange story of a plague of the animals on the edge of the Turkana escarpment. It was told to me by the game warden at Moroto in Karamoja. He said that among the Karamajong there is a belief that at night the *Imuron*, the tribal witchdoctors, can either turn themselves into hyenas or travel from one place to another on the backs of the animals. *Imuron* are not among the most popular members of the tribe.

During the great drought in East Africa the cattle began to die in thousands and hyenas became a menace. With an abundance of carrion they increased in numbers and, instead of scavenging in twos and threes, a pack of thirty or forty animals would gang up together and attack living animals. The warden killed them by pouring a tin of cattle dip into the stomach of a dead cow and leaving the poisoned carcass in the bush. In this way he sometimes collected twenty or thirty dead hyenas in one night.

After one successful onslaught his chief scout told him with evident satisfaction that he had killed an *Imuron*. Among the dead hyenas they found one animal decorated with the sacred ear-rings of the soothsayers. They could not have been put on after death. The bone rings were embedded in the pierced ears and the flesh had grown around them. The animal was also wearing a sacred necklace and its chest was painted with the characteristic stripes of the medicine men. The warden could offer no explanation for the decorated animal but the tribe considered he had done them a good turn.

Karo did well to call the Laisamis the home of the hyenas. The animals scurried about in the dark, snuffling and whining and showing up fitfully in the light of the fires. Towards midnight one of them began to call insistently from a ledge of rock about twenty feet above the camel lines. Lelean picked out the grey beast in the light of a torch and I shot it in the chest. It was so heavy that we had to leave it where it fell.

Turkanaland

At the top of the Laisamis the next morning we came across a group of tired Turkana stretched out under a plam tree, pretending to be fast asleep. An old man with an ivory ball pegged to his lower lip gave a deep sigh which tailed off into a dog-like growl; another grunted and flicked a fly away, a third rolled over on his stomach. They all gave the impression they wanted to be left alone. This I considered discouraging. After walking for several hundred miles I felt we deserved a welcome on our return to the lake. We had travelled full circle round Mount Kulal, braved the Chalbi and now, after crossing the scarp for the second time, we were intent on novel achievement. Apprentice days were over. It mattered little that we were in one of the hottest places in the world. I was determined to enjoy every minute of the remainder of the safari. I was Marco Polo. But among the Turkana it seemed that I was not appreciated.

I said, 'Tell them we have come here from Wamba'. Mezek put it into three crackling sentences. For a moment there was silence and then Ivory Ball said 'Aiee' but he said it with no apparent curiosity. Wamba meant nothing to him. It might have been Huddersfield or Honolulu. I tried North Horr. He was not interested.

'Say we have meat,' I said. 'Argri.' It was one of the very few words I knew in Turkana. The response was noticeable but not overwhelming. When they had eaten four tins of meat loaf, very slowly, I discovered that they had recently devoured a very large sun-baked perch.

I had hoped that we should be able to buy some camels from the Turkana. About twenty animals, most of them cows, were browsing in the scrub but I could make nothing of Mezek's explanation of what they were doing at the head of a mountain pass at eleven o'clock in the morning. His gestures were conspicuously erotic and he repeatedly used the word husband. I couldn't understand what he was getting at. Grinning hugely he tried again.

He clenched his fist and with his elbow pushed into his hip he slowly raised his forearm as if he were lifting an invisible weight. I took this to signify virility but failed to see what it had to do with the sleepy Turkana. I suggested disputes over bride-wealth or an initiation ceremony. He shook his head. After more grotesque pantomime I realized that the Turkana were waiting for the arrival of a stud bull. One of them had gone to fetch the animal from a nearby homestead. Their intention was to water the herd in the lake and then put the bull among the cows.

The bull arrived in such a state of perturbation that I feared for the safety of our own animals. It was a large lion-coloured beast with a fringe of black hair along its spine. As soon as it saw the herd it broke away from the man who was leading it and tried to savage the rival bulls. The animals scattered, the Turkana grabbed their sticks and we began to move down the escarpment in a procession that was often a running fight.

If the waiting cows were supposed to whet the bull's appetite the manœuvre was ill-judged. The animal was aggressive, not lustful. Perhaps it was frustrated. Although haltered and held down by two men, it roared and grabbed at any form of flesh within reach of its frothy jaws. I am inclined to think that camels are far more docile than they are reputed to be, but I had heard that a bull on heat can bite off the top of a man's head and I kept out of its way. It ground its teeth, rolled its eyes and blew an enormous pink bladder out of the corner of its mouth. This is the palatal flap, a distensible piece of skin like an elongated balloon. It denotes *musth*, the periodic fervour that also afflicts the elephant.

In the camel the sexual instincts of the males are suppressed for the greater part of the year but when *musth* overtakes them they have on occasion to be chained down. The Turkana bull broke free for the second time and when we last caught sight of the herd it was far below us and the cows were galloping down the slope. I was not sorry to see them go. It was cool on the heights and we had time on our side.

The path down to the lake was unusually steep but the going was easy; the fact that the track between the lava boulders was regularly used by camel trains meant that we were unlikely to run into trouble and within three hours we were again bathing in the bright green waters of *Basso*.

South Island stood out like a fortress. Farther north was the pyramidal outline of Porr and behind it a smudge of the Longon-doti Hills. This is where we had been. Through field-glasses I stared at the ashen-grey volcanoes at the south end of the lake. This is where I planned to march on foot, without the camels. The first step was to find a site for a base camp on an extensive and largely unbroken platform of painfully hot rock.

The Turkana from whom we had hired the big Gabbra said that he knew of a *lugga* 'not very far' where there was both shelter and browse for the camels. This struck me as wildly improbable and I was tempted to return to the foot of the escarpment where at least we should be in the shade. Lelean disagreed. The Turk-ana, he said, came from a tributary of the Kerio river to the west and could find shelter 'like a hyena'. This was a variation of a stock Samburu joke. Hyenas are called 'the sheep of the Turkana' and in times of famine they are said to eat them. I decided to take a chance on the man's knowledge and for two hours we marched over rocks on which a bad time was had by all. The surface was not only hot and so brightly polished that the sun flash hurt the eyes, but the ridges of the lava were exceedingly sharp, and cut into the soles of my sand shoes.

Despite the usual dire forebodings the Turkana led us into a deep *lugga* bounded by vertical banks of lava. It was compara-tively sheltered; a tree provided an identifiable place for my bed and the men hacked a snug out of a large bush. I was delighted with the place and in honour of my own *manyatta* I wrote 'New Hampstead' on one of the blank portions of the local map.

A drink at sundown was interrupted by a familiar bellow. To my dismay I saw that the Turkana camels were coming. Still pursued by the somewhat exhausted bull, the herd was advancing on the best patch of browse in New Hampstead. Shouting to Goiti to head them off, I greeted Ivory Ball with another tin of meat loaf and we talked for about an hour.

The outcome was that the Turkana camels were useless for our purposes. They had not been trained to carry loads. The tribesmen used them as a source of blood and milk. The cows supplied about a gallon of milk a day if they were in good condition, usually it was far less; the bleeding process varied in accordance with the number of animals in one *awi* or tribal stall. From references to my pint mug I calculated that the blood yield was not more than a gallon a month from a bull. The Turkana extracted it by putting a tourniquet of bark rope around the camel's neck and piercing the jugular vein with a spear. The blood is mixed with milk curdled with urine. They poured out some for me. It looked like raspberry jam and I indicated that I might drink it later.

Before the Turkana walked off into the night the stud bull made one last and laborious conquest. For some time it had been wandering from cow to cow with no success and considerably less ardour than I had expected from its earlier behaviour. Taking advantage of a couched animal he flopped down beside her and prevented her from rising by placing his head across her neck. When the cow threw herself forward in an effort to rise, the bull took advantage of her upturned hindquarters and covered her, adroitly, uttering an exultant bellow. The cow lifted her head up and began to bleat like a goat. The noise had an extraordinary effect on the rest of the herd. Bulls and cows crowded round, snuffling and grunting until the coupled animals were entirely hidden from view. The commotion was over in about ten minutes. The bull disengaged himself from his dog-like posture and got to his feet with surprising alacrity. The cow was disinclined to rise and had to be flogged until she rose from her knees and lumbered after the rest of the herd. It seemed a sad end to a brief encounter.

Our first whole day in New Hampstead was remarkable for the intensity of the heat. This bald statement needs some explanation. We had been pretty hot on previous occasions. At Loiyangalani the shade temperature had reached a hundred and eight. Once or twice in the Chalbi I thought we had reached the point beyond which all life becomes extinct, but I had other things to think about when the sand blew down on us. In short, hardship was never as bad as I thought it would be. The problem at New Hampstead was that I had nothing to do but think and I usually thought about the heat. As a shelter the tree was about as effective as the bare ribs of a parasol. The rocks became untouchable and the whole *lugga* quivered angrily. I had the feeling that we were about to be vaporized.

For want of something better to do I tried to work out the time of the day from the length of my shadow, but became irritated because I couldn't cope with the arithmetic. At nine o'clock it was almost exactly equal to my own height; at ten o'clock it was a little longer than half my height and at precisely ten minutes to twelve I had no shadow whatever unless I stood with my legs apart or jumped into the air. I have this on the very best of evidence: I tried it. Mezek looked surprised. I don't know what he thought I was doing. At the time I didn't care. I didn't care about anything except the heat.

During the late afternoon I set off on a combined hunting, fishing and bird-watching expedition contrived essentially to relieve boredom, but as the Rift Valley has been called the future playground of Africa it may be of some value to give a strictly factual account of the latter part of a day's holiday in an unexplored bay of the Jade Sea.

We set off at four o'clock. Lelean carried my rifle and a rucksack; I followed behind with a shotgun, a fishing rod and a packet of salt tablets. He wore only pants and sandals; I was similarly dressed with the addition of a hat and two pairs of sunglasses. It was very, very hot. I have said this before and I shall say it again.

Our intention was to go back, up the *lugga* towards the scarp and then strike west, returning to the lake in what I assumed would be a parallel valley. The intention was excellent and the assumption established although the scenery was undistinguished. We found another *lugga* littered with the wrecks of trees and the leavings of the Turkana. In their camel watering forays the pastoralists set up temporary *awis* and stay until they have cut down every tree and eaten up every spike of thorn. There is little enough to attract them in the first place; they leave behind almost nothing but bare dust and rock. Here, indeed, was the Waste Land.

> . . . the dead tree gives no shelter, the cricket no relief
> And the dry stone no sound of water . . .

Nor beast nor edible fowl. Lelean thought he saw buck and he may have been right. Faint dots that might have been gazelle danced on a distant hillside but I refused to follow them up. As ever his mind was on meat; mine on the necessary minimum of exertion. It was, as I have said, very hot.

I used to imagine that I could always find something of biological interest in a new place but this was before I ventured into the Northern Frontier District. After an exhausting hour of peering and probing the total bag was one grasshopper, one dead beetle covered in ants and a spider-like animal called a solifuge which I rescued from a wasp. This is not altogether surprising. At high sun I was informed that the temperature of deserts is sometimes within sixteen degrees of the boiling point of water. The only bird we saw, a large pippet or a long-claw, cheeped among the lava boulders while a flat grey snake coiled even deeper into the shadow of a rock.

There was more to be seen beside the lake. As soon as we reached the shore, intent on a swim, the crocodiles took to the water like rats. Some dived five or six feet off the rocks; others slid in on their bellies. They were not large animals but they were numerous and I wondered if there were big ones in the deeps. Lelean seemed quite unconcerned by the prospect of mixed bathing and found a shallow pool where he said we should be quite safe.

Floating on my back I became conscious, as I so often did, of a sense of total unreality. The lava, the crocodiles and the violent sun seemed to be a fragment of a strange but not unpleasant dream. Even the colour of the sky and the unctuous touch of the soda-laden water appeared foreign to experience. The sky was dove-grey; against it a spiral of soaring pelicans became white motes, like falling cigarette ash caught in a beam of sunlight. It was a storm sky and as I waded out and took the rifle so that Lelean could wade in, a whiplash of lightning cracked across the cinder cone behind us.

Lelean called it a 'M'vua m'kubwa' but it was not a big rain. It was a big wind bearing a large amount of ashen-grey dust. Count Teleki did well to name the lake after his unpredictably temperamental patron. Within a minute the sultry afternoon was blown away by a wind of cyclonic force. A cataract of dust poured over the escarpment; it blotted out the lower slopes of the hills and swept over us as we ran for the shelter of the rocks. For about half an hour there was an almost constant play of lightning but only a growl of thunder. The flashes were accompanied by a noise like the tearing of a sheet.

The storm died away almost as quickly as it began. A few gusts furrowed the centre of the lake but around the shore and in the bays the surface was calm, powdered with dust and unbroken except for inky splodges left by the sluggish rolling of fish. As we walked back to the camp I scooped up a handful of the dust and wondered whether it had come from the Chalbi, the Karoli or one of the arid plains beyond Kalacha in the Huri Hills. It looked unlike anything I had seen in the vicinity of the lake.

Mezek came to meet us and from his expression I knew that the camp had been hard hit. He said that a few things – most of them mine – had been broken but, worst of all, the little white one was missing. This affected me far more than his elaborate description of the damage done by the wind. I am not sentimental about domesticated animals, certainly not pack animals, but I had very real feelings of affection towards the little camel. It was gentle and responsive and as I usually got her ready myself; we were on the best of terms. Mezek said that Goiti and Karo had been driving the unhaltered animals up from the lake when the dust cloud swept down the *lugga*. The animals panicked. Two of them, including the white one, ran ahead; the others were found in the lee of an overhanging rock. When the men got back to camp with the remaining six they discovered that one of the missing animals was already couched, awaiting them; it had run home. The white one had evidently run on and Goiti and Karo were still searching for it.

To say that the camp had been flattened by the wind would be an exaggeration: my folding table and chair were still standing although both, as Mezek put it, had 'been for a little safari' on their own. Most of the damage had been done by a pile of rocks which had been used to weigh down the foot of a groundsheet immediately above my head. This was one of Mezek's bright ideas. He had rigged up a windbreak. As the bed was in a depression at the foot of the tree, he had tied the groundsheet to the upper branches and stuffed the lower end under a veritable tumulus of lava boulders. When the wind blew the sheet had split and the bed was immured. I managed to excavate shaving gear, some bent plates and cups, the gun-cleaning material and *Lives of the Desert Fathers*. We had also lost two mosquito nets, some washing and what the army used to call the unexpired portion of the day's rations. They were soaked in paraffin. I knew that it would be a waste of time even to try and find out why the tin was unstoppered when it was blown over.

Goiti and Karo returned about eight o'clock to say that they had lost the tracks of the camel at a place where the spoor merged with the spoor of the Turkana herd. It seemed to me unlikely that the stray would venture up the escarpment alone and in the dark but I saw no reason to doubt the men's story. I thanked them and told them to continue the search the next morning. Up to that moment I had hoped that it still might be possible to lead the whole caravan across the lava into Turkanaland. But now that we had only seven camels and two of them in bad shape I knew that it would be foolish to try.

Supper that night was an exotic affair of roast plover and tangerines – the birds a present from Lelean who had knocked them down with a stick; the fruit all that remained of a small store of tins kept for special occasions. I ate the meal with a map on my knees and calculated how far we were likely to get into Turkanaland on foot. As there seemed to be no point in spending another day measuring the length of my diminishing shadow I told Lelean to be ready at dawn.

During the night the wind backed from east to north and however many times I re-arranged a wind-break of ammunition boxes I could not escape the dust. Towards dawn the wind started to blow from the west. Sparks from the fire showered down on my bed. I got up and hunched over the glowing embers in a blanket. I was not only tired and somewhat disconcerted by the turn of events; I remember that it was the first time in the desert that I felt cold. Before long I began to speculate unprofitably on why I had returned to the lake. It was certainly not to catch one of the big fish. Nor were the volcanoes any more spectacular than those we had passed on the way. As far as I could unravel motive from a tangle of romanticism, I was intent on walking through the worst country I had seen, but to what end was not clear at that hour of the morning.

We set off at half-past six. A walk of about three hours brought us to the foot of the cinder cone of Nabuyaton. To reach it we followed the shoreline as far as the red cliffs of Lotar where, after an unsuccessful scramble among the rocks and the crocodiles, we found ourselves confronted by a sheer face of lava and a long narrow inlet of iridescent green water. It was necessary to strike inland and approach the cone from the rear.

Nabuyaton lies with its feet in the lake. With its smooth, improbably symmetrical flanks it resembles a gigantic worm cast. Most of the volcanoes on the edge of Von Höhnel's Bay are considered to be of a type known to geologists as explosives, that is they erupted suddenly, possibly when lake water poured into new fissures and vaporized in the heart of the volcano. It is likely that Nabuyaton is a subsidiary cone, a valve on the periphery of the main vents. Among nine craters to the south I could see the stark outline of Teleki's volcano. When a traveller called Strickland visited the region in 1897, nine years after the discovery of the lake, he was surprised to find the whole face of the country altered; the only sign of volcanic activity was several miles from where Teleki had placed it. I saw only smoke rings and plumes of steam from unidentifiable points to the west. After dark, vents of burning gas glowed momentarily.

That night we slept under a rock with a rucksack for a pillow. I was uncomfortably aware that the sand was richly impressed with crocodile tracks and as a form of protection I should have preferred something less flimsy than a mosquito net. But it was a quiet night. Birds called, wavelets plashed reassuringly and the milky light of a massive moon softened the outlines of the cinder cones. The next morning it was plain from an abundance of tracks resembling the impressions of human feet that we had been closely inspected by several crocodiles as we slept. During those days on the Turkana shore I sometimes got within a few feet of large ones. The only sign of aggression came from an animal that swung its tail round so violently that it lost its grip and gyrated on its back legs. However, I had no wish to get within snapping distance of an animal in the lake and I took care to keep out of their way as they plunged headlong into the water.

If the Turkana were surprised to see us they kept their feelings to themselves. In one sandy bay we came across five naked men industriously hammering out and tempering the tinplate heads of fish-spears. They looked up but said nothing and went on with their work. I suspect that Lelean's khaki cap tended to inhibit cordiality. It represented an authority that has never been noticeably successful in the country between the western shore of Lake Rudolf and the Uganda border. Over a period of forty years the Turkana have been directly or indirectly concerned in one of the most ludicrous and least-known aspects of Pax Britannica. Primarily herdsmen, the Turkana are also raiders who have tied down whole battalions of the King's African Rifles. In fights with their hereditary enemies, the Dodoth and the Karamajong, they have cost the British government more money than it would have taken to rejuvenate large tracts of the wastes of Turkanaland.

As I had been in Dodoth country at the time of one of the biggest raids in recent years I wanted to find out what the other side thought about this protracted war, but Lelean was not much help. He knew only a little more Turkana than I had been able to glean from a missionary's glossary.

We asked the fishermen where they came from. The answer was a series of grunts and some imprecise waves towards the west. It might have been the Turkwel river not far to the west; it might have been a hundred miles away on the Uganda border. I tried another tack. Had they got much food? An old man whose job it was to drop the bits of hot metal into a tin of fat with seemingly fire-proof fingers pointed to the rocks on which were spread yellow strips of fish and said 'Not enough'. I took up the cue. I told them grandly that I would catch some fish. Feeling as if I had to uphold the reputation of the Fly Fishers' Club, the Casting Club de France and the Leeds and District Amalgamated Society of Anglers, I walked out to a headland and began to flick a silver plug into the soupy water.

In an hour of hard work I caught seventeen fish weighing about three hundred pounds. This is not a boastful statement. With the exception of the inedible tiger fish, the perch gave themselves up as if they were only too anxious to leave the lake, although by Rudolf standards there was not a big fish among them. None the less, they were wholly acceptable to the Turkana and for two days I became the Lord of the Fish and the Father of Food.

The tribesmen were still not prepared to say very much about where they had come from. They hinted at an *awi*, a dwelling 'near the hill over the big river' but this could have been anywhere on the banks of the Turkwel or Kerio. Asked what they were doing beside the lake they said they had lost many cattle in the *akumu*, the long dry season which I took to be the phenomenal drought of 1961. After more questioning it transpired that a band of Dodoth had raided their Big House, the *awi napolon*. Men had died, the family had split up and some of the poorest members of the tribe had wandered towards the lake in search of food. They said the Dodoth had come down the 'big hill' at night. This, presumably, was the great Oropoi Pass into Uganda. The Dodoth had guns. The Turkana had no guns and they lost twenty-three men. This was not surprising. From official figures I discovered that in a year and a half, that is from February 1960 to October 1961, the Turkana had lost a hundred and twenty men and seventeen thousand cattle in raids and, during that time, they had killed a hundred and forty-four of their enemies.

Nobody knows when the Karamoja war began. It is fought between inter-related groups of tribesmen who are known collectively as the Karamajong Cluster. They are the Toposa, the Dodoth, the Jie, the Karamajong, the Suk and the Turkana. All but the Suk and the Turkana live in Uganda to the west of the massive escarpment that runs from north to south and effectively divides Karamoja from the great plains of Turkanaland.

To describe the inter-tribal relationships briefly would be like trying to unravel the branches of the Hapsburg and Bourbon families in half a dozen sentences. Enough to say that although nobody can identify the aboriginals, in his thoughtful book *The Family Herds** Dr P. H. Gulliver reckons that a tribe in the centre of the group – the Jie – split up and one section remained on top of the escarpment, that is to the west of the wall, while the remainder, the secessionists, clambered down the mountains and started to expand from the Tarac valley on the eastern side. They are the Turkana and he believes the split probably occurred at least two hundred years ago.

Since that time the individual tribes have been industriously engaged in an endless series of cattle raids. The Jie, with the hostile Dodoth to the north and the Karamajong to the south, have been repeatedly attacked and have staged equally repetitive counter-attacks. As a variation, the Karamajong attack the Jie's allies, the Turkana, and the Suk attack the Karamajong.

* *Routledge & Kegan Paul* (1955).

The raiders are not sneak thieves who run away when challenged; nor are they violent robbers with a blurred sense of guilt. They are warriors, engaged in 'noble' expeditions carried out under the command of the tribal elders. Cattle are their common currency. Without cattle they can neither marry nor hold an honoured position as a tribal elder. Their women-folk incite them to raid since without a surplus of cattle they are unlikely to get a husband.

Custom permits a man to live with a girl and have children by her until he can steal enough cattle to buy her or until another man comes along and buys her over his head at a slightly reduced price. If another man buys her, he buys the children as well. If boys they become his sons and herdsmen; if girls they are accepted as his own daughters and eventually sold off in marriage. As the boys who are sold with a mother on a 'sale-or-return' basis cannot claim a share of the foster-father's cattle by right, they are obliged to make several raids before they can even think of marriage. Among the Karamajong the disinherited sons are known as the Wild Ones (*N'girengelemwo*); they raid more frequently and are more daring and more ferocious than those who are only in the raiding business because everyone else is. The girls with whom they live are invariably anxious to become respectable; they urge their impoverished suitors to go raiding and tease, taunt and eventually pour scorn on them, if they do not go. Respectable courtship on the western side of the Jade Sea is a complicated, expensive affair. Fathers usually ask for fifty cattle or camels and up to a hundred sheep or goats. Concubines are free; they are fairly common but by nagging they usually attain respectability after they have borne a few children.

Lelean affected a profound disdain for the 'barbarians'. This arose in part from his service with the King's African Rifles when, as far as I could discover, he shot at Turkana and Karamajong alike, convinced that they were all *washenzi*. He must have been aware, too, that our hosts were not too fond of a man with a khaki cap and a rifle. The Turkana had also become his tribe's enemies. In their southward drive into the N'dotos and Matthews, the 'Turks' are still driving deeper and deeper into Samburu country.

He announced in an offhand way that the barbarians were prepared to guide us back to New Hampstead, adding that we should have to feed them on the way. For two days we walked and fished and ate *posho* pancakes and drank a little camel blood and milk. At the end of it I became tired of the surly Turkana, the blinding sun and the crocodiles and decided that it was about time we set off for Wamba.

Landslides on Ajuk

A morning for song. The sun shone, the lake shimmered and we were packed and ready to go at half-past six. I took a final look round the camp. Mezek threw sand on the fire; Lelean put on his Game Department cap and jacket before he came up to salute and say that all was prepared. I said good and he said good, and then, as he always did, he took off his jacket and tossed it over the *herio* of the leading camel. Karo smacked the animal on its backside with something not too far removed from affection and we moved off towards the escarpment to the tune of the Soldiers' Chorus from *Faust*.

This is a strictly factual account of the start of our journey home. To say that we sang the chorus would be inaccurate. I don't know the words. After bawling a vulgar parody of the song, an expurgated version of which is 'Beer boys and bother the Band of Hope' I lapsed into an equally stentorian *Daah* (pause) *dee dee, tiddly-dee-dee-daah* which was soon picked up by the men. Old Conrad advised me to sing to the camels at the beginning and the end of each day's march. I had tried 'Marching Through Georgia' with considerable success; the Chorus was even better. The rhythm fitted the rolling gait of the camels. *Daah dee dee, tiddly-dee-dee-daah!* Dear God, I was happy! This, indeed, was the very essence of safari.

There were eight of us. The company included the old 'Turk' from the Balessa Kulal, a young guide and a sick man. The old 'Turk' whose camel we had hired would no more part with us than he would part from his camel, but on the problem of getting over the escarpment he had a one-track mind and the track was the Laisamis, the home of the hyenas. He had heard of other tracks but he could not imagine anyone wanting to use them. I was unwilling to go back east when our course lay due south. Besides, we had crossed the Laisamis. And the Serima. I wanted something new.

172

I don't think we should have discovered the Kakorinya track had not Ivory Ball turned up the previous evening with news of the little white one. The camel, he said, had been found in the hills by a family travelling south. They knew it was both a Rendille and a stray. They had taken it along with them and would probably leave it at one of the homesteads in the Sugata valley. Although this is simple enough to relate, it took me half an hour to unravel the facts through interpretation and a map drawn in the dust by the light of a lamp. I had no reason to doubt that the camel would be well looked after: in connection with anything relating to property I had a great respect for the integrity of the up-country African. What concerned me was how to get over the lava wall without going back on our tracks and where we should find the missing camel. In the day-light it was easy enough to point to the notches in the escarpment but I had planned the journey in the dark; I had waved, vaguely, into the tremendous night and hoped that my finger-drawn map bore some relationship to reality and the comprehension of our some-what puzzled friend.

The outcome, as I thought about it again that morning, was that the escarpment could be crossed at a point almost immedi-ately ahead of us. A narrow track certainly, but Ivory Ball sounded confident. He said it was 'good' for camels. 'Little trouble that way.' It led to the great cinder cone of Kakorinya; beyond lay the salt lake of Namakat at the head of the Sugata valley. The valley, I had heard, was a confusion of hot springs, mud flats and vents of burning gas. The toothy contours on the map marked the uncertain position of six large volcanoes. I had been advised to keep away from them. Ivory Ball disagreed. He said the Turkana family had gone through the gap with many camels and we could do the same. We agreed that his son should accompany us as far as the brow of the scarp. The other addition to our company was a cheerful little man who sweated profusely from what he called 'the strong fever of the fly'. As I failed to make him understand how to take anti-malarial tablets in pro-gressively diminishing doses there was nothing for it but to take him along and dose him on the way.

At nine o'clock we were high above the lake and still in the mood for singing. The track, like New Hampstead, is not on the map, but unlike our windy home by the lake it was wholly serviceable the whole time. It zig-zagged backwards and forwards in such a deceptive manner that on one occasion when I lagged behind to take a pot-shot at a bird the camels were almost above me on another layer of the track. For those who are keeping the score of what I missed with the gun I must say here that I missed again.

As I describe a few of the incidents of these wholly pleasurable days it might be thought that our time was wholly preoccupied with outstanding spectacles or minor drama. This is far from the truth of the matter. There were days or parts of days when we did nothing except get from one place to another as quickly as we could. The need for food and water and the urge to see something of the desert, the lake and the mountains had turned us into Ishmaels. We were constantly on the move. This is the curse of nomadism. Like the safari ants and the migratory gazelle we could not stay in any one place for long. Circumstances drove us on.

At Wamba it had been the need to cross the mountains to replace the camels at Rodosoit. This done I wanted to cross the lava wall beyond South Horr and spend some time by the lake. Once there I was obliged to hurry on to the Ballo *lugga* to meet The Warden. More moves: Ballo to Allia Bay, North Horr, the desert, back to the Balessa for water, another glimpse of the lake, New Hampstead, Turkanaland. Where next?

Wamba was about a hundred and thirty miles away. We could have done it in six or seven stages had we stuck to the main track over the Laisamis and marched smartly down to South Horr. But the Laisamis had been outflanked. For some reason which was no doubt largely snobbish we were heading south on an unexplored track. With any luck we should reach a point in the Sugata where we could get back on the high road south. The snag was that between the Sugata and South Horr there were mountains. But, as I have said, it was a morning for song and the camels looked as if they could have crossed the Himalayas. I sang noisily and the men added some bass and treble bits which if anything were an improvement on the original.

I forget the name of the son of Ivory Ball, a short-legged, athletic youth, but I remember that he went up the track like a mountain goat. The only other thing I can remember about him is that he developed an extraordinary passion for Mezek. There was something quite touching in the way they hustled along together, hand in hand, chattering in Turkana. Whatever Mezek did, his friend tried to do likewise. Mezek brought me a squeaking cricket; his friend proffered a little coloured stone. I asked Mezek for the camera; his friend immediately offered to carry it and anything else I could give him.

After a stage of four hours, carried out at an unnecessarily cracking pace, we stopped to regain our wind and look at the scenery. We were near the brow. The track ribboned backwards and forwards, always climbing until, like a rearing snake, it suddenly flung itself across the top of the scarp. To the south a disorderly arrangement of bare hills with no hint of the promised hell of the Sugata. I turned to take my last look at the lake: vast, undisturbed and too green to be wholly real. To have seen it was a privilege but to say good-bye was not a lasting sorrow. Good-bye Basso. I waved, turned again and hurried after the men who had not troubled to look back. Why should they?

During the early part of the afternoon Lelean and I got lost in rather ridiculous circumstances. We had stopped at midday for the usual brew of tea and a rest. The men had eaten nothing that day and they tended to linger over their *posho* and scraps of dried goat. The way ahead seemed clear enough. After a word with our guide about a tryst on a distant hill, Lelean and I marched on with the intention of finding a good camping site before it grew too dark to hunt. I had the feeling that a day so well begun should end with a feast of gazelle.

It was a hot, still afternoon. The sun played freakish tricks with the most ordinary objects. A hill became watery at the base and eventually disappeared as if it had been washed away. A lone acacia tree followed suit. To look at it was like looking through a tear. This disconcerted me because I had been watching the tree and hoping that we might rest. In the presence of dissolving mirages I was sometimes tempted to think I was suffering from hallucinations. Lelean's grin was reassuring. Looking back we saw the smudgy line of the caravan winding towards us; it was farther away than I imagined and, as it sank from sight in a depression, we decided to wait in the shadow of some rocks until it caught up with us.

175

We dozed. An hour passed. Still no caravan. We walked back for half a mile only to discover that there were at least half a dozen routes through the little hills. I turned down the suggestion that we should go back farther, because I felt that by striking south we should be able to intercept them. Lelean went off to reconnoitre from the top of a pile of rocks while I tried to take a photograph of a mirage.

How I managed to lose my way when I tried to rejoin him is difficult to explain, but in an effort to cut off a corner I had strayed into a little canyon. I walked back angrily to where I imagined we had parted and heard him call. The shout echoed and added to the confusion of direction. I called back and eventually fired a shot. In the utterly still air the echo sounded like a fusillade.

The incident ended on the usual note of anticlimax. As I climbed up a hill towards a patch of scrub, intent on lighting a fire (I had read somewhere that this was the thing to do), Lelean (who had been watching me) climbed swiftly round the other side. We met before I could start the signalling operation. He had seen the caravan far to the south and Mezek and his friend had come to look for us. They were waiting at the foot of the hill, still hand in hand. As we walked towards them I remembered that it would have been difficult to light a fire. I had no matches. Perhaps I could have made a burning glass out of the front lens of my field-glasses. I looked at them. It was impossible to remove the lens without a special tool. If there had been any wood at the top of the hill I'm pretty sure that it wouldn't have burned.

It took us about an hour to reach a camp expertly laid out on high ground by Goiti. As I drank dark brown tea, made from the last drop of water from Lake Rudolf I am ever likely to taste, I watched the steam vents coil into the air from the crater of an unnamed volcano. We had outflanked Kakorinya. This was the Sugata, the valley of the volcanoes or, to be more exact, it was a ridge above the Sugata valley, for I was unwilling to venture far into the salt flats. It was an empty but by no means dramatic landscape. The impression was of the still-smoking ruins of a bombed and burnt-out city. After paying off the guide I strolled off to bang away (unsuccessfully) at plover and dikkops and (unsuccessfully) at snipe. The sunset was extraordinarily vulgar. I remember it for two reasons.

Lelean and I discovered that birds on the ground could be picked out in the light of a torch. (Sportsmen can make what they will of this: we were hunting for the pot.) During a stroll over a patch of stony ground on our way back to the camp I heard a high-pitched sizzling noise almost at my feet. It was nearly dark. Thinking I had disturbed a bush cricket I bent down and called for the light. To my intense surprise I found that the noise came from a saw-scale viper not a yard from my foot. It repeatedly hurled itself forward but for some reason it never pressed home the attack. In the light of the torch it curled up and retreated backwards in a curious, side-winding motion. This was the only occasion during the whole trip when a snake showed any signs of attacking us, but fortunately it did so with no especial resolution.

I remember the night for another reason. At one point the wall of rocks around us was broken as if by a city gate. About half a dozen flat-topped thorn trees grew in the gap. As we drew near to them we noticed that the trees harboured a small flock of hooded vultures. They squatted motionless on the uppermost branches with their gaunt heads drawn back into a ruffle of neck feathers. Silhouetted against the flaming sky they looked like wardens at the gates of hell.

During the night the roast plover began to quarrel violently with a substantial tot of South African brandy and I was obliged to take a chance with the saw-scaled vipers in the moonlit bush. On the second or maybe the third noctambulation I tripped over a guy rope on the return trip and swore so loudly that the camels rose like a *corps de ballet* and hopped about on three legs, grunting unsympathetically.

After an effective but rather dull breakfast of coffee and kaolin powder we set off about nine o'clock. I felt hollow and peevish.

A dreary day by any reckoning and I tried to console myself by remembering how good the previous one had been. If that is philosophy it failed and I was not cheered up by the men's repeated mime of how I fell over in the dark. Shrieks of laughter: theirs not mine. They were too good by far at these impersonations. With an indelible feeling of embarrassment I can still recall their account of how I once tried to hire a chief's testicles (*pumbu*) instead of his donkeys (*punda*). They all had a version of this. The best was Karo's who used to finish his act by running away screaming, his hands over his crotch. Another good story (from their point of view) was how I once sat very briefly on a wasp. Nobody quite like the *effendi* for brightening up a dull day.

On our way towards the mountain barrier we were overtaken by a flying circus of migratory storks. For three hours the birds sailed overhead in flights of thousands, gliding east on outstretched wings until they lost height and slowly spiralled up the aerial staircase of another thermal.

Of more substantial game there was a distinct lack. My efforts at knocking down a gazelle by a long-range bombardment provoked nothing but a good-natured laugh. The shot blew a cloud of dust off a ledge high above us. It smacked into the ground about five yards from an old baboon who leaped into the air and fled uttering falsetto barks.

At a deep hole of dirty water in what I took to be the Lenchukuti *lugga* we had an awkward argument with a Rendille goatherd. No doubt such incidents are commonplace in the life of the Game Department staff, but it surprised me and there came a point in the heated discussion when I thought we should have a spear thrown at us.

The man was watering his goats at the bottom of a hole about six feet deep. In an effort to get down to the last drop of water the herdsmen had dug out a narrow cutting capable of holding no more than one goat at a time. As several goatherds were waiting to take their turn, the Rendille shouted and flicked his animals across their flanks with a long leather whip. Lelean asked to see it. The wand of leather was neatly sewn up from the haft to a flexible tip. 'This,' said Lelean, 'is made of giraffe skin. Where did you get it?' Far from being abashed at being caught in possession of a piece of almost sacred skin – the giraffe is a carefully protected animal – the man lost his temper. As far as I could follow the torrent of words, he asked what business was it of Lelean's and reached for his spear. I took possession of the weapon, told him to sit down and for half an hour we went over the involved history of the whip.

If it could have been established that he was the owner the chances are that he would have got six months in gaol. The game laws are extraordinarily strict. The Rendille went through the usual evasions. He said the whip was not his. He had found it. At least he had not actually found it; it appeared that he had borrowed it from his brother. The case seemed to hinge on whether or not the brother, if there was a brother, had got a permit (*cheti*) for the skin. But I couldn't remember the word for permit and the Rendille's *manyatta* was several miles away. Lelean looked at me and raised his eyebrows. The man glowered, furiously. He was a very angry man. I shrugged my shoulders and said 'Confiscate the whip'. At this Lelean cut the thong into three pieces and gave them back to the man. He followed us for about two miles, shouting and shaking his spear. I took the precaution of walking behind him.

From Lenchukuti we travelled west towards the mountains at a faster pace than we had ever marched before. The safari seemed to be gathering momentum. I was by no means anxious to get back to Wamba and the dreary routine of city life but I had a passionate desire to get through the Laralok Pass, the last major obstacle we were likely to meet. Events were running smoothly, perhaps too smoothly. I had got the hang of things. But I had some doubts about whether tired camels could be driven high up into the mountains. Afterwards, or so I imagined, we could afford to dawdle. I wanted to see something of the Delectable Mountains through which we had hurried on our way up to the lake. I told Lelean that if he could find a good camping site in the Matthews I would stay there for a week. There would be much meat and cokes from the *dukas* of Baragoi. He seemed impressed and said he knew a good place.

After a stage of six hours we lost ourselves in a maze of sand dunes and had to retrace our steps for four miles. I steered by compass on what might be described as very general principles. Given a choice of tracks I chose one with a westerly component and hoped for the best until we reached high ground and could see where we were. General principles let us down twice and I had to send scouts ahead and wait patiently until I got a signal to press on or fall back. Karo was the best scout I had. He knew that I could watch him through field-glasses and he usually waved us on from afar.

'What news?' I asked as he loped back like a wolf.

'Bad!' he would answer with a disarming grin; 'the road is *that* way' and he pointed in the direction we had come. The camels had to be turned and we ambled down another featureless track. Without a guide we had constantly to return to Square

One in our efforts to get to Kimbat, at the mouth of the pass. Or so it appeared from the map. Some people put unfaltering trust in maps. After using some of the Kenya sheets I am not among them. Yet on that afternoon I should have preferred to have known where we were going.

In the evening, burnt, bloodshot and very tired, we slanted down to the last whaleback of a dune-chain to find Kimbat immediately below. It looked as good as it proved to be: a bright green strip in a fold of bare hills. Parched as I was, I stared, fascinated, at the first flowing stream I had seen for nearly three months; then I waded in and drank with far less decorum than the camels who had waded in with me.

The sudden translation from stark desert to exuberant oasis is such a transcending experience that I can liken it only to the silence that follows the switching off of a pneumatic drill. I walked about aimlessly, conscious only of the pleasure of assuagement. Tall trees dappled the sunlight; the musical chatter of water mingled with the burbling of doves and the twitter of bulbuls. Kimbat, unmarked as ever on the map, was the metropolis of the Ajuk Hills and we spent several days there. At night I strolled up the hillside and watched eerie fires burning in the Sugata. Seen from our haven the desert and the volcanoes might have been on another planet.

The problem of getting a reliable guide for the climb through the pass occupied the best part of our last evening in Kimbat. There were several candidates for the two-shilling commission. Karo produced a shifty character to whom, I suspect, he was in debt; Lelean's nominee was more presentable but rather vague about whether it was possible to get through the pass after the storms of the previous year. I settled on a haughty Samburu who said he would get us through the Laralok in two days, perhaps in one. It transpired that he would have said anything to get the job, but this I did not know at the time and I went to sleep under a fig tree satisfied that I had chosen well.

After one or two minor ceremonies we were off again at dawn. Regretfully, I paid off the old 'Turk' from the Balessa. Unobtrusive and hardworking, he had a feudal sense of loyalty which would have made him a first-rate man to have had for the whole safari. Unfortunately, he had no clear idea about where he was going and there would have been the problem of what to do with him when we got back to Wamba. He trudged off into the Sugata, wearing one of my old pairs of khaki shorts, his massive camel striding out, looking as fresh as it had looked the night we hired it in the Karoli. Before we left Kimbat the haughty Samburu announced that overnight he had developed the kind of fever that might respond to a handful of tobacco. I put a crushed aspirin on his tongue and painted a swastika on his forehead in iodine; this was to draw out heat undetectable by a clinical thermometer. I told him he could have some tobacco when we got through the Laralok. He marched off chewing the less soluble bits of the aspirin with a wry expression and we followed him, hopefully.

At the foot of the first pass we nodded and smiled with all the smug assurance of old hands at the mountain-storming business. I took charge of the second camel and tried to pretend that each vertiginous bend in the narrow track was the worst and the last. It was, of course, neither one nor the other. After many vigorous efforts at ramp-making and rock-shifting on the lines of lessons learnt on the Ol Canto, I tried to make sense out of what the guide said and found that, whatever other qualities he may have had, he was an unashamed liar. He said that the biggest boulders had been washed into the stream bed since he had last walked through the gap. Two black marks here for deceit.

A reconnoitre showed that we were not climbing through a pass or a gap; it was a corrie or blind valley. We were coming to a dead end. Moreover, the majority of the heavily embedded boulders looked as if they had rolled into the bed of the stream at least a century earlier. We swung round and made our way back over gangways of stones laboriously laid down to take us in the opposite direction. After seven hours of hard work we got back to the point where we had congratulated ourselves on reaching the last obstacle. Another palaver with the villain of a guide convinced me that he knew little more about the mountains than we did. He had crossed them only once in his life and on that occasion he had been driving goats.

Did he know the *dukas* of Baragoi or South Horr? He said yes. We asked him how he reached them. Even from his vague gestures it was evident that he marched round the periphery of the foothills and had rarely if ever crossed the middle of the range which stretched for about twenty-five miles on a north-south axis.

By this time we had nosed into a point near Ajuk, apparently the highest peak in the western wall. If the range could be crossed I was determined to cross it. I sent the self-styled guide back to Kimbat with Karo who had instructions to hire another one if he could. We pitched camp on the spot and allowed the camels to browse at the end of long, pegged-down headropes. There were elephant tracks in the gorge. Mezek stuck his big toe into a dropping to see how warm it was and said that two or three young bulls had left shortly before we arrived. At four o'clock Lelean and I trudged up the easiest-looking slope we could find to see what we could see from the top.

Clambering up I became aware of a new dimension to the world. It was clouds. What interesting things they were after long days in the desert. Two Bateleur eagles banked overhead soaring on motionless wings and remarkably deficient in anything resembling a tail.

Lelean pointed to a pinnacle of golden granite towering high above a flock of lesser peaks. It rose sheer with a slight nose-like over-hang towards the top. Under the oblique sun it was an improbably bare sliced-off section of a cliff, vast and seemingly invulnerable. 'Iko Ajuk,' he said. During the time it took to smoke a pipe we traced the dark lines of deep-cut gorges through field-glasses. It was like trying to follow a tortuous forest trail from a low-flying aircraft with the double disadvantage that we were fixed and relatively low down among a labyrinth of canyons. We talked, earnestly, about which way we should go but I was conscious of a suggestion of a sneer in the upturned nose of Ajuk.

Certain features were clear. The western series of peaks were sharply divided from the Nyiru massif by a long valley. Only one pass seemed to lead to the valley, and this, presumably, was the Laralok. All the others tailed off into corries or got lost among the peaks. Once we reached a point to the east of Ajuk we could afford to take it easy; we should be through; we could see the trail ahead without the help of glasses. After wearing the edge off that useful word *labda* (perhaps) we agreed on a route which, from our superior height, seemed to have no obvious disadvantages.

I shot a little antelope, a duiker, on our way down to camp; the meat did something to take our minds off the elusive Laralok. Mezek served it up with what he called Turkana beans; these were acacia seeds which had been induced to germinate and which, when boiled, tasted like little broad beans. Karo came back to say that he couldn't hire another guide; Kimbat was almost deserted and the Samburu had made off down another valley before he got there; it looked as if I had hired the only stranger in town.

Far away an elephant screamed. A shooting star drew a chalky line across the immensity of the night and I went to bed. There was nothing else to do.

Things went badly with us the next day. Two camels went lame and had to be towed along like empty barges; we got lost several times and finished up at night scarcely three miles from the point where we started at dawn. In between our inauspicious start and belated arrival we did about fifteen miles, at least half of them clambering down what we had already clambered up. If this sounds frustrating I have succeeded in describing how I felt for the greater part of the day. What I did not realize until I had several times thought of returning to Kimbat was that, although the majority of the valleys ran from east to west, they wound about in such a serpentine manner that we often had to march several miles north to gain a few hundred yards to the east. The first valley we tried looked as if it would take us straight through to the Laralok but, at a point where the walls on both sides were almost vertical, the floor was blocked by a landslide. Trying to forget how long it had taken us to reach that point we crawled back, thrashing the shivering camels and unloading to get them over the worst of the obstacles. Some of the piles of boulders were as high as the camels

More trouble in the next valley. It was waterlogged. A stream meandered through a series of peaty-brown pools; it was rarely more than two or three feet deep but lined with slippery mud. The camels skidded, crossed their legs and flopped down on their rumps, dousing their loads. We jogged along, cursing and swiping at king-sized horse-flies.

In normal circumstances I might have admired the high enclosing walls, the moss-hung grottoes and the garish flowers in the stream bed but I found it uneasy going all the way: one big rock and we should have to turn back. Lelean and I went ahead, gauging progress from the echoing roars behind. Around a sharp bend the rock changed from black to golden-red: towering above us was the south face of Ajuk, the nose more disdainful than ever from directly below. A mile farther on we met a rock which took four of us to send it rumbling into the stream bed. We camped, late, under an overhang and let the camels roam free to browse on what the men hacked down from the tops of bushes. There was plenty of water, an obsessive number of flies, but little timber and no meat. As Mezek made tea I wondered whether to eat rice and soup, rice and dried camel or just rice. Providentially, supper flew in out of the night. Sitting in my chair I heard a twitter overhead and the first of several groups of sandgrouse skimmed down to a pool scarcely ten yards away. I fired point-blank from the chair and got three or four with each shot. We spitted a dozen and I ate my share with a thick stuffing made of *posho*, acacia seeds and red pepper. In Swahili pepper is called *pili-pili* and hot pepper *pili-pili ho-ho*. To judge from the fire on the roof of my mouth the stuffing was unusually *ho-ho*. More trumpeting in the night but far away and strangely musical. The camels groaned, nightjars bubbled, and Ajuk partly masked the moon.

Tension at breakfast the next morning was relieved by the sound of a distant shot. I had sent Lelean forward with orders to signal if the way ahead seemed clear. It was our starting gun. Scattering the crows as they staggered forward, the camels were a sorry sight: two were lame, one had a cut pad which marked our progress with a reproachful print of blood, the others were uneasy with saddle sores. Mezek packed so quickly that he left me standing with a mug of tea in my hand. I drank it slowly, lit a pipe and walked over to the camel that carried my own gear. There was no need to hurry. As I knew only too well it would be some time before the others got very far.

Together we lashed down the first *herio* and made a platform behind the hump. Two other mats were placed farther forward. I pushed the coupled sticks under the animal's belly so that they could be spread out like a big V, two on one side and two on the other. They were secured fore and aft to the neck and to the girth wrapped round the first *herio*. This was the saddle of sticks and matting to which the sacks holding the loads were tied. Working together the whole process from the first mat to the last loops which held the canvas water bags took about twenty minutes. On my own it would have taken me about three-quarters of an hour; I knew because I had tried several times. Hauling on flat girths of bark rope had toughened my hands and given me a red patch on my groin which I suspected was mange. I loosened the head rope and scratched the animal under its chin with the back of my knuckles, an action which it loved. I said 'Giddup!' The animal rose and we ambled after the others.

When we saw them about an hour later the impression was one of desertion; it looked as if the staff had run off into the hills in different directions. Goiti was high up on one side of the valley, energetically flogging two camels that appeared to be lying down. Karo was on the other side, hauling a string of three. Both men were too far away to be hailed. Through glasses I saw Lelean striding down towards me, his camels nowhere to be seen.

He related what I had feared: we had run up against another landslide. A substantial portion of rock and earth had blocked the track for about half a mile. He thought it would be impossible to get over it; he had tried to take his own camels up on to the crest and over into the next valley but they had come to grief on a steep track. Their loads were too heavy. I asked him where they were. He said two strangers were looking after them. So there was a *manyatta* near by. Could we get help? He thought so.

The outcome of the affair was that we hired the services of fifteen Samburu to act as pathfinders, load-carriers and camel-shovers. As members of a tribe not remarkable for hard work they were perhaps unique. Four were sent off immediately to the aid of the beleaguered Goiti. What happened could only be guessed at from the bellows that echoed across the valley. We didn't see Goiti again until we met in the Laralok late that afternoon. Karo did better than anyone else and was near to the top of the crest before we reached him with extra hands. Lelean had run into trouble but was unwilling to admit it and go back and follow in Karo's footsteps; there was always some rivalry between them. My camel was unloaded and the sacks carried up by hand. When the animal flopped down on a sticky patch and refused to budge, a mild-faced youth came up to me to ask for matches. He said it was necessary to light a fire under it. Fortunately, it was susceptible to flogging.

There is not much more that I care to say about the rest of the morning on the brink of the Laralok except that it was a horrible experience. Feelings of responsibility towards the company were mixed with apprehension and qualified compassion for the camels – qualified because there was not much I could do for them.

At one point Karo's leading camel slipped on a soft patch and rolled over sideways like a shot rabbit. I though that was the end of it, but to my intense relief it staggered to its feet, unharmed, and began to clamber up the slope again, shakily but with surprising agility. The other camels roared incessantly. By this time I had become accustomed to the noise and thought I could detect the note of anger and indignation rather than the bellow of pain.

Goiti was nowhere to be seen. Karo and Lelean had joined forces under a difficult overhang about fifty feet below the crest of the ridge; Mezek was surrounded by so many Samburu that I had the impression that both he and the camel were being carried up a gully.

At four o'clock we were over the ridge and facing the broad downward sweep of the Laralok. Goiti trudged up with an unconcerned expression as if mountain climbing with a string of camels were part of his business. His camels were as muddy as rats and dabbled with froth but they were in better shape than any of the others. We greeted him with a warmth that obviously surprised him.

That night we feasted the tribe on three sheep, twenty pounds of *posho* and a potful of raisins. Before I sat down to the boiled mutton and onion sauce, I wandered round the busy camp, puffing at a little cigar and listening to the sound of bulbuls by now as familiar as the twittering of starlings in Trafalgar Square. Life had its ups and downs but on the whole it was good.

The Delectable Mountains

At the foot of the Laralok we swung on to a hard, straight track and headed south for Baragoi. It was the sort of morning I like to remember: the air keen and the mountains high. Birds twittered, the men sang and the water sloshed about in the jerricans with a musical rhythmical *ker-plash-ker-plonk*. As often happened we seemed to be making up for a temporary setback with an extra burst of energy. All the derring-do of the previous day was over and done with, almost forgotten. Ahead were the Delectable Mountains. Yet time was running short; I reckoned it would take us about three days, maybe four, to reach a mountain camp in the Matthews where I hoped to rest, to put the whole journey into perspective. I wanted a brief respite before we marched down into Wamba. The problem was whether we could get there in time to set up a worthwhile base camp. A few calculations based on divisions by the almost mystical number of two point seven five – the speed of a camel in miles per hour – convinced me that it was about time I started to relax and enjoy myself then and there.

We stopped for lunch under a peak called Porlera but not for long. The urge to move, to keep up with that fearful, that ridiculous thing the schedule, was irresistible. To march as far as we did I had always to be somewhere at a certain time. But even Ishmael wanted tea at twelve o'clock and I refused point blank to go out with the gun; distant gazelle could safely graze. A few Samburu turned up with the excellent news that a stray camel that was almost certainly the little white one had been left at Baragoi by a band of Turkana. Tobacco changed hands and I was asked if I wanted to buy a goat. A very good goat, said Karo, and cheap, too. They wanted twelve shillings for it but we got it for eight and before I had tied up the bag of coins and locked them in the ammunition box the animal was dead and partly dressed.

The deft, unemotional way in which this was done never failed to appal me. But only briefly. It was all done so quickly. Karo grabbed the animal and held it down on its back while Mezek cut its throat with a casual upward flick of a knife as if he were striking a match. Then both men jumped clear as it kicked, violently. In ten seconds it was motionless. The knife was re-inserted in a fold of skin below the throat and drawn towards the genitals in a bloodless cut. The skin was then literally punched off. Mezek pulled it back, gently, with both hands while with his knuckles Karo pounded the milky-blue undersurface of the skin at the point where it peeled off. In twenty minutes the animal was skinned, gutted, dismembered and ready for the pot. I ate the liver and kidneys, fried; the rest was lightly boiled and promptly devoured by the men. We slept for an hour. The camels browsed. Our visitors squatted on the ground, massaging their gums with fibrous twigs and indolently waving off flies. At half-past two we were off again.

During the afternoon we had a bit of trouble with an exceptionally pretty girl. I don't know where she came from but she obviously had her eyes on Mezek. She jingled along beside him, mocking him playfully. This embarrassed the always boyish Mezek who moved up to Karo who was leading the second string of camels. The girl followed. Karo was delighted but Lelean became jealous and joined them. The last camel started to lag behind. I ordered Mezek to look after it and Lelean, the girl and he fell back to the rear of the caravan. This annoyed Karo who shouted abuse over his shoulder. I don't know what he said but it was clearly uncomplimentary and directed at Lelean. It probably had something to do with the fact that he was not a particularly big man. On one occasion when we stopped to adjust the load I thought it was going to be necessary to separate them. I made a prissy speech; pointed at the sun and made the old crack about hot hours and hot heads. Continued scowls. I reminded them that pay was due at Baragoi. No concord, no Cokes. Begrudging nods all round. I scowled at the jingly woman and we marched on.

The only other occasion when jealousies of this kind arose was at South Horr on the other side of Mount Nyiru. As Nyiru was almost exactly due east of us I began to wonder whether there was something endocrinally significant about latitude two degrees five minutes north. However, when everyone began to ignore her the girl slipped away.

The sinking sun brought out the cicadas. Above the hiss of the insects, Karo heard the noise of a Land-Rover, high up in the hills. Eventually he said he could see it. In fact, everyone saw it except me. I asked whose it was. They said B'wana McKean, the white hunter who was looking for Buffalo. Asked how they knew, they reminded me that he was the hunter who had said good-bye to us at Wamba on the day we set off for the Ol Canto and they knew it was his Land-Rover because a slight cut on the edge of his front tyre left a distinctive track in the dust. They said we had crossed his tracks earlier in the afternoon. Who else could it be but B'wana McKean? The African's ability to remember a detail of a print or track is scarcely less remarkable than their powers of reconstruction.

Once in the Chalbi, Karo pointed out the spoor of a solitary hare. The word *sungura* was new to me but I understood what he meant when he crouched down and gave a pretty fair impression of the animal. The track persisted for about a hundred yards and then vanished. When I asked him what had become of it he pointed to the sky and grinned. Incredulously I asked him if he meant it had flown away. Still grinning, he flapped his hands like wings and then slowly brought them together as if they were claws. On either side of the place where the hare tracks disappeared was a smudge of smoothed-out sand where the wings of an eagle had brushed the ground as it swooped down and picked the animal up. Two little black pellets of dried blood confirmed his interpretation of what had happened the previous night.

On another occasion he pointed out the tracks of a big bull elephant which were so large that I stopped and measured them. They were eighteen inches in diameter. At intervals the tracks were interrupted by impressions like quarter moons made as the animal's trunk swept the ground from side to side as it had ambled along, contentedly. After a time the regular impressions were replaced by a scrabble of deep tracks. By raising his arm in the manner of a fascist salute Karo showed how the animal had stopped and sniffed the air with its trunk. When the tracks continued, the distance between the individual prints was noticeably shorter. The animal was hurrying towards a distant tree where among a great deal of disturbed sand we found the more delicate impressions of a young cow elephant.

Before we pulled up for the night I began to run after a large ungainly bird, a bustard, which was clever enough to keep within gun range of the leading camels. This amused the men but annoyed me. After vainly trying to flush the bird to a point where I could safely fire, Karo chased after it and the bustard rocketed like a pheasant. The men shouted, I cursed and eventually shot it down into some bushes where it took us a quarter of an hour to find it. Karo volunteered to cook the bird in a distinctly original way. He chopped off its head and legs and tossed it into the glowing ashes of the fire. To my dismay my supper burst into flames and became an almost indistinguishable lump of carbon but when it was eventually fished out of the fire the skin and feathers had formed a hard shell around a perfectly cooked bird. The trick seems to depend on getting a mound of ashes hot enough to seal up the bird in one explosive flash.

Goat soup and roast bustard taste good but if my feet are young my stomach has become middle-aged and for the remainder of that evening I belched like a camel. When the big beetles began to clatter on the lamp glass I crawled under a mosquito net and, still hiccuping, tried to sleep on a nightcap of bismuth powder and water.

Towards dawn it started to rain, at first gently but with increasing force until I had to get up to make sure that everything was under cover. Lelean's voice came out of the darkness, sleepily, to say that all was well. The next morning I discovered that everyone, that is four staff and five hangers-on including a woman, had crawled under a mound of sacking and ground sheets. Except for one protruding leg they were all completely covered. They crawled out like worms, stretching and sniffing the cool mountain air. I was surprised they had not suffocated.

I see from my diary that the night of the rain and the succulent but indigestible bustard flambé was spent on the banks of the Losergoi *lugga*. The place and the date in mid-February are of a personal importance because it was here we began to stride through the mountains in a series of day-long marches unchecked and with increasing momentum. After much talk with

Lelean I had chosen as our major objective a place in the Seya valley about a hundred miles to the south. I intended to stay there, enjoying myself and doing nothing in particular. At the rate we were moving it is likely that we could have made it in a week and this account of varied safari would have ended on a self-satisfied note. What stymied us was the weather and a little brush with big game at a time when I thought, morbidly, that a snake or a scorpion had done for me.

Our first day out of Losergoi was the longest of all. We did thirty-two miles. This was Lelean's home country, the region which he patrolled in search of poachers and I took his word for it that we could reach the mission station at Baragoi in a stage of eight hours. With a break from half-past twelve until two o'clock it took us more than twelve. We enjoyed the halt. McKean, the white hunter, drove up in his Land-Rover with three American clients. As the men had foretold they had been hunting buffalo and the vehicle had a distinctive front tyre. Handshakes all round. I talked airily of the journey we had started the previous year (Christmas had fallen providentially in mid-safari) and offered to give them a haunch of gazelle. Admiring waves from the Land-Rover and they left to look for kudu. I hauled up my tattered pants and strode after the camels. To speak English again was a curious experience after the curt imperatives and short factual sentences of up-country 'Ki-settler'. What had I said? That I would meet them all in Nairobi? Under the twin peaks of Kowop and Poitikal that bright afternoon I took no pleasure even in admitting the exist-ence of a city. Yet as the afternoon wore on it became too hot and too bright for comfort.

Rain was in the air and the sun overloaded with *uma* – that over-worked word that meant forks, stings, bites, aches or pains. Karo's close-cropped head was partly covered by a cap made of fig leaves; Lelean wore a rolled-up vest like a turban and Mezek a piece of sacking. Only Goiti strode out, perspiring freely but uncovered. I put on two pairs of sunglasses and felt the *uma* through my shirt. The downpour the previous evening had provoked extraordinary activity among the local beetle popula-tion. The black soil heaved with industrious dung-rollers, seed hoarders and bumbling burrowers into carrion. They cracked underfoot and attracted large numbers of storks and slow-flying buzzards. When the rains come to the wasteland, life springs up overnight. Every gully is lined with thick-leaved succulents like monstrous brussels sprouts and bushes with flaming flowers. Lelean waited until I caught up with him and then announced with the air of a man imparting the secret of life that Baragoi was not very far. This made me unnecessarily annoyed. I had not asked him how far it was and if I had, I knew perfectly well what he would have said.

By five o'clock we had covered the better part of twenty-five miles and the *uma* in my neck had shifted to my skull. The aspirins left an unpleasant taste in my mouth and I tried to take an intelligent interest in the landscape. It was dull: an empty plain relieved only by shallow *luggas* where someone, a giant or the like, appeared to have left a lot of old stonework about. To judge from the distance to the next shallow crest, Baragoi could not be less than five miles away. Depressing thought. Dusk fell unnoticed and we still jogged on.

Memories of that evening walk still come back like the fragments of a half-forgotten dream. The camels looked as if they were slightly drunk; the top-heavy packs took up the momentum of this rolling motion, and threatened to throw them off their feet. Although I carried virtually nothing I was very tired. We had been on the go since dawn and the effort of pushing one foot in front of the other was purely mechanical. I seemed to be affected by a kind of creeping paralysis. Worse than the business of physical endurance was the quite irrational feeling that we were being forced to march to a destination that constantly moved farther away. I was not wholly convinced that Baragoi really existed but it was easier to doubt and march on than endure the complications of a night in the open bush. Or was it?

It is extremely unlikely that we should have been in any danger had I called an immediate halt but I was still mildly obsessed by the formalities of safari life. It was not the sort of place the Warden would have approved of. Too much cover by far. We could have been surprised in the dark. Close at hand came a noise like the sawing of wood. *Uh-uh-uh.* 'Leopard,' said Lelean. No especial danger there (I hoped). Twice I heard what I thought were lions, a sound somewhere between an asthmatic cough and the note of a bassoon. The men said the noise was made by birds, probably hornbills. For the third or perhaps the fourth time that night I decided to walk on for just another mile.

At the top of a ridge we were accosted by an old woman who shook her fists at us and shrieked so violently that the camels shied. She may have been a little mad or a little drunk; perhaps both. I pretended to ignore her. Not so the boys. They greeted her like an old friend. Karo pinched her cheeks playfully until she stopped yelling and began to smile. I was puzzled and somewhat humbled by this performance; an example, I thought, of the African's profound respect for human idiosyncrasies. Lelean pointed to her enthusiastically. 'An old woman,' he said. I nodded. She was indisputably a very old woman for whom I had no particular regard. 'An old woman,' he repeated. 'From Baragoi. We are *there*.' Faintly, from the valley below, came the sound of mooing, the braying of donkeys and the cries of children. Lights appeared and then huts. At nine o'clock at night we stumbled out of the bush and into a world of sanded roads, lamp-lit stores, groves of eucalyptus trees and, on a hill, a well-built church and mission school as trim as a cathedral close. I have never felt nearer or more warmly disposed towards a concrete expression of Christianity.

With a nice sense of propriety Goiti couched the camels at the foot of a petrol pump and I walked into the big *duka* to order beer, Pepsi-Cola, chewing tobacco and a dozen bars of chocolate. An unctuous Somali brought out a chair; the men lay on their backs with their knees bent and for half an hour we did nothing except relax, drink, nibble and enjoy the admiration of the citizenry of Baragoi.

Father Stallone, they said, was probably in church and with a horde of children skipping ahead I walked up the hill towards it, unsteadily. The rhythm of sustained movement had gone, leaving nothing but a painful sense of rigidity. Knees refused to bend; from the thighs downwards my legs seemed to be encased in splints. We walked past lines of fire-lit huts. 'Jambo,' said everyone. 'Jambo sana,' the double greeting. Past a little hospital, a school, the guards of the police post. More jambos, more waving. How far was the church? It was, of course, not very far and Father Stallone was not in it when we got there. It was lit by a small altar light under which a young black girl prayed passionately, audibly. I tip-toed out, thanked my escort, dismissed them and knocked on the door of the seminary. It was locked. I tried another, got lost in the dark, called out and was conducted to the wing of a house where a cherubic little man rose from a table laid for two. 'Welcome,' he said. 'Welcome. I was expecting you. Please sit down. Forgive the simple meal. It's Friday.'

Events showed that the march to Baragoi was by no means the end of our trials but our arrival there was a major milestone on the homeward journey and we stayed for two days. Father Stallone pressed me to stay for a week. He was an extraordinarily nice man. A member of the Consolata mission that believes in grace through works, he has built a little city around his church. He had not seen us arrive that night but sitting on his verandah at dusk he said he had first hoped and then felt that someone would arrive. He confessed that work at the station was a little lonely at times. Expecially at night. 'It is like a holiday when a friend comes to talk of outside things.'

I slept out in a guest house with a spectacular vista and ate more luxurious meals (out of tins from the well-stocked *duka*) than Thesiger would have approved of. In an instructive talk in London the explorer of deserts told me that in the bush he lived mostly on rice with a little meat. I had lived on rice, too, and I was heartily tired of it. At Baragoi I ate grilled hams from a wart-hog on a foundation of tinned pineapple, and when I followed it up the next day with guinea-fowl, tinned asparagus and cream, I provoked indigestion of an embarrassing violence. This is a convenient place to mention that because of sinus trouble I have lost much of my taste, but as far as I can tell my greed is unimpaired.

The day before we left the hospitality of the mission, which was a Sunday, there occurred a memorable event; the little white one returned to us with excitement befitting the return of the Prodigal Son.

At mass that morning Father Stallone provided me with a seat at the back of the church where the red-skinned European in tattered shorts was relatively inconspicuous among the cocoa-brown-skinned Africans in immaculate blankets. Relatively is perhaps an understatement. Feather-decked heads peered round, girls giggled and white teeth flashed in enormous grins. An elderly coloured Sister marched up and down the aisle, seating late-comers, swiping the talkative and cuddling the kids that started to bawl. It was all very human and very Roman. Apart from the familiar rhythm of the Lord's Prayer which begins 'Baba yetu . . .' I could make very little of the service.

Afterwards as we waited for the Prodigal to arrive from an outlying *manyatta*, I endeavoured to entertain the villagers. They sat cross-legged around the little radio and seemed fascinated by a Sunday-morning talk on Bartok by a man with a flutey voice in London. The camel turned up at midday accompanied by a jolly mob who used it as an excuse for a procession. To judge from the current literature about otters, lion cubs and bush babies, most expeditions these days seem to adopt an animal, preferably a small furry one, somewhere along the route. Mine was an exception. Far from greeting me like an old friend, the little one vomited green cud and showed no pleasure whatever in rejoining her old companions in hardship. Perhaps camels remember. I tried to humour the animal with two packets of Smith's Potato Crisps but got no more than a half-satisfied rumble as it grabbed at the discarded paper and wandered off chewing it noisily.

I wanted to start at dawn. I should like to be able to say that we swept out on to the El Barta plains with all the panache acquired during the trip but somehow it didn't work out like that. Trivialities tripped us up and Goiti was chiefly to blame. At five o'clock in the morning the old scoundrel had to be fished out of someone else's hut. I neither knew or cared what he was doing there; in their search for him the men aroused all the hut occupants in the vicinity of the compound, especially the widows, the orphans and the unattached and this was a heaven-sent opportunity to delay our departure for another hour. The men didn't want to leave; they were irritable and obstructive; Goiti was quite unrepentant and I tried to suppress my indignation by slowly articulating threats in Swahili. When I said that we should have left hours ago, Lelean was quick to point out that I had made a mess of harnessing the little one. I had omitted to lash down one of the sticks and the belly girth was clearly too slack. He untied everything with such malicious patience that I walked off and gave Goiti another good dressing down. It was not, as I have said, a good start but we strode down to the plains before the sandgrouse had flown off and it was some comfort to know that we were back on the map we had started with.

For the remainder of that day and for several days thereafter we travelled fast and uneventfully over the soft green of sage bush, stopping only when the camels tired. The route was due south to Swiyan and the great waterhole of Barsaloi where over a thousand cattle were watered daily. Clusters of zebra, oryx and gazelle ran ahead of us, wheeling, turning, gazing and then running on again. The air was bright and clear, the mountains blue and rain never far away. At Barsaloi we went up the wide *lugga* that divides the Matthews from the N'dotos, remembering that it was not far from here that we had run into the red elephants on the outward journey. But we saw nothing of them this time and, to judge from the old droppings and the distant squeals at night, they had gone up into the mountains to mate. The men pestered me to shoot everything we saw, four-legged and feathered. For various reasons, particularly digestive ones, I managed to confine the slaughter to spur-fowl. They were less arduous to chase at dusk than gazelle; they cooked quickly and they tasted good.

In one dilapidated *duka* above the Barsaloi I was surprised to see half a dozen brassieres hanging from a nail in the door. In colour they were a hideous fluorescent orange, distinctly small in capacity and fitted at the back with spring loops instead of a strap. A girl who could be described as handsome and well-built fingered one curiously. The proprietor urged her to try it on. Hesitating less from modesty than distrust of the unusual she lifted out one breast the size of a melon and snapped the twin cups on either side of it. Giggles all round. A friend tried to explain the principles of western uplift but her bosom being the size it was she failed to cap both nipples. The girl bought the dreadful thing for about a shilling and went out into the sunlight, proudly pinched up on one side. In the road it fell off where more helpful friends tried to defy the rule about the impossibility of putting quarts into pint pots.

In the Barsaloi we met another well-known white hunter. He walked into our camp at dusk, hand outstretched cordially but clearly a man with a lot on his mind. He refused a drink, said he couldn't stay for supper. 'I'd like to,' he said, 'but I've got to get back to put my client to bed. We're just round the corner. The old boy's a German businessman. Bit of a queer chap, turned seventy and nearly stone deaf. I give him a couple of pills at eight o'clock and stay with him until he wakes. I feel like a bloody nursemaid but it'a written into the contract.'

The German, he told me, was terrified of the dark. This did not deter him from shooting elephants and buffalo. He flew to Africa once a year and spent about two thousand pounds on a month's safari. I felt sorry for him. I felt sorry for white hunters. Their profession ranks among those most productive of stomach ulcers. Apart from the quartering problems of a luxury safari, they are usually on reconnaissance at night when their clients are full of liquor and fast asleep. They have an elaborate system of scouts; baits have to be laid out in areas where they are permissible; game movements need to be checked against permits to shoot in blocks allocated by the Game Department and they are obliged to keep in touch with those who direct the industry from offices in Nairobi. The intricate planning goes on behind a façade of nonchalance. The client has the impression that he is being conducted through a teeming jungle where one animal after another providentially pops up in front of his sights. For this he is charged a basic fee of about fourteen hundred pounds a month which doesn't include the cost of shells, liquor, extra licences and the hire of guns. Remembering that my own men were each paid three pounds a month, I thought of the deaf old man and the price of sophistication. The white hunter said he was only interested in elephants and buffalo and yet he was afraid of the dark. Afraid of what? Probably the unknown. Had I been scared during the journey? I thought of the wind and the blown sand and, carefully tip-toeing round the word 'scared', I decided that I had been distinctly anxious on several occasions. A faint voice asked whether there was any difference between fear and anxiety. Anxiety, as I thought about it in the dark, referred to a fear whose object is non-specific and difficult to identify; a fear, nevertheless, which is at times overwhelmingly powerful and always unsettling. It seemed to me that before Freud complicated matters, fear was a relatively simple affair, an admission of anxiety. Now it seemed to be linked up with a raven-brood of inhibitions including the threat of castration and memories of the birth trauma. As I tried to unravel these matters a hyena called in the dark. I remembered how I felt when I first saw hyenas limping up to the camp in twos and threes. I knew perfectly well that they rarely if ever attacked a man and yet . . . another hyena called. That night the great grey dogs came nearer and I became aware once more of the little cats of fear.

We followed the Barsaloi as far as its junction with the Seya and Lodowar *luggas*. What little water there was here and it was poor stuff – tepid, bright green with scum, and fouled by baboons. Lelean said that if we managed to get to the top of the Seya *lugga* the following day we could climb into the Ngeng valley and set up the camp I had thought about since the day we left the lake. I nodded with no particular enthusiasm.

It was vindictively hot. The air was heavy with thunder and, instead of the clear-bright mountain vistas I had hoped for, the Matthews were hung about with leaden clouds. The camels, too, wore a defeated, downtrodden look. Unless we could give them a substantial rest it was unlikely that we should get more than a dozen miles a day out of them. Our own store of energy which I had thought virtually inexhaustible was also running down. Time to look at the map. Wamba was about sixty miles away by the direct route and more, perhaps half as much again, if we went up into the Ngeng. I chose a site on an island in the dry stream bed and decided to stay there for at least a day. The site which I remember for a number of reasons, one of them painful, was called Ndumoteserem, the Meeting Place.

That night a horde of Samburu with a variety of ills converged on us as soon as we settled down. Dysentery was rife and to treat them all with sulfa drugs would have been impossible: I was down to a handful of tablets. I doled out tablespoonfuls of kaolin and threw in a little sulfa for the worst cases. Candidates for iodine were lined up for group therapy; suspected malingerers received an aspirin each in return for half an hour's wood-gathering or fodder-cutting and the constipations and the colly-wobbles got varying amounts of Epsom salts. Among this group was a markedly pregnant woman whose time, she said, was overdue by nearly two weeks. I gave her a stiff dose, hoping that if it worked, it would not work then and there. I had no wish to add midwifery to common quackery. She walked off pretty smartly I thought.

During surgery hours a phenomenal number of crows flew in. Camps always attracted a few birds but when Mezek carelessly threw away some rotten meat we got more than our tolerable share. Tiring of the incessant clamour, I remembered a successful trick of earlier days and to the great delight of my waiting patients I shot one (one of the birds I mean) and tossed the corpse into the fork of a nearby tree. The effect was the very reverse of what I intended. Crows flew in from all sides; wheeling and turning they dived down on to us and their dead companion making a dreadful noise. Scarcely able to hear what the next patient said I told Lelean to select three bad cases as the surgery was about to close. *Kabissa*. It was nearly dark.

The first had pleurisy or pneumonia; I cannot distinguish between them but I prescribed sulfathiazole and Lelean explained how the tablets were to be taken in a diminishing sequence. The next was a gross post-circumcisional infection for which I had scarcely enough penicillin powder and no clear idea about how to apply it. The third man was sent packing; he had, he said, a very sick cow. Doubting whether I had done a ha'p'orth of good to anyone I sat down to a kettle of tea only to find the inevitable – the last importunate patient on the edge of the lamplight. She was a young girl who said simply that she was ill. 'Mimi m'gonjwa.'

Anticipating triviality I asked where the pain was. She untied a bandaged foot to disclose the dead flesh of leprosy or a similar disorder far beyond my understanding. It was fearful to look at. I gave her a note for Father Stallone in red ink which was calculated, I hoped, to impress the truck driver who went past her *manyatta* once a week while Mezek, unbidden, gave her a pot of tea.

I awoke the next morning to find a young gazelle scarcely ten yards beyond my feet. It sniffed the air, wrinkling its nose, and made off, bounding away like a Lilliputian charger. Flocks of yellow wagtails ran under the feet of the browsing camels, hopping into the air to snatch at flies. I decided that it was a good morning to be alive and put the gun back into its case.

At eight o'clock a tracker arrived who knew so much about the ways of game that I hired him to introduce me to the local inhabitants. I discovered later that he was sent to gaol for six months for an offence under a section of the Wild Animals Protection Ordinance. He was, in fact, arrested that very day and I felt rather sorry about it; I had no idea that I had hired a poacher when we set off for a morning's game-watching but Lelean, it seems, had his eyes on him from the start.

I remember a chirrupy fellow with a large wart on his nose who called himself a bee-keeper. Starting from the back of my bed he told me through Karo, who seemed to be the only man who understood his dialect, what had happened during the night. I had been visited, it seemed, by two hyenas and a jackal distinguishable by its jointed toe-pads. The animals had snuffed about near my pillow. A fat-bodied snake had slithered into a hole near the cookhouse. He yanked it out with a stick and let it go again because, as Karo said, it contained no forks. Another snake, a huge creature, probably a python, had left a track like a drain-pipe across the sand. The trail disappeared into some thick grass where I thought it prudent to follow it no more.

We picked up the triangular spoor of the leopard near the scummy water and followed it step by step as it slunk towards the camp. At one point the pad-marks deepened and showed the impression of claws. It had paused to spring; 'At what?' I asked, wondering if one of us had had a narrow escape. 'At a mouse,' said the tracker and from the flurry of tracks it looked as if the mouse had skipped out of the way.

Although there were no visible marks among the stones, the tracker was insistent that the leopard had crossed the *lugga*. I asked him how he knew. He looked puzzled and Karo said he could 'see' the marks it had left behind. It was my turn to look puzzled. After re-phrasing the question several times he pointed out a little stone the size of a sixpence that was 'lying on its back'. Normally, I gathered, it would have been lying the other way round but the leopard had brushed it with its paw as it stalked past. Several other pebbles had been dislodged and here and there the leaf of a plant – a single leaf – had been crushed as the leopard slunk forward. The tracker followed unobvious marks and, just as he foretold, we picked up indisputable tracks in the soft sand at the other side of the *lugga*.

There is a sad end to this story. While we were on the trail of the leopard Lelean tracked the tracker back to his hut where he found an antelope skin that couldn't be accounted for. The tracker was arrested and for the remainder of the journey he travelled with us, escorted by a man from his own village.

I am, in ordinary life, a light sleeper; little noises immediately wake me up. I have boasted that very few people have seen me with my eyes closed. In Africa my sleep was lighter than the stuff of dreams; it was practically ethereal. The marvel is that I got any sleep at all. During our last hours at Ndumoteserem I must have awakened a dozen times.

About midnight I dragged my bed to the foot of a huge acacia only to find the topmost branches tenanted by an industrious family of snuffly, lemur-like animals who also seemed to be suffering from insomnia. They kept up such an infernal chatter that I leaped out of bed and hammered on the tree with the back of a mess tin, an action which had the effect of rousing the whole camp. The men thought I had been attacked.

There was peace for about ten minutes. Then more snuffling and a rhythmical rasping noise and the animals gnawed at the bark. Something wet and sticky fell down on to my face; as I wiped it off another drop fell on to the pillow. Sitting up in bed I examined the drops with a torch. Curious. Blood! My bed clothes and ground sheets were spotted with unpleasant red stains.

Lelean wandered up, sleepily and naked and not at all surprised that I had been spotted from on high. The tree, he said, was an 'Ulimbo nyekundu,' and he explained, slowly, that when the bark of a certain kind of acacia was cut it exuded a bright red gum. I had been sleeping under a red gum tree.

I shifted my bed for the second time but for the rest of the night I had to put up with a quarrel between the lemurs and anything else that tried to alight on the top of the tree. As far as I could determine from the hooting, yelping and squeaking, the disputants included a large owl, several kites and a party of homeward-bound bats. I got up at a quarter to five and started to dress in the dark.

The faint pleasure that I always felt at the beginning of another day's journey was short-lived. I vaguely remember that the lid of the steel box in which I kept my clothes was partly open. After the incident of the snake in the haversack Mezek had orders to keep the box not only shut but locked. I put my hand inside and fumbled for a pair of shorts. Something promptly stung me on the inside of my left thumb. It happened so quickly and the immediate pain was so violent that I was more curious than alarmed. My thumb felt as if it had been hit with a hammer. I looked for puncture marks and seeing none I called for Karo. He pointed to a slight film of moisture on the inflamed surface and said I had been stung by a scorpion. Considerably relieved I smeared it with an ointment containing an antihistamine drug and gave orders for the camels to be loaded immediately. The pain by this time had subsided considerably. I strongly recommend a preparation called Histofax but I noticed that as I washed and shaved with my right hand the face in the mirror was the colour of a lettuce.

It was not a good day. As we shambled up the Seya I felt slightly sick and I was obliged to put my left arm in a sling. Karo, who assured me that everyone had been stung at one time or another, said it would be eleven o'clock before the sun 'began to pull the forks out'. This was a pretty accurate prediction and it is likely that I should have been sitting under a tree, sipping tea at that hour had it not been for the rhino.

We saw our first at ten o'clock. It went off like an express train, leaving a corridor of dust in its wake. Realizing that some high-grade wildlifemanship was called for, I sent the prisoner and his escort forward on one bank of the *lugga*; Karo was ordered to take the right bank while Lelean and I walked about two hundred yards ahead of the camels. I felt rather exposed.

Karo drew the second rhino at half-past ten. When the animal ambled out of the bushes he bawled so loudly that it took fright and plunged down the bank towards us. Lelean raised his arms and shouted. To my relief it turned in its tracks and pounded away upstream, away from us. I thought this would effectively scare away all the other inhabitants of the *lugga* and limped along looking for a rhino-free resting place.

The third rhino differed from the others in that it had an undeveloped horn and a distinctly undeveloped instinct for flight. It looked at us for so long from a range of eighty yards that I thought it would turn round and make off. Instead, it put its head down and charged. It was as simple as that.

My recollection is that I half-turned to run towards the oncoming camels. Lelean, I remember, knelt down and slowly took aim. I heard the bolt slam home and the pounding of the animal's feet, but the brief, foreshortened view I had of the rhino deplorably close was blurred as my leg gave way and I fell flat on my back. The animal scraped me on its first run and then swung round and tried again.

Rhinos are protected animals. Although I had to write a report about the incident for the Game Department I cannot say at what range Lelean fired. I dimly remember that his first shot turned the animal and his second caught it obliquely. It staggered, recovered and ran off into some bushes.

Lelean and Karo ran after it, following the blood spoor for several miles. They returned at dusk and went out again the following morning.

In the afternoon they came back to say the rhino had only been lightly grazed and had last been seen making off into the mountains. This, as it turned out later, was a lie. When the animal had got on to rough ground they had lost the spoor but by that time I was on my back with my arm and leg on two supports cunningly devised by Mezek out of an old pair of pyjamas.

This is the cue for some stiff-lipped heroics about cold sweats and partial paralysis. My diary records 'curious hallucinations' but these may have been aggravated in part by the whisky I drank. Sufficient here to say that, apart from nausea, I felt as if I was suffering from a combination of toothache and pins and needles from my shoulder to my left ankle.

Two incidents stand out from the Seya episode: the first is that notwithstanding our fires a party of elephants wandered into the camp late on the first night and trumpeted at us peevishly. Had they arrived when I was less concerned with other matters I should say more about the sudden appearance of large animals with large tusks in the moonlight. We scared them off by shouting at them.

The second incident is that when I had nothing better to do than lie on my back and look at the sky I discovered how to play an acacia tree. Some species are protected by a palisade of double V-shaped spines arranged spirally around the bark. Mine was such a tree. I twanged one of the spines. It gave out a musical note. By breaking off varying amounts from the points I found that it was possible to make enough notes to play the 'Blue Bells of Scotland' and the first bars of more pretentious works. On the third day I arranged another early morning start. I felt fit again and it was high time we took the road to Wamba.

The journey to the lake and back had taken us just over three months, a leisurely excursion by Thesiger standards but notable, as far as I was concerned, for the amount of unnecessary gear I had brought with me and the number of things I had done wrong. Part of the pleasure of the remaining days derived from giving the gear away and organizing simple camps with the maximum of comfort. The camels had accounted for the pressurized lamps, the Primus stove and other fragile inessentials: the dispensable *bakshishi* included cutlery, crockery, kitchenware, jerricans, a host of knick-knacks, nine pairs of tennis shoes (I kept two and threw one away) and a pair of much-travelled suede boots which are known in Nairobi as brothel-creepers. All this dilapidated stuff was divided up into lots and drawn for on the morning that Waraguess, the peak above Wamba, popped up over the horizon. This seemed to be a reasonable excuse for a party and I shot two bushbuck for the occasion. They went down at fairish range. One thing at least I had learnt from the safari and that was how to use a rifle.

The next problem was to find a suitable site for a feast; I wanted it to be a memorable occasion since it was probably the last time we should spend a leisurely night together. I pulled in to an arid tributary of the Ngeng and parked at the foot of a grassy knoll for no better reason than that it bore a striking resemblance to Parliament Hill on Hampstead Heath. But it was obviously not the sort of place for a quiet night's sleep. The bark of an encircling necklet of trees had been rubbed bare by elephants and the ground was criss-crossed with hyena tracks. I decided to eat in the shade and move on up to the top of the hill when it grew too dark to see far into the surrounding bush.

My memory of the Ngeng that morning is stirred by the thought of butterflies. Countless thousands of little green-and-white insects fluttered over us like chains of flowers; they rose in showers from the pools of chocolate-coloured mud and re-settled, quivering, on the camel dung. In the tropics, where many butterflies have a predilection for dung, especially human dung, it is difficult to maintain the European notion of the insect as a symbol of delicacy. I walked towards the cookhouse where Mezek was dressing one of the bushbuck. The other animal lay on its side with mouth agape and one white butterfly vibrating tremulously on its glazed eyeball. The sight of a little spark of life on a corpse was startling. The attraction, presumably, was moisture. It reminded me of earlier days in Uganda where a warden told me of a similar occurrence.

He said that one morning his headman came to tell him that a young girl had been found dead in a nearby forest glade. She had been raped and strangled. She lay on her back with one arm thrown back above her head. Her posture, the warden said, was so peaceful that for a moment he thought she was asleep. What astonished him was the sight of her eyes for below the lid of each a large blue butterfly slowly opened and closed its wings.

News of our feast had travelled fast and far. So many strangers turned up that I began to wonder whether we should have enough to eat; yet it was soon apparent from the bleating of goats and sheep that several of the tribesmen had brought their own rations. We feasted at midday and not at night because I had discovered that Africans soon get drunk on a surfeit of meat; it usually takes about eighteen hours for the effects to wear off and I wanted to start early the next day and reach Wamba before dusk.

As far as I can accurately recall the *chakula kingi*, the afternoon of the emperor-sized feast, the last guest went home about six o'clock, the time when I awoke in a bower of euphorbia, heavy with food and sleep. The sun was sinking into the Samburu Hills and the camp seemed strangely quiet.

I called to Lelean. Nobody answered. I got up to find Mezek asleep under a bush still clutching a half-eaten leg of meat. He got up drowsily, his face shiny with grease, to say that Lelean, Karo and Goiti had gone off to a *manyatta* about three miles away. Apart from the prisoner and the escort we were alone in the camp and likely to remain so for the remainder of the night. After carefully arranging a midday feast I had completely overlooked the possibility of reciprocal hospitality.

The situation irritated me. Instead of a leisurely stroll around the camp and a drink before dinner we should have to work hard to get the gear up to the top of the hill before dusk. Holding the leg of meat like a club, Mezek went off to round up the camels while I folded the table and chair and put them on a ground-sheet.

After innumerable journeys up and down the hill we organized a hilltop camp on the pattern of Custer's Last Stand. The camels were double-hobbled and couched inside a *boma* of thornbush; the prisoner and his escort lay down beside them while I chose a patch of ground on the summit for my bed, table and chair. Very neat and trim, I thought. Mezek kept to his cookhouse at the foot of the hill but he made it clear he had no intention of spending the night there.

At dusk I was surprised to see him running up towards us. Breathlessly he explained that the lions were coming up. He had heard one 'very near' and had seen 'many many hyenas' among the trees. The lion, to the best of my knowledge, was fictitious. We heard one or two during the night but they were far away. What he had not exaggerated was the number of hyenas. Through field-glasses I saw them limping into the shadow of the bushes below and in the light of the torch I picked out many pairs of emerald-coloured eyes.

In a belated tour of inspection I found that the bushes at the back of the place where the men had feasted were littered with entrails and discarded bones. Instead of burying the remains the men had thrown them away without thought. From the chorus around us it was plain that the blood and guts were attracting every carnivore in the neighbourhood.

We threw all the offal we could find on to the cookhouse fire and went off to look for trees that would burn. In the light of the torch it was difficult to distinguish between live wood and dead; all the trees had a ghost-like appearance. Three old hulks on the ground were obviously ripe for arson; we piled brushwood around them. Four others seemed less combustible but by the time we had buttressed them with dry timber I reckoned that seven matches would be enough to raise a Siegfried-like ring of fire. We walked back up the hill where I drank a large Scotch convinced that we had done all we could.

At eleven o'clock that night we appeared to be surrounded by hyenas. They fought for the scraps and the chorus of howls gave way to yelps and squeaks. When groups of the animals began to run up the hill, snuffling round the uneasy camels I gave the order to fire the trees. As a piece of stagecraft it came off superbly well. The moment the trees blazed the chorus sank to an occasional whimper, offset now and again by the deep note of lion.

For two hours we sat in the centre of a circle of flame. I wondered if the men would see the fires from the *manyatta* on the other side of the valley. No doubt they were still eating for, as Lelean had said, 'All was nearly over.' Yet of the four he had most to look forward to. As a trained game scout he would eventually become a sergeant and send his own men out into the foothills of the Matthews. Mezek, too, had been promised a job. The young warden at Wamba who had done so much for me before he went home on leave had said that if he behaved himself he would be hired as a cook. Mezek had certainly behaved himself.

Goiti, the camelman without a flock of his own, would probably wander back to the Balessa Kulal, looking for odd jobs among the vagrant Samburu and Rendille. Karo had said that when I paid him off he had nowhere to go and he gave me the impression he didn't care. As for our prisoner, the poacher who understood the ways of animals only too well, there loomed the prospect of a long stretch in gaol. He was certainly not looking forward to the end of the safari. As for myself, I knew the journey was all but over when we swung into the Ngeng that morning. In the light of the burning trees I thought of the camels swinging back towards the lake and the winds and the sands. In imagination they were already far away

Little remains to be told. Back in Nairobi with nothing to do I wandered about, uncertain whether to fly home or spend a few days up in the Aberdares, trying to put my thoughts in order. The problem was simply one of acclimatization to the chronic boredom and slow corruption of respectable life. The store of energy built up during the trip seemed irreducible. I began each day by walking up and down Delamere Avenue at least twice, sometimes spending a little time in the Coryndon Museum, checking my disorderly notes with the people in charge of the collection of plants, insects and stuffed animals. In the afternoons I strode round the outskirts of the town, looking into the government buildings, button-holing geologists, meteorologists, anyone who could be persuaded to talk about winds and the rocks of the Northern Frontier District.

Let nobody imagine that business worries or a broken heart drove me into the desert; boredom certainly had a lot to do with it and that boredom had been wholly replaced with a reservoir of self-confidence, based on a brief affair with a lake. Anything that reminded me of that lake was a pleasure.

I saw Rudolf once more from a height of forty thousand feet. The time, near midnight, the Comet laden with dozing passengers travelling at hundreds of miles an hour. On the flight deck the navigator assured me we were almost directly above the Turkan shore, but in the light of a quarter-moon I could see almost nothing below. The pilot flicked over the switch of one of a bank of dials and the precise outline of Rudolf appeared eerily green in the centre of the radar screen 'Looks a grim place,' he said and switched it off.

I went back to my seat and we flew on towards Khartoum. The journey was over.